Faith and Science in an Unjust World

Vol. 2: Reports and Recommendations

FAITH AND SCIENCE IN AN UNJUST WORLD

**Report of the
World Council of Churches'
Conference on
Faith, Science and the Future**

Massachusetts Institute of Technology
Cambridge, USA, 12-24 July 1979

Volume 2: Reports and Recommendations

Edited by Paul Abrecht

FORTRESS PRESS
Philadelphia

Cover design: John Taylor

Library of Congress Catalog Card Number 80-81141

ISBN 0-8006-1391-0

Printed in Switzerland 1-1391

Table of Contents

Introduction 1

PART ONE: REPORTS OF SECTIONS

  I. The Nature of Science and the Nature of Faith 7

  II. Humanity, Nature and God 28

  III. Science and Education 39

  IV. Ethical Issues in the Biological Manipulation of Life 49

  V. Technology, Resources, Environment and Population 69

  VI. Energy for the Future 88

  VII. Restructuring the Industrial and Urban Environment 105

  VIII. Economics of a Just, Participatory and Sustainable Society 125

  IX. Science/Technology, Political Power and a More Just World
      Order.. 135

  X. Towards a New Christian Social Ethic and New Social Policies
      for the Churches 147

PART TWO: ADDITIONAL REPORTS AND RESOLUTIONS

  I. Science for Peace: a Resolution on Nuclear Disarmament...... 169

  II. A Critical Statement by Participants from Africa, Asia, Latin
     America, the Middle East and the Pacific 171

III. Report on the Science Students Conference.................. 173

APPENDICES

Officers of the Conference 195

List of Participants... 199

Introduction

In his introduction to Volume 1 of this report, Prof. Roger Shinn dealt very fully with the conference programme and work. I therefore need to add only a few remarks, especially on the findings and recommendations of the sections whose reports are included here in Volume 2. I also want to take this opportunity, as organizing secretary, to offer a few comments on the rationale for the meeting and how this influenced the programme and organization of the sections.

In the thinking of the planning committee, three imperatives were uppermost:

First was the need to put the ecumenical discussion of science and faith and science and society in a world perspective. Modern science and technology developed in western industrialized countries, and the majority of scientists and technologists are from these countries. The debate about science and technology has therefore been largely influenced by their views and oriented to solving their problems, and there was an urgent need to examine the issues from a worldwide and truly ecumenical perspective. Many western scientists argued that the scientists of the new economically developing nations were not yet experienced or competent enough to contribute to a genuine debate. The question was also raised whether scientists from Africa, Asia, the Middle East and Latin America, largely trained in the scientifically and technologically developed countries, would have anything distinctive to contribute. Such arguments tended to be self-serving and to delay a worldwide discussion which was becoming increasingly urgent. In planning the conference at MIT, it was decided that the ecumenical contribution to resolving the situation would be to ensure the widest possible participation of scientists and non-scientists from all parts of the world. The topics and the organization of the sections were designed to provide for an examination of the conference topics from this world perspective.

Second, there was also the need to relate the new concern for ecological and technological sustainability to the continuing ecumenical concern for justice and participation. Sustainability as a goal had emerged in the ecumenical conference on Science and Technology for Human Development in Bucharest, in 1974. This new goal had aroused suspicion especially among third world Christians because it seemed to run counter to the ecumenical commitment to social justice. The WCC Assembly in Nairobi, in 1975, asked that the relationship of justice, participation and sustainability be studied further, especially in the context of a continued rapid spread of science and technology throughout the world. In 1977, the WCC Central Committee appointed an Advisory Committee on the "Search for a Just, Participatory and

Sustainable Society" (JPSS), consisting of twelve members drawn from the Central Committee and representing all programme units and a selected number of sub-units. Their task was to look into the implications of the just, participatory and sustainable society for all ecumenical social thought. The report of this committee was presented to the Central Committee, meeting in Jamaica in January 1979, which concluded that "more clarity and fuller articulation were needed especially regarding the sustainability aspect" of the JPSS theme. It was "urged that the JPSS emphasis be further reflected upon and enriched by some of the forthcoming major WCC events, namely the 1979 World Conference on Faith, Science and the Future...". The concern of the conference planning committee was to discover how best to explore this complex of inter-relationships as it is manifested in key areas of industrial and technological development, giving particular attention to the concern for a sustainable society, as the newest dimension of ecumenical social thought.

The third aim was to develop a critique of science and technology in terms of faith. Until relatively recently it had been assumed that science and technology would be ultimately beneficial in all situations. However, the obvious predicament of societies increasingly dependent upon science and technology was leading to a questioning of this assumption and of their role in human affairs. Fears about the future of scientifically and technologically organized societies had become very real. It was clear that an evaluation of the direction such societies were taking would require a deeper analysis of the methods and ultimate goals of science and technology than could be provided by a purely sociological or political approach. The planning committee therefore decided to give a large place to the theological and ethical critique of science and technology, and include not only the Christian perspective but interpretations of the problem from the standpoint of other living faiths and ideologies.

The balance between plenary and section meetings

The programme structure and participation were planned to meet these three imperatives. In the programme great emphasis was placed on plenary sessions to provide ample opportunity for the presentation of a wide variety of viewpoints. There was a demand at the beginning of the conference for additional plenaries in order to allow for an even wider presentation of opinion. It is true, perhaps unfortunately, that what reaches most people via the press reports, secular and religious, is what is said in conference plenaries and not what comes out of the sections, which is reported only later.

The choice of plenary topics and speakers was made in light of the fact that the issues of science and technology were to be uppermost in the conference, and it was important for the churches to listen to the scientific community which thus far had had little opportunity to be heard in church circles. This specific focus explains the exclusion from the programme of such topics as armaments, transnational corporations and the New International Economic Order, for which there are other WCC programmes of study, consultation and action. It also determined the composition of the conference: about 50% physical and natural scientists and technologists with social scientists, political thinkers and others making up the rest. The challenge throughout the conference to this specific focus made its work difficult, especially in the sections, where there was an effort to interpret the conference mandate so as to broaden its scope and give more attention to the political and social issues in the application of science and technology. The officers and steering committee did everything possible to accommodate this wider expectation within the limits of the time available.

The planners had not foreseen the interest which the conference aroused and the number of requests to participate. Originally participation had been set at a total of about 350. In the final months plans had to be changed to accommodate more than 900, in the following categories: church-nominated participants; WCC-nominated participants, including science students; observers; accredited visitors; press; and staff.

This expansion multiplied the organizational, financial and staffing problems. The results of this were felt most seriously in the sections where the lack of preparation and understaffing created problems greater than is normal in an international ecumenical meeting. Plans had been made to have ready well in advance a detailed programme for each of the ten sections and also to provide an opportunity for section leaders to meet together prior to the conference. Because of lack of time and staff (and of finances to employ more staff), these plans could not be implemented, and it was only possible to make final section agendas available on the day before registration!

The task of the sections

The issues facing the conference were difficult and controversial and the tension and conflict naturally focused in the sections. Since more than three-fourths of those participating were attending their first major ecumenical conference and had little experience of the problems of ecumenical procedure and compromise, some of the sections had great difficulty in agreeing on the agenda for their discussions, and even more in producing a final report. Nevertheless, the reports show the substantial work of intellectual and ecumenical understanding that was achieved.

It could be argued that it would have been better to limit the numbers attending the conference and to have concentrated staff time and resources on section preparation. But the World Council of Churches can hold a study conference of this order only once in about ten years and the planners felt it right to err on the side of opening it to as many people as possible while at the same time keeping the international balance and the competence desired.

Some of those who look back to the WCC Conference on Church and Society in 1966 feel that the reports of the 1979 conference at MIT are less clear-cut and specific in their ethical conclusiveness. As the organizing secretary of both conferences, I see the reports as expressive of two contrasting situations.

The conference of 1966 came at a moment when the churches were ready for decisive speaking and action on the issues of world economic development, racism and social and political liberation. That conference succeeded in proposing some definite ethical guidelines.

The conference of 1979 faced an entirely different situation. The issues of science and technology are more complex and controversial and there is much uncertainty in both Church and society about the future of technologically organized and controlled social systems. Science and technology raise ultimate questions about the relation of faith to science which many churches, in both technologically developed or technologically developing countries, have only begun to consider. All present political and economic systems have made assumptions about technological and economic planning which require rethinking. The scientific-technological world-view has come under challenge and with it many previously accepted social goals. The 1979 conference could highlight the problems—it could not resolve them. It could, however, help the churches understand the immense promise and threat of modern science and technology, the challenge these present to traditional Christian thinking, and the desire of many scientists to work with the churches in determining their social responsibilities.

Editing the reports

The reports were discussed, amended and voted by the conference. In each case the action was "to receive the report for inclusion in the general conference report; and to adopt the recommendations for transmission to the World Council of Churches and its member churches for their study, consideration and appropriate action". The amended texts were then entrusted to an editorial committee appointed to complete the editing process.

The section reports are published in the order in which they were presented to the conference, but the reader may find it helpful to begin by reading the report of Section X which met in the final days and which was constituted of representatives from all the other sections. Its report therefore represents a kind of interpretation and summing up of the ethical issues emerging from the work of all the sections and from other conference discussions.

Special thanks are due to the officers of all the sections (see page 195) for their work in drafting and editing, and also to my staff colleagues Janos Pasztor, Peter Scherhans and Gordon Schultz for their great help in the detailed editing and checking of the reports.

It is hoped that the churches will respond to the challenge and move in the new directions defined in the findings and recommendations of the reports and resolutions of the conference at MIT, or propose alternatives.

P.A.

Part One
Reports of Sections

I. The Nature of Science and the Nature of Faith

1. THE RELATION BETWEEN MODERN SCIENCE AND CHRISTIAN FAITH

Our underlying concern with respect to science and faith

We do not come to the theme of "Faith and Science" only out of disinterested curiosity, nor will we be satisfied with academic abstractions as an aid to our understanding. As we peer into the future we glimpse much that fills us with fear and dread, but we believe that the future is God's, and we know that he is preparing the riches of his Kingdom for that future. In this position, seeing what we do, we are concerned to live as Christians in this world in a way that is consistent with the work of God and his Kingdom. We are well aware that there are differences among us as we approach the challenge of the future. Some of us see science and technology as flawed, earthen vessels, but vessels that nevertheless can be made fit to express God's love towards his world. Some probe the relation between science and faith in order to gain more insight into how science can be brought into obedience to the calling we hear from God in faith. Others place the science-faith issue in the framework of political and economic questions, holding that it is the political-economic context which provides the character and direction of science and technology. Still others are doubtful as to whether either faith or the best political economic system can prevent or control the harmful effects of science and technology. They believe that inherent in the character of science and technology itself is a dynamic which operates independently of social will, and consequently they are wary of granting to science and technology a Christian blessing. The following historical, philosophical and existential description emerges from this situation in which we stand with our hopes and doubts.

Historical and contemporary origins of our concern

Historical background: Modern science as we encounter it today is the contemporary form of a development that has deep historical roots in Mediterranean and Eastern cultures (Greek, Arab, Persian and Indian). It is a historical fact that the concept of science, in the form we now recognize by that term (see below), arose in the matrix of western Christian civilization about four centuries ago. This emergence of empirical science was possibly influenced by the Judeo-Christian doctrine of creation that affirmed the contingency of the created order and de-divinized nature.

Nevertheless, the institutional Church in the famous case of Galileo acted outside its proper sphere and failed to recognize the inadequacy and inability of its received traditions to answer the kind of questions being raised in the new experimental philosophy (i.e. empirical science).

Historians disagree on the extent to which Christian beliefs *per se* can be regarded as a "cause" of the flowering of the natural sciences. In the creative, initial phase of science, Christian faith played a significant role. On the continent of Europe in the sixteenth century, Kepler drew upon a medieval Christian mysticism, whereas Bruno was part of a Christian revitalization of classical humanism. In seventeenth century England, the new "natural philosophers" were devoutly motivated to read the "book of nature"[1] which they regarded as written by God alongside the Holy Scripture. The story of the gradual rupture of this early harmony between scientific endeavour and Christian devotion, that had its roots in the unity of the medieval outlook, has often been told. Science was characterized by an increasingly mechanistic view of the world, generated by the very success of the "new philosophy" in solving its first major problems—understanding the motion of objects on the earth and subsuming planetary motion under these same laws. (Remarkable for this period were also the introduction of very abstract concepts like "inertial mass", "gravitational mass", etc., and formal mathematical descriptions of observed phenomena, such as motion.)

In the eighteenth century distance increased between the adherents of the "book of nature" and those of the "book of faith", the Bible; between those holding that nature is a realm of strict mechanistic causality and those believing that nature is a theatre of divine intervention and action. This gradual distancing has been regarded by some as a purification of the faith, by the abandonment of any pretence to offer a cosmological explanation of the world. Be that as it may, the achievements of Galileo, Kepler, Newton and their successors led the way to the eighteenth century deistic concept of God and of his relation to the world. God was regarded by Laplace as an unnecessary "hypothesis" for explaining (for example) the periodicity of the perturbations of Jupiter and Saturn, and he seemed to be finally expelled from the world when Darwin proposed and justified a natural explanation of the presence of the multitudinous biological species on the earth. Darwin's discovery seemed to many at the time to give the *coup de grâce* to the then popular understanding of the doctrine of creation, which had already been undermined by the realization that the earth was immensely older than was, in that period, inferred from the Bible. The interpretation of the Bible itself changed rapidly at about the same time under the impact of scientific-historical investigations.

---

[1] A phrase made familiar by Francis Bacon but going back to St Thomas Aquinas.

Nevertheless, many scientists (a word not coined until the nineteenth century) continued to be Christian believers, and many believers continued to practise the Christian faith apparently unperturbed by these discoveries. On the other hand, the term "agnosticism" was first used in this same century to describe the state of mind of many former believers. Attempts were made to integrate science and faith, but profound though some of these were, they had little effect on scientists and Christians in general. In the first half of the twentieth century, very drastic changes occurred in the concepts and theories in physics (e.g. quantization of energy and other properties, the uncertainty principle, the theory of relativity), but the theologians, in contrast to philosophers and Marxist theoreticians, were generally not interested. Indeed, until well into the second half of the century, there was an uneasy truce between science and faith. But in recent decades tracks have appeared across the no-man's land separating these two forces.

Scientists, after a period in which they were adulated as the high priests and magicians of a progressing technological society, have had to face the consequences of the social significance of science and technology. Developments in the history and philosophy of science, and indeed within science itself, have led them to accept that their fundamental understanding of the natural world is not as absolutely certain as they had previously assumed.[2] For example, our knowledge of certain properties of sub-atomic systems cannot, it now appears, be more than "probabilistic". Physical scientists have had to recognize increasingly the limitations of their models which are, at best, only approximations of reality.

Christian theologians, too, have had to move out of their ivory towers. The mounting world problems in which Christians are engaged are seen increasingly as involving human life and society with the natural world, and thus with science and its methods and results. The attempt by some to confine divine revelation to the Word of God in the Scriptures or to Church teaching has been challenged by a critical age, whose scepticism has been enhanced by the success of science in prediction and control. At the same time, Christian theology has not been willing to capitulate to secularist views which claim God to be merely a projection of human hopes and fears or the content of a purely subjective experience. The new situation to which science has contributed has freed the Christian churches to recognize that if God as the Creator is the all-encompassing reality that Christian faith affirms, his presence, influence, and purposes have to be traced and unveiled in both human society and nature.

This is the background to our consideration here of Christian faith, modern science and the future of a society radically changed by science and its offspring, technology. From the time of Francis Bacon, the development

---

[2] See report on the 1977 WCC Cambridge colloquium on the Ideological and Theological Debate about Science, *Anticipation*, No. 25, 1979, pp. 5-8.

of fundamental science has been closely, and often self-consciously, linked with serving human needs in the prediction and control of nature. So economic pressures have shaped the technologies that science has generated, and these technologies have themselves influenced scientific developments, particularly through the invention of new instruments and experimental techniques. Today science and technology are intimately connected, so that it is difficult for society to distinguish between them. For this reason, a mechanistic understanding of the natural (including human) world drawn from a hazy fusion of science and technology is becoming the dominant world-view of our time which all religions and philosophies have either to oppose or appropriate.

In our discussion of science and faith, we recognize that many non-Christians are challenging the Christian faith by suggesting that other religions provide a better system of ecological values for meeting the impact of science and technology. For this reason, as well as for all the others adduced at this conference, an examination of the relation of Christian faith to modern science is urgently needed.

Contemporary experience of science: A knowledge of the historical background of contemporary science is important and helpful for any attempt to understand it. However, it is often the existential situation in which we live under the impact of science and technology that directs our quest for understanding.

The character of this existential situation is too complex to describe adequately here, but we can illuminate some of its major elements. For millions of people, the point of departure is a sense of being governed, even oppressed, by societies that are permeated by scientific endeavour and technology.

For persons in the developing nations, this coercive power of science carries with it marks of an alien culture, that of the West, including values and even religious motivations that are not indigenous to the non-western world. The sense of oppression is widespread in the developed nations as well, even when the science and technology are home-grown products. Both the developing and the developed nations recognize, however, that they require science and its benefits. This sense of need, combined with scepticism and sometimes anger, presses people to reflect upon science, to analyse it and its methods, what it means, and whether it could exist in any other form. For many of the non-western nations, this includes reflection upon the relation between science and indigenous traditions in their culture. One of the frontiers of reflection is that of determining how the practice of science could be altered or rendered more beneficial by relating it to cultural patterns different from those of the West in which science has been developed. In the socialist countries, the prevailing world-view is one in which a dynamic scientific picture of the world is accepted as obviously correct, and as the most beneficial for society. For Christians in these countries, the task is to understand how faith with its sense of the holy is compatible with science and yet autonomous in its basic assumptions about God and his will for human life.

In the countries of western Europe and North America the scientific enterprise is fully as decisive for life as in the socialist lands, but alongside those who are enthusiastically committed to the scientific picture of the world are others who take a strong "counter-culture" position. They fear that life will be stifled by what they perceive as the depersonalizing, mono-dimensional picture which science enforces. On the other hand, there is also a substantial movement of those who consider scientific humanism a better philosophy of life and system of values than traditional religion. Many western Christians are engaged in an apologetic debate with this humanist philosophy.

We see as one of the major challenges to the churches that they undertake to reflect seriously upon the consequences of beginning an analysis of science from these experiential situations. The preceding historical sketch would prove useful in such an endeavour, but it is very likely that an analysis proceeding from the existential situation would in fact result in an expansion and even the rewriting of the history of the rise and flourishing of science.

"Modern science" and "Christian faith"[3]

By "modern science" we mean that manner of addressing questions to nature that consists, on the one hand, of empirical inquiry, under defined conditions, into the repeatable phenomena of the natural world; and on the other hand, of the interpretation of the observations so obtained with conceptual schemes ("models", "laws", "hypotheses") which, if not provable, can at least be accepted or eliminated by their ability to predict observations as yet unmade. That is, the purpose of propositions in science is to describe and understand natural regularities.

The growth of science has been closely related to social and economic demands for the solution of problems in the prediction and control of natural events, so the foregoing account of the more intellectual, exploratory character of science must be supplemented by a careful appraisal of the effect of the wider social nexus, in which scientists operate, on their ability (indeed even their desire) always to live up to the ideals delineated. There does, indeed, seem to be a continuous spectrum from the "fundamental" scientific activity, whose character has been described in Prof. Hanbury Brown's address,[4] to the kind of "industrialized", applied science that is a captive of military, politico-economic power structures.

Many scientists would recognize that fundamental science is influenced by the social context in which it is pursued and as its ideas are exchanged in peer groups. All could agree that the spectrum of scientific activity cor-

---

[3] For brevity, in what follows, we shall often refer to "science" and to "faith", meaning specifically "modern science" and "Christian faith" in the senses elaborated above.
[4] See Volume 1, p. 31.

responds to and is at all times inter-related with social life and its activities and structures.

By "Christian faith" we mean trust in and obedience to God who has revealed himself in the life, death and resurrection of Jesus Christ, and who allows us to participate in the liberating and reconciling power of that revelation. The task of the Christian theologian is to reflect on the faith and life of the Christian community. The activity and receptivity of faith have been variously elaborated, e.g. as acknowledgment and acceptance in freedom of the gifts of God (creation, redemption, the coming kingdom), and as "evidence of things not seen" (Heb. 11:1), and thus always involving trust. For some this reliance is sufficiently firm that the content of the experience of faith can be described as "knowledge", that doctrines of faith (e.g. the Trinity, the incarnation) are to be placed on the same level of certainty (and of uncertainty?) as those provided by science. Christian theologians have variously distinguished, and continue to do so, between two aspects of Christian faith: between "believing in" and "believing that" (*fides qua* and *fides quae*); between faith as a condition or state of mind and the content of faith; between awareness, existential apprehension of and commitment to God, on the one hand, and knowledge, on the other.

Faith is not simply a single individual's belief and trust in God. It exists primarily in community with other Christians who share a common body of belief. Perhaps it can best be understood if we stress the mutual *participation* of believers and God in the Holy Spirit. Participation *(koinonia)* can then be regarded as a kind of transintellectual, extrasensory "knowing" and not merely as "involvement in decision-making". But this participation is not only between God and each believer but also between all believers in the community of believers, which in this context is appropriately regarded as the Body of Christ.

The continuity and identity of this Christian community were for many centuries embodied in a common propositional expression of faith (the creeds) and a common cultus (Holy Scripture, ministry, sacraments, liturgy).

But the East-West schism of the eleventh century and those of the sixteenth century and later disrupted the communal unity which might have served to identify "Christian faith". The ecumenical movement in the twentieth century, including post-Vatican II Roman Catholicism, has begun to restore this sense of a common faith, in spite of a plurality of theologies. The WCC is both the instrument through which the churches express their common faith in Christ, and also the arena in which different theologies and articulations of the faith encounter each other.

The praxis of modern science and of Christian faith

Both modern science and Christian faith can and should be judged by how they are living up to their respective ideals and best intentions. At this conference, there has been an emphasis on the shortcomings in the praxis of science and technology, but we must also draw attention to the shortcomings of the Christian churches in the praxis of their faith, not only in the past but also today. Sensitivity to these failures should render Christians less holier-than-thou in their approach to science and technology, more ready to heed the injunction about extracting the beam from one's own eye before calling attention to the mote that obstructs the vision of another.

There are different perspectives from which we may view both science and faith. An example from the present discussion: one could speak from the perspective of inner integrity which proceeds from what the self understands of itself, and one which considers the concrete actual impact of the self upon its world as essential to the self. One of the major preoccupations of our times has been to bring such different perspectives into a synoptic view. Since the community of faith and the community of science overlap in the lives of many individuals and in our churches, it is important that we, too, address this task of bringing the two perspectives together.

Many would regard this conflict in perspectives as sterile for the future fruitful interaction of science and faith. Both science and faith want their internal integrities to be taken seriously. So, too, the respective communities in which faith and science are nurtured insist that their own understandings of what they are about be respected. On the other hand, perhaps in the conviction that faith is too important to be left to the churches, just as science is too important to be left to the scientific community, our cultures today insist that both faith and science allow themselves to be enlightened by the actual impact which they have on the world about them. Both faith and science are disturbed by what this second perspective reveals. The community of faith and the community of science see that the inner visions to which they hold themselves accountable have implications for the affairs of this world, some of which they themselves abhor. Both have become in some sense captive to ideology,[5] with the result that the essential vision of each is used in a distorted manner for purposes that it recognizes as alien to its integrity. We acknowledge the appalling scope of such distortions and their consequences. Faith can be the "glue" which holds society together, and therefore it is not surprising that humans have in a perverse way used it as a tool for manipulating (consciously and unconsciously) people in the interest of ignoble causes. Many would insist that in recent times science has become so wedded to the technological-industrial manipulation of nature and human beings that it has, in fact, become in many places the dynamic centre of materialistic and destructive exploitation that threatens our entire planetary ecosystem.

Consistent with our common goal of bringing both our faith and our

---

[5] See the report by M. Hesse of the 1977 WCC Cambridge colloquium on the Ideological and Theological Debate about Science, *Anticipation*, No. 25, 1979, pp. 4-8.

science into conformity with God's will, we do not wish to permit either of these perspectives on faith and science to overwhelm the other. Rather, we insist that the two perspectives be allowed to interact with each other and point the way to a new situation. The interior visions of faith and science constitute the norm to which their praxis must be held accountable. Since the impact upon the world of our faith and of our science cannot be denied, we call for the correction of our praxis by the vision that we proclaim to be essential. We acknowledge that God is supreme over both science and faith. Therefore, the process of correction is nothing else but our attempt to be more obedient, in both our science and our faith, to God's will to consummate his creation.

In the context of this conference and its theme, we join in calling ourselves, as people of faith and as scientists, to exercise a faithful critique of faith and science so that their praxis may promote the just, participatory and sustainable society. In so doing, we intend no violence to the authenticity of the inner visions of faith and science. Rather, we remind ourselves that the communities of science and faith which hold these visions certainly have no wish to tolerate a praxis that in effect contradicts, and even calls into question, the truth and power of such visions.

This call for faithful correction of faith and science serves several purposes for us. It enables us to bring together into one meaningful framework both the sharp criticisms of science and the passionate defences that we have among us. Furthermore, our perspective calls for both parties in this controversy to recognize the degree of validity of the other argument and to engage in constructive conversation which will result in a new path for both science and faith. Our view reminds the churches that the criticism made of science, that it has lent itself to ideological and practical abuses, can equally well be made of the community of faith.

Ways of relating modern science and Christian faith

Modern science and Christian faith are currently being related in a variety of ways. This variety is rooted in the plurality of ways in which the churches regard the faith and conceive of God's relation to the world. As a result of both this theological plurality and the wide range of scientific activity, multiple interactions between modern science and Christian faith are to be expected. There is a need for extensive and careful theological and philosophical analysis of this complex inter-relation, an analysis which recognizes that science and faith share a deep sense of the mystery that underlies them both and which is rooted in human nature and the reality of God.

What follows is only a broad indication of some of the inter-relations that are proposed. It does not intend to delimit or prescribe what this relation should be and we strongly urge the churches to promote the study of these issues in universities, theological seminaries, and church-related colleges.

i) SCIENCE AND FAITH DEAL WITH TWO SEPARATE REALMS

In this formulation of the problem, the area of revelation, redemption, christology and human life constitutes the realm of faith, while the order of nature constitutes the realm of science. The strength of this foundation for formulating the science-faith relation is the power that stems from its recognition of God's revelatory and redemptive activity and of the centrality of Christ. Its weakness is that it tends to assign, by default if not explicitly, a degree of unreality and a relatively low significance to the natural world. It does not take adequate account of the God-given potentialities and openness of the natural order.

ii) SCIENCE AND FAITH ARE INTERACTING APPROACHES TO THE SAME REALITY, SO EACH MAY MODIFY THE OTHER

This is, broadly, the common position of many who otherwise differ markedly in their theologies. Although it is shared by a number of thinkers, it requires manifold modifications in the interpretation of the Christian faith, not to mention attitudes to science. It seems to commend itself as a common shared starting point because of its realistic view of the natural world, its inclusion of humans in the natural order, its consistency with the assumption of both science and faith that in their respective activities it is reality that is being discerned or unveiled, and so its accord with, and respect for, the activities of both, its implicit confidence that the Christian faith is relevant to truth wherever found (scientific truth in this context), and its deep foundation in the doctrine of the incarnation. Its disadvantages include the heavy burden of stringent, continuous, intellectual and theological inquiry it places on the Church as it tries to reformulate its position in a viable manner; the heart-searching it produces when it asserts that doctrine can be modified; and the temptation, to which it is particularly subject, of overlooking the ultimate transcendence of God with respect to *all* our conceptual schemes.

Those who hold this view of the science-faith relation need to give further attention to the distinction between faith and theology on the one hand, and between science and technology on the other. For some would urge that science can modify our interpretation of the Bible, but not faith itself, and that faith can modify the application of science, but not science itself.

iii) SCIENCE AND FAITH ARE TWO DISTINCT AND NON-INTERSECTING APPROACHES TO THE SAME REALITY

According to this view, science deals with observable qualities while faith seeks to indicate ultimate goals and forms of understanding. In other words, science answers the question "how?" and faith answers the question "why?" In our time, however, scientific accounts of man and nature increasingly give rise to "why?" questions and have always asked "what?" as well as "how?" Moreover, theology is increasingly asking "how does God create, act in the world, etc.?" as well as "where?" and "when?"

iv) SCIENCE AND FAITH CONSTITUTE TWO DIFFERENT LANGUAGE SYSTEMS
They have different imaginative and symbolic contents, so they do not conflict with or indict each other. This view is based on Wittgenstein's understanding that each kind of life generates its own language "game" which is valid and intelligible in its own sphere and for its own practitioners, but which cannot be related to those of other kinds of life. This view has been adopted by many modern philosophers who wish to take religious discourse seriously. Its advantage is that it allows clear autonomy and freedom to both faith and science in their own spheres and so ensures that faith cannot reproach science, nor science cast doubts on faith. Perhaps it is not surprising that it is adopted by academic philosophers of religion, as well as by some devout pietists and strict confessionalists. Its disadvantages are that it tends to trivialize both faith and science as is perhaps indicated in the appellation "game"; it does not clarify how either can make *true* statements; and in the end it seems to degrade both science and faith into useful fictions.

v)   FAITH AND SCIENCE COMPLEMENT AND PENETRATE EACH OTHER
Since science cannot finally prove its concepts, it is also basically a confessional enterprise, characterized by "faith" in the intelligibility of nature, in the orderliness of the universe, etc. At the same time, it is an intellectual discipline which is subservient to its object and can therefore be defined only in relationship to that object. In that sense theology can also be called a "science". In any form of understanding, therefore, there is a faith factor and a science factor which complement one another.

vi) THE INTEGRATION OF FAITH AND SCIENCE IS REALIZABLE
There are those who believe that with every scientific-technological advance, the gap between reality and human understanding is widening. But others believe that scientific advances, especially in molecular biology, modern physics and chemistry, are consonant with the Christian perspective enshrined in the Bible and elaborated by early theologians. According to this view, Holy Writ and the theology elaborated by the Church fathers and early ecumenical councils cannot be discredited or discarded, for it is claimed that they too contain much scientific truth which is only gradually becoming apparent through the insights being elaborated by science. Some modern scientists thus tend to rely increasingly on metaphysics and theology to provide answers to baffling problems posed by their own findings as, for example, on black holes and the origin of life, to mention only two examples. If this alternative is taken, this necessitates a new appraisal of the whole dialogue between the two enterprises. This is important for those theologians seeking to establish a scientific foundation for faith, who desire to formulate the relevance for humanity of a divine revelation and religious dogma, as well as for those scientists seeking to provide answers to some of the questions raised but unanswered by science itself.

2. THE VERIFIABILITY OF SCIENCE AND FAITH

In all areas of human knowledge, the problem of verifiability is crucial. We all need assurance that our knowledge corresponds with reality. We wish to be protected from gullibility and superstition and above all from making a deep personal commitment to an illusion. This need in turn gives rise to a search for methods of discovering and rejecting false knowledge as we strive to approach ever closer to the truth. We want our knowledge of reality to be, if not certain, at least credible, to function in enlarging and deepening our understanding of ourselves and our world, and to fulfil and liberate our lives in it.

Experimental science

The immense fruitfulness of modern science has resulted from the possibility of carrying out observations and controlled experiments with instruments of ever-increasing sophistication, and of reflecting on their results. This route to knowledge, although seemingly limitless, is nevertheless applicable only to those aspects of the natural order which satisfy certain conditions which themselves are not universally agreed upon by scientists and philosophers of science. We note two which emerged in our discussion. The first is that the objects of investigation must either *(a)* be made up of members of the same kind (electrons, atoms, DNA molecules, current or fossil members of a biological species, etc.), or *(b)* persist for a sufficient length of time to permit repeated observations (a galaxy, a geological stratum, etc.). Those holding this view believe that it is not applicable, for example, to instances of Extra Sensory Perception (ESP), Unidentified Flying Objects (UFO) or the abominable snowman. The other condition discussed in our group is that it must be repeatable in the same way on demand so that anyone, anywhere, at any time can repeat the experiment. Yet, even this seemingly self-evident assertion of repeatability is controversial. For example, scientists study the origin of the universe and the conditions of the universe that existed billions of years before the planet earth. These studies are based upon both experimental research and mathematical and theoretical reasoning. They are certainly scientifically credible but the phenomena of which they claim to have knowledge assuredly are not repeatable, neither do they persist into the present. There is no *a priori* reason why the universe as a whole should satisfy our conditions for knowledge, but the fact that it does is a gift which we do not deserve but for which we must be immensely grateful.

Fundamental religious knowledge is not gained in this way because it is primarily concerned with the nature of a reality which transcends space and time and with transcendent action (acts of divine grace, salvation, judgment, creation, incarnation) which cannot be produced at will for demonstration by anyone, anywhere, at any time. This domain of the totality of human experience and external reality is as substantial as that portion of the natural order subject to experimental science, but we must employ other means to assure ourselves of the validity of our knowledge of it.

Public versus private knowledge

Science and religion are often contrasted by the assertion that knowledge of the former is public and of the latter private. This assertion is demonstrably false. Knowledge of both is possessed in community.

Never in ancient Israel was knowledge of God a private possession of individuals. And from the fourth to the sixth centuries part of the universal public knowledge of the Greco-Roman Empire was that proclaimed by the four great Patriarchates and the first seven Ecumenical Councils. From the seventh century on, the universal public knowledge in Islam, knowledge based on the Prophet and the Quran, has been universal and public. From Charlemagne to the Reformation, Catholic Christianity was part of the universal public knowledge of western civilization. Only in the nineteenth and twentieth centuries has scientific knowledge become universal and public knowledge in the West, and increasingly in this century in the whole world as well.

In order to verify knowledge in science, one has to commit oneself to the enterprise of science, become a member of the scientific community, and submit oneself to its discipline and its canons of inquiry. It is the same with religion. Only committed and dedicated Christians in the community of a church can verify for themselves knowledge of the God and Father of our Lord Jesus Christ and the grace and power of his Holy Spirit. Who in the public at large can verify the non-conservation of parity in beta radio-activity or the fact that the genetic code for the amino phenylalaline is three thymines or uracils? Popularization of science for the non-scientific "public" has the same limitations and inadequacies as Christian apologetics had in its day for the pagan "public". The knowledge within either community is public in the sense that any member of the public who wishes to share in it and make it his own is welcomed with open arms. In this sense, but only in this sense, is our present knowledge of either nature or Christ "public" knowledge.

Individuals in either community may advance and defend explanations or theories which the community as a whole then tests against the common experience. In time, after due consideration and trial, the community may be forced to reject these as false. The attempts to reconcile the fact of Christ with the unity of God expounded by Sabellius, Paul of Samosata and Arius were logical, but had to be rejected by the Church in favour of the more difficult understanding of the single being of God in three distinct persons. The antinomy of fully human and divine natures in one person was adopted at Chalcedon against the more rational and understandable explanations of Apollinarius, Nestorius and Eutyches. There are numerous examples of the same process of rejection of false or inadequate theories by the scientific community. Both communities operate not so much by verifying truth as by falsifying error.

In both communities the individual finds meaning, acceptance and fulfilment from participation in them. This is the inner, subjective, deeply personal element in both. Individual Christians bear witness to the power, the joy, the sanctification and the redemption they experience from their life in Christ. Individual scientists bear witness to the personal satisfaction and fulfilment they derive from science and their enthusiasm for the value, importance and nobility of the enterprise in which they are engaged. Individuals in both communities are from time to time assailed by doubt and a dark night of the soul only to be caught up by new surprises of joy and unexpected vistas of meaning. Participation in both communities is a pilgrimage, an adventure of discovery and a journey in faith, rather than sharing of a completed system simply given and received; it is "new every morning" for each pilgrim on the way.

The current situation

Science now finds itself locked in between the Big Bang before which there was no before and the Big Crunch after which there will be no after. The universe it investigates is unimaginably vast, mysterious and beyond our grasp; it is on a one-way journey into an unknown future. It seems to overwhelm and dwarf us into total insignificance. Yet there is a strong case for the proposition that it had to be as big as it is in order to be a home for the human creature. If it had been smaller there would not have been enough opportunity for the generation of elements essential for life and the subsequent evolution from DNA to humanity. The chance of our planet earth being duplicated in another stellar system is probably much less than one in a million. Yet if there is such another place, it has been created by God in the same creative process that he used on earth, not as a matter of necessity, but of his freely choosing consistency in his creative acts. Science has arrived at mysteries which can only be dealt with, if at all, by theology.

At the same time, Christian theology is confronted with basic challenges to its traditional formulations, posed by new understandings from science. Traditional doctrines of creation must be restated: rather than emphasizing a single creative act at the beginning of time, stress must be laid on the creative activity of God in time; God who patiently, step by step, in a long continuous process brings forth ever more intricate and amazing wonders out of those which came earlier. Moreover, evey new work of creation emerges within a complex fabric of interdependence with all other elements of the created order. Traditional doctrines of the omnipotence of God must be rethought and reformulated. Biblical scholarship forces upon theology new approaches to an understanding of revelation and of the intercourse between humanity and God. New ways of expressing the authority of scripture, tradition and magisterium need to be found. In a cosmos which is 16 to 20 billion years old, where is the eschaton to be located on the axis of time?

In the midst of this intellectual ferment in both science and theology, there is the prospect of a new and more comprehensive vision of reality. In both science and religion in different ways it is a vision of a wider truth and coherence which lies within our reach if each could find a way to free itself from the sterile conflicts and protective armour characteristic of their past relationship. There would be no such prospect at all if each were not convinced that it had achieved at least some portion of the total truth. But for both communities the task is complicated by their present fragmentation into numerous and frequently non-interacting sub-communities: of science into a broad spectrum of disciplines and increasing narrow specialities, and of the Church into an equally broad spectrum of denominations. The process cannot be forced or hurried, but the goal slowly becomes more visible as we peer into the mists which shroud the future.

One final thing needs to be said about the current situation. The credibility and validity of every human institution—governmental, industrial, academic, religious or scientific—stands ultimately under the judgment of the society at large. As has been emphasized earlier in this report, science and faith both claim to be accountable to a larger vision that deserves the respect of all people. But the credibility and worth of both visions are falsified and negated if the two enterprises, each in its way, do not promote love, translated in the present discussion into concern for the just, participatory, sustainable society.

We have heard in this conference a great deal of criticism of science because of its links with exploitative technological enterprises. We believe that the true and legitimate purpose of this critique is not to destroy science nor to violate its integrity. Rather the purpose of that critique is to press home the conviction that unless science serves the purposes of love, it betrays its own vision and also the hopes of the world. This critique applies equally to the Church. In this sense, love and its corollary, the just, participatory and sustainable society, constitute the public criterion of verifiability and falsification. Our earlier discussion has concentrated on the internal sets of criteria applicable to science and faith, and these are essential. The chief and distinctive concern of this conference is, however, this broader societal and exterior criterion.

3. A CALL FOR INTERACTION BETWEEN THE WORLD-VIEWS

A significant feature of science since the sixteenth century has been its development of world-views which differ from those of established religions and cultural traditions. This process continues today. The clash between the scientific and pre-scientific world-views has had the effect of making it more difficult to be credulous, to accept faith too easily, and has made us more aware, and perhaps more critical, of our religious, cultural and historic points of view. Scientific studies have been applied to various aspects of the life of the community of faith and to the traditional sources of Christian revelation with results both helpful and disturbing.

There have, moreover, been two subtle effects of the rise of science on the articulation of the faith itself: on the one hand, there has developed a tendency to reduce the scope of theology to the history of human existence and a divinization of the transcendent element of faith, leaving out any consideration of the natural world and of cosmological developments. On the other, there is a tendency for some theologically oriented scientists to regard consideration of the natural world and of cosmological development as of compelling significance for awe and faith. This conflict in approach is especially unfortunate for twentieth century theology and is related directly to the concerns of this conference.

The scientific point of view is not to be regarded as arbitrary; although it is admittedly coloured at any given time by the social context within which it is developed, it represents the scientists' best information about the world within a limited domain of validity. It is because its validity has been so thoroughly tested by observation throughout the history of science that scientific knowledge has been established as reliable public knowledge. The wide range and reliability of the knowledge given by science have led to the dominance of the scientific world-view and thus has deeply affected not only human self-understanding but also the interpretation of faith itself. "As for the great mysteries which stand in the shadows of all human thought, such as the origin and the purpose of the world, modern science cannot be accused of sweeping them away."[6]

But in what way does the scientific world-view affect the articulations of our Christian faith and almost all dimensions of our self-understanding? One example of the former is the reformulation of the doctrine of creation in light of, and in terms of the theory of evolution. An example of the latter is the way in which modern science has given new meaning "to an old and powerful idea, to the unity of human beings and their environment, and to their need to live in harmony with it".[7]

Another is the new understanding of human health provided by modern medical science. It is precisely its relevance to practical affairs that has produced rising expectations of science and has fostered the dominance of the world-view of science in almost all areas of human experience.

However, although modern science points to the unity of humanity with its environment, this discovery does not embrace the whole of reality or, in other words, the total environment of human beings. For it does not and cannot take into account its relationship to a transcendent reality. The relatedness of humanity and its world in God constitutes a deeper and more complex "environment", which is not included in the scientific world-view. The discovery of this relatedness is not just a matter of an arbitrary individual point of view or of private belief.

---

[6] See Hanbury Brown's address in Volume 1, p. 40.
[7] *Ibid.*, p. 38.

In recent years, our experience of the applications of science has led to new and unanticipated consequences. Under the shadow of science, faith has come to see itself as limited to a subjective experience without knowable relevance to the world, people are regarded as little more than machines to be repaired or improved, cultural or social relations are regarded as structures to be shaped and rebuilt. It has become increasingly difficult to find words to express the intrinsic values of life; the only language which seems relevant to human existence is technical language; community life and its goals are dominated by anonymous technological power structures.

Speaking of the Christian faith in terms of expectation and hope we have to give account of the content of our expectation and of the goal to which our hopes are directed.

Since we affirm faith in terms of expectation and hope, there are certain critical questions which we must direct primarily to ourselves as Christians. Why has science had such a tremendous effect not only on the world we live in, but also on the Christian faith? Are we ready to accept that God has revealed the meaning of his creation through science as well as through his other actions in history? And is it not correct that through science and its consequences we have been taught a new lesson about our shortcomings? Questions such as these challenge us to develop a world-view in which humanity's relationship to God is perceived as an essential dimension of reality. The explication of the cosmological meaning of faith and theology is necessary not only for apologetic reasons, but also to ensure the coherence of theology and Christian witness. This entails serious attention to the formulation of a strong theology of nature and a reassessment of the doctrine of creation. There cannot be one single theological approach to the problems posed to us. Ways must be found to articulate a theology of nature in terms of a new ecological sensibility. Christian theology must not be reduced to naturalism nor, on the other hand, can it retreat from science into religious feeling. Our theology must emphasize our responsibility for nature as God's creation, a responsibility which accepts the duty given to us by God to care for this world.

4. SCIENCE AND TECHNOLOGY: ARE THERE MORAL LIMITS?

Technology and science: their relationship

Technology may be described as the systematic way of doing work normally involving tools and techniques. It is a purposive activity. Science is a disciplined way of thinking (it has been described in Part 1 of this paper).

There is an important distinction and a reciprocal relationship between science and technology. When we consider the roles assigned to human beings in the creation account, the duty of naming the other creatures could be seen as parallel to the activity of science and the exercising of dominion as parallel to that of technology. However, as is evident in the account of the fall, there are limits to both our dominion and our knowledge.

From the biblical perspective, human wellbeing depends upon our living in faithful obedience to God within the limits our Creator determines for us. Science, assisted by technology, as our way of knowing the natural and social dimensions of our existence, makes it possible for us to act with understanding towards each other and our environment. Faith provides us with the spiritual and moral values which should guide and regulate our application of science and technology. To gain an understanding and an appreciation of the mysteries of creation reverently fulfils the human spirit. To use this understanding irresponsibly leads to great suffering, destruction and the brutalization of both those who wield the power and those against whom it is directed.

Contemporary technology makes it possible for human beings to exercise power over nature as a whole and over other human beings. The temptation to use this power for personal gain and self aggrandizement is great. From the Christian point of view, the greater the power, the greater the responsibility and service required.

The origin and nature of the problem

The general discussion of the conference reflects the growing awareness of society that there must be some limitations, stemming from considerations of human values, in the exercise of science and technology. On the other hand, science and technology can be of great theoretical and practical utility in the attainment of a just, participatory and sustainable society and it is often claimed that any outside interference or limitation reduces their ability to achieve these aims.

The general problem manifests itself in two, inter-related dimensions, the theoretical and the ethical.

Theoretically, we know that freedom is essential for the fruitful development of science and technology. The argument for this freedom of inquiry is rooted in the basic openness of science: it cannot know ahead of time the relevance of its observations to fuller knowledge of the world and hence must be free to follow its own internal logic, if its understanding is not to remain incomplete. Moral limitations on science and technology represent intrusions from outside its own internal logic and are considered by scientists and technologists as an obstacle to a full understanding of the phenomenal world.

At least three positions have been taken vis-à-vis the tension generated by moral constraints on science and technology. They argue that:

i)   Science is the description of the world; moral considerations stem from understandings derived from areas of human experience which do not intersect with science.

ii) Science is intimately associated with technology; even the process of inquiry in the fundamental sciences is conditioned by the social context, which makes the proper goal of science the solving of the problems that confront humanity. Since all areas of scientific and technological activities intersect with human aims, a consideration of values in relation to those activities is valid.

iii)   The frontiers of scientific knowledge have advanced to the point that few areas of scientific inquiry remain where knowledge may be sought for its own sake without massive (and costly) technological support. Consequently, questions of the potential human value of any proposed research must be raised. The ethical issue is the allocation of finite resources to maximize human good.

The ethical dimension of the problem is posed in the question: How are ethical values to be applied on the activities of science and technology? We must discover and validate ethical criteria, properly structure their application to the various sciences and technologies, and understand how the Christian churches can share in their ethical task.

a) *Ethical criteria:* Ethical criteria are derived from moral positions which have found support in human experience. For Christians the basis for these positions is in scriptural and doctrinal teaching and in the historical events accepted by the community as revelatory of God and his purposes in creating humans. These have been authenticated in the collective experience (history) of the community. We suggest that the following moral positions derived from the Christian revelation are applicable in the human activities of science and technology:

i)   God has granted every human being freedom to develop his or her own potentials, informed by the freeing, creative qualities of life in Christ. Whether or not this freedom may be invaded without the informed consent of the person involved is itself an ethical problem. There is a moral burden of insuring an acceptable level of understanding of possible hazards of scientific research by the human subjects/participants and this obligation is not lessened by their physical or mental condition, social or cultural context.

ii)   All elements of the Lord's earth are his creation and are to be treated responsibly. The ethical relation denoted by the Christian term "stewardship" should apply. Decisions affecting hopes for a sustainable future are to be made in this context. When living organisms in the Lord's world are affected by scientific or technological activities, there are additional ethical imperatives beyond those obtaining in the utilization of inanimate elements. Biblical tradition recognizes that taking of life (animals) is not in accord with the true will of God but it also recognizes the facts of human existence. Therefore, while the flesh of animals may be used for human good, animal "life" may not be taken. We interpret this distinction as recognizing the need to use animal and plant life in the human food chain including related experimental and technological activities, but that man wantonly obliterates animal or plant life for other purposes to his own peril.

iii)   There will always be instances of proposed scientific or technological activity which seem to violate the ethical requirements. In those instances, the burden of proof of ethical acceptability is on those proposing such activities. They must show clearly that their projects can promote a sustainable future for humans in their ecosystem.

b) *Methods for applying the ethical criteria:* As important as the criteria for moral intervention in scientific and technological activities is the methodology by which those criteria are actually applied. The structures for intervention should vary according to the scale of the activity, the foreseeable effects of the activity on the possibilities for a sustainable future, and its intrinsinc nature. Three elements may be suggested:

i)   Individual moral control by the scientist or technologist. Individual scientists and technologists can exercise essential and powerful ethical control in the realm of their activities. They are the most intimately involved and the first to be aware of new knowledge and its implications. They know best the subtle qualities of the activities which may be crucial for the future of a sustainable society. Consequently, it is of vital importance to educate, assure the moral competency and enlist the cooperation of the practitioners of science and technology.

ii)   Ethical control of scientific and technological activities by peers. The collective moral perspectives of groups of scientists or engineers engaged in the same or similar kinds of scientific and technological activities is a necessary component in the structures of ethical intervention.

iii) Ethical control of scientific and technological activities by society in general and its agents. The right of society itself to intervene in activities of science and technology and the acceptable methodologies of such intervention are more controversial. We affirm the right of the society to exercise ethical control of scientific and technological activities. We further affirm that when the ways the moral decisions to be made and executed are determined, the varying interests and views of all persons who might be affected by the scientific and technological activities should be adequately represented. Safeguards should be provided against corruption of the ethical control system by undue pressure, by greed or favouritism. The way in which this ethical control is structured gives substantive meaning to the phrase "participatory society".

c) *How should the churches share in the ethical control of scientific and technological activities?* The churches can and should play a key role in the ethical control of scientific and technological activity. Reassessing ethical positions in light of changing circumstances in the world and improved theological understandings of the faith is a major task of the Church.

Churches should foster a heightened moral awareness among their members engaged in scientific and technological activities. They themselves should participate in and should promote representative participation in the discussion of ethical issues raised by technologies and their implementation. The churches and their members should call in question immoral or amoral behaviour in scientific or technological activities. This questioning is a continuation of the traditional prophetic role of the Church in society.

At the same time, the churches must give rigorous attention to the way they interpret the demands of their faith in relation to new technologies. On the one hand, they have no reason to fear free inquiry; they should not encourage the repression of valid technologies. On the other, there seem to be activities of a technological nature which must be completely forbidden on moral or rational grounds. The use in war of powerful chemical poisons, virulent biological agents or nuclear weapons must be banned. The paramount moral issue of our age is how nuclear disarmament is to be achieved in ways that will lead to a just, participatory and sustainable society.

One particular aspect of the problem of the control of scientific and technological activities invites the urgent attention and support of the churches. These activities are so vast and require so many elements of expertise and special languages that timely, effective, integrating communication is an almost insurmountable obstacle to the wise exercise of moral control. It may be a crucial contribution of the churches, united in moral concern, to reduce resistance to communication through the trust engendered by the invisible fellowship of the faithful, and through an awareness of the action of the Holy Spirit in the world, and thus to form a network of communication equal to the problem posed.

5. EPILOGUE

We have discussed the nature of science and of Christianity in terms of the history of their development, the nature of each as a source of knowledge, and the validity of the claims which each has made for the truth of that knowledge. At each stage of this history, however, individual Christians have made a commitment of faith involving not only academic or philosophical assent but profound personal belief and conviction. Columbus not only felt he could defend the proposition that the earth was a sphere as a likely hypothesis; he staked his life on its truth. Indeed for both science and Christianity faith is a prerequisite for understanding; *credo ut intelligam*, I believe in order that I may understand.

Christians who are scientists at any stage in the history of the last two centuries, as we have briefly reviewed it, have experienced the tension between their faith in Christ and the convictions of non-believing colleagues. For many of the latter any belief in a reality transcendent to the natural order was an illusion and a betrayal of their faith in the adequacy of science to provide an all-embracing access to truth and a sure hope for the future of mankind. Today tension is intensified by the prevailing agreement among the non-scientific general public in many parts of the world on the superiority of scientific over religious faith.

In the remaining two decades of this amazing and fateful century, scientism or the exclusive faith and hope in science is certain to decline, as the realities of an exploding population of the human species confined to a finite planet with dwindling resources become clearer to all. The limited ability of science to cope with the situation and the reality of divine judgment on the self-centred profligacy of humanity are becoming starkly evident to all, as numerous addresses at this conference have shown. The industrial revolution spawned by science has given us a two-century joyride which was exhilarating and materially satisfying while it lasted. But the joyride is almost over and we face with deep anxiety extremely painful adjustments to a life of increasing austerity and hardships. Science will continue and we will depend on it even more crucially than we do now. But more and more we will assent to the ancient proclamation "Our help is in the name of the Lord", as we cry "Kyrie eleison, Lord have mercy".

We Christians in this latter quarter of the twentieth century should be humbled by the sturdy examples of our brothers and sisters of a century ago who loved and served the Lord Jesus Christ as Lord of Lords and King of Kings in a milieu in which mechanistic and deterministic science reigned supreme and such faith was far more difficult to maintain and defend than it is for us today. Let us above all cling to Christ and witness in our lives to the joy and confidence that is within us, as we journey with our non-believing friends and colleagues on the awesome pilgrimage of judgment which lies ahead.

6. A RECOMMENDATION

Appreciating the experience of this conference, we recommend to the WCC that the present meeting be followed up by smaller meetings devoted to issues in the relationships between Christian faith and modern science as described in our report, and urge that these meetings include active scientists who do not share the assumptions of Christian faith, and allow enough time to develop mutual understanding, clarification of the concepts employed, and careful identification of the critical issues.

II. Humanity, Nature and God

The ecumenical movement must set the struggle for a just, participatory and sustainable society in a broader context: the relation between God, humanity and nature. This has been made clear to us by the crises in our scientific and technological world, the anxious questions of scientists, and the new inquiry about the biblical message for this situation.

The revolutionary social processes of the present must be viewed together with the problems of the scientific and technological revolution. It is not sufficient from either a theological or an ethical point of view to consider human history and society with their conflicts apart from their relationship to the non-human creation. God's creation is as indivisible as are justice and peace, values which are themselves applicable to nature, humanity and society. The crises in our scientific and technological world, seen in the light of the Bible, call for a holistic approach in which the relationship between God, humanity and nature is developed in relation to contemporary problems.

It must be stressed from the outset that these relationships are not static. Humanity and nature belong within God's history with his creation in which justice and injustice, even life and death, are in conflict. But this history is also under the promise of God who will fulfil it in justice and peace. It is from this perspective that we see the future and commit ourselves to it.

This struggle to which we are summoned as members of the ecumenical movement is also indivisible. In our discussions, the commitment to justice and to ecological sustainability has been marked by different and even opposing emphases. We have tried to understand the connection between them, and to learn to participate in the urgent needs of others, in order to be able to cooperate in the struggle for a just, participatory and sustainable world society.

The main structure of the report is as follows:
— a description of the situation in our scientific and technological world out of which our questions arise;
— a presentation of the biblical message we seek to understand;
— the relation between the two;
— the relation of Christian perspectives to those of other faiths;
— a number of recommendations arising from these reflections.

1. THE RELATIONSHIP BETWEEN GOD, HUMANITY AND NATURE IN MODERN WESTERN THOUGHT

Opposition and epistemological dualism are characteristic of modern western thought; subject and object, matter and spirit, knowledge and belief, intellect and feeling, the whole and the individual, are set over against each other.

Along with this opposition between humanity and nature, God vanishes from the view of modern science[1] and humanity emerges as a substitute god over against nature. This happens despite the fact that God has been regarded in the Christian tradition as the One who holds humanity and nature together.

Modern science and technology have achieved great success in the knowledge of nature and its use for humanity. However, the technological treatment of nature made possible by modern science has increased humanity's oppression and exploitation of nature to a degree previously unimagined. At the same time the oppression of other human beings—the poor (especially in the Third World) and women—has been intensified. Furthermore, science and technology, by reducing non-human nature to the status of a mere object, have denied the intrinsic value that inheres in every creature because it comes from the hand of God.

Modern western Christian theology put up little resistance to this development. Indeed, it undergirded the opposition between nature and humanity by making the uniqueness of humanity the predominant theme of its doctrine of creation. Yet the trinitarian doctrine of Christian theology runs counter to the dualistic tendencies of modern times: it makes impossible both a naturalistic and an idealistic reduction of the relation between God, humanity and nature; it presents the relationship between God, humanity and nature as a differentiated unity.

There have also been other counter-currents in western thought, for example, the romantic movement, Schelling's philosophy of nature, Whitehead's process thought and the dialectic of nature and society in Marxist thought. But even these counter-currents had no more success in countering dualism than the elements of resistance in the Christian tradition.

This dualistic tendency is what distinguishes western theology from the theological thought of the eastern churches. Orthodox theologians have constantly taught "union-participation" not only between God and humanity in Christ but also between humanity and nature, and the Church of the East in its worship has practised this participation of humanity in the universe.

Modern western science is understood by many of its exponents as a pure search for truth. The sincerity of those who hold this view is unquestionable.

---

[1] The English word "science" is usually restricted to the natural sciences. The German term *Wissenschaft* is broader and also includes social sciences and theology. It was not possible to discuss this question of terminology in depth.

Yet it is no accident that the growth and development of the natural sciences accompanied that of the capitalist system. Knowledge is power. In its self-interpretation, science has all too often ignored its social impact as an instrument of those in power.

2. THE RELATIONSHIP BETWEEN GOD, HUMANITY AND THE NON-HUMAN CREATION IN BIBLICAL THOUGHT

Western theology has introduced the above-mentioned opposition even into the interpretation of the Bible: creation and salvation have been separated; either the theology of salvation swallowed up the theology of creation, or creation was treated in isolation from it.

Today, by contrast, we need to point out the numerous ways in which the Bible connects creation and salvation in Christ, eschatological hope and obedience, and justice and sustainability. The following gives an idea of how this might be done.

i)   The story of the flood constitutes the centre of the primal history in Genesis 1-11. In it the saving of humanity and of the animals and the preservation of the threatened creation are presented together. This story can serve as a symbol for us in our seriously threatened world. It shows clearly that the creation stories in Genesis 1-2 answer not simply the question of the origin of the world but the question of its continuing existence.

ii) Despite the rift which runs through the whole creation, all human communities, their work and the non-human creation (Gen. 3-11), God upholds his world, does not allow chaos to break into it again (Gen. 8:22). Despite the failures of humanity, God wills to bring his creation to its goal. Despite the disruption of all communion (including that between humanity and the non-human creation), God promises the persistence of basic continuities and rhythms (Gen. 9:1-17). These are the object of natural scientific knowledge; only because of them does natural science have an object.

iii) *Imago Dei* (image of God) is the biblical concept which indicates both humanity's relation to God and also the relation of humanity to the non-human creation. As God's image, humanity is to rule with care over the non-human creation and in this way share in the preservation of earthly creation and further its development. Humankind as a whole has been created in God's image without distinction of sex, class or race.

iv) As God's image, humanity also mirrors the communion in God (Trinity): human beings live in the community of man and woman, brother and sister, in families, tribes and peoples. Language equips them for fellowship both with each other and with God through prayer. Language also brings them into relationship with the animal world in that it is by language that creation is named (Gen. 2:19 ff.).

v) In speaking of human dominion (dominium), Genesis 1 distinguishes between the subjection of the earth and rule over animal life. A hierarchical gradation is unmistakeable: humanity is more closely related to the animals by their common possession of life in the blood (Gen. 9) than to the earth and its plant cover. By their work (e.g. farming) humans exercise dominion over the earth. On the day of rest, however (Gen. 1; Ex. 20), humanity—like God in the creation account—is to desist from work, leave it behind and rest (self re-creation) and contemplate the miracle of creation.

vi) The divine commission to human beings has not been cancelled out by sin. But the great rift in the whole of creation makes humanity's relationship to the non-human creation laborious (Gen. 3 ff.) and fills it with violence (Gen. 3:16). Conflict arises between human and non-human creation, and also among human beings themselves (Gen. 9:1-7).

vii) God does not abandon his creation even in its conflicts. The prophets and the psalmist testify that He bestows justice *(sedaqa)* especially on the poor, the weak and the oppressed—whether human or non-human. He creates justice on the basis of faith, the personal covenantal relation with him. Through human beings He allows justice to be shared by his non-human creation. This obligates humanity to solidarity in conflict.

viii) God entrusts the land to his covenant people, as a loan. This land is not their possession; even strangers have a right to live there. Every seven years the land, too, is to rest (re-creation) (Gen. 23:10) and then every fifty years be redistributed and equally shared out (Lev. 25). This is a reminder that the earth is not humanity's property and that we are only tenants of it as God's guests.

ix) In Jesus Christ God renews his covenant with the whole of creation. In becoming human, God comes down to the lowly and makes use of his power for healing and salvation. Since He becomes incarnate not only in the spirit but also in the body of a historical human being, He allows the material world also to share in his saving work. The bodily resurrection of Jesus Christ opens up for the whole of creation the possibility of new life out of death. In contrast to all dualistic or spiritualistic pictures of hope, humanity and the non-human creation thus remain intimately bound together in an open-ended history: the promise of fulfilment applies to the whole creation. However, the Risen Lord remains the crucified One, and the whole creation continues to suffer (Rom. 8).

x) But the common suffering of humanity and world is, according to Paul, a sign of hope because it is an expression of the clash between the unsaved world and the salvation of God. It shows that the spirit of the Risen One is already at work in the world. Once again—as with the *dominium*—human beings have here a duty towards the non-human creation: human beings who bear God's Spirit are the sign of the great promise of freedom for all creation (Rom. 8). They have a duty to alleviate the suffering in creation and so to be signs of the coming Kingdom of God.

xi) In the eucharistic meal of the Church, many of these strands come together. Here, in the bread and wine—elements of the non-human creation which have been fashioned by human labour—God meets us as servant. The "parable of sharing" here becomes reality: each equally receives the bread and wine. There is no waste of resources: each receives no more than necessary and the elements are handled with care.

xii) Thus in the eucharistic meal, human beings and things are set free to serve one another. At the same time, the eucharistic view of the world shows that our Christian hope for human beings and the non-human creation is not unfounded. These are foretastes of the coming kingdom of freedom.

All these biblical concepts show *(a)* that society (human relations) and ecosystems (non-human creation as humanity's home) are intimately interconnected and may not be separated, and *(b)* that the justice and the sustainability of creation are also interconnected. Justice always means concern for the oppressed, the exploited and the weak, whether these be human beings or the earth.

3. GOD, HUMANITY AND CREATION:
THE BIBLICAL TESTIMONY IN THE CONTEXT
OF THE SCIENTIFIC AND TECHNOLOGICAL WORLD

The testimony of the Bible (see above) must be related to the thought and situation of our scientific and technological world. It must be interpreted in terms of the problems and modes of thought of this world so as to help transform the world.

Structures and elements of a language must be sought for this purpose—a language in which scientific and theological thought can communicate and so become dialogue partners in the struggle for a just, participatory and sustainable society. It is important to recognize here that faith and science both depend on metaphorical and symbolic linguistic elements. Science and technology, no longer sustained by an optimistic belief in progress, need especially symbols of meaning and hope which set their programmes within a horizon which provides both meaning and direction.

As Christians we speak of humanity and nature in the context of the work of God as Creator and his goal for his creation. By the term "creation" we mean the entire universe in its relationship to God. It includes therefore both humanity and nature and the disciplines which study them, whether the natural or social sciences or the humanities. God remains free in relation to his creation. In his faithfulness He grants it continuity and permanence. He is always at work in creation, enters it in Jesus Christ, and purposes to complete and perfect his communion with it. This cannot be deduced from a scientific view of nature but only from our knowledge of God in the history of Israel and through Jesus Christ. But it gives the work of science and technology a basis, meaning and direction.

The cultural context has radically changed since biblical times. In the biblical period humanity was confronted with an overpowering nature. The command to rule the animals and to subdue the earth delivered people from fear and from the temptation to divinize or demonize nature, and encouraged them to overcome suffering and to build culture. The power relations have since been reversed by science and technology. A desacralized nature is in the power of humanity which is now able to destroy its own species and perhaps even all life on the earth. Our own technological inventions and our social process are threatening to get the upper hand and to become as overpowering as nature once was. What needs to be emphasized today, therefore, is the *relatedness* between God and his creation rather than their *separateness*. The dignity of nature as creation needs to be stressed and humanity's *dominium* must be bound up with our responsibility for the preservation of life.

Humanity is part of nature yet at the same time transcends it. We intervene in nature, bear responsibility for it, restore it. But we must never forget that this transcendence is itself rooted in nature and that in the exercise of it humanity remains part of nature. This is shown today by the human sciences. Their scientific view can be assimilated by the biblical concepts of the *imago dei* and the *dominium*.

The biblical concept of *dominium* is developed today in various ways. Two such ways can be distinguished: humanity as the maker *(homo faber)* and humanity as the cultivator.

i) Men and women are makers in that they use nature as raw material and as instrument. This conception accords with the role of humanity in traditional science and technology.

ii) Men and women are cultivators in that they preserve and develop the life of the earth. In this view, instead of confronting nature humans share as partners in its life and accept responsibility for the sustainability of the total system. This conception has an affinity with certain biological conceptions that view evolution primarily as a process which brought forth humanity.

What we need is a view which integrates these two approaches, sets a limit to the maker and opens the way for creative imagination, a view in which the reshaping of nature is embedded in cooperation with nature. Such creative and cooperative relationship with nature can be a parable of God's own activity as Creator. This, too, is included in the *imago dei*.

The need to protect and preserve nature should not make us forget that according to the biblical witness, nature must be reshaped by humanity and adapted to human needs. In this respect, the situation of the rich countries of the earth is completely different from that of the poor countries. In the rich countries nature has been so thoroughly reshaped that humanity lives in an artificial world, whereas in the poor countries it has not yet been sufficiently adapted to human need and there is still much work to be done (although not necessarily in the pattern of the rich countries).

As God's creature, humanity is above all a receiver. In modern times, to the detriment of all creation, this dimension of our relation to God and nature has been hidden by the one-sided emphasis on *homo faber*. To counter this, it must be emphasized that, even in making and cultivating, humanity is a receiver. This emphasis relativizes the importance attached to "making" for the fulfilment of human life. If taken seriously it would enable the production process to be organized in a more human way and the exploitation of nature to be diminished. The institution of the sabbath for humanity and the sabbath year for the earth points in this direction. We are constantly reminded of the dimension of receiving by festival, celebration, worship and art.

The *imago dei* and the *dominium* are the birth-right of all human beings. The knowledge and cultivation of nature and the enjoyment of the fruits of this labour must therefore be shared by all. Therefore both science and theology must be public and critical, and the establishment of priorities in scientific research and technological development must be subject to democratic control. The increasing specialism, secrecy and mystification of science and technology are an aspect of sin, which instinctively seeks to hide itself and avoid discovery. These abuses are present in theology as well.

If participation is to be a reality, the people affected by the negative consequences of science and technology (e.g. the victims of the existing economic system and the transfer of inappropriate technologies; peoples and cultures threatened with extinction; the victims of inappropriate medical techniques) must be consulted, heeded and involved. Since nature cannot speak for itself, we human beings must make ourselves its advocates and defend its right to live.

This implies a willingness on our part to be alert to and share suffering in order to alleviate it. The cross of Jesus Christ points to the way of participation and the creative transformation of suffering. This is one aspect of following the cross in our scientific and technical world.

The Christian hope sets science and technology in the open-ended process of God's history with his creation. In this way it seeks to save us from the temptation rooted in either fear or titanism, to plan and determine the future exclusively on the basis of the present. This would make us prisoners of our existing structures and—biblically speaking—anxious about the future.

From the perspective of the Christian hope for the consummation of the whole creation, science and technology should contribute to the human responsibility to preserve life and keep the future open. Those who look for this hope must not pervert it by exploiting the future to the advantage of the present. In the light of our hope, therefore, the concept of justice must be extended and applied to actions which affect future generations.

The Christian hope enables us to accept the boundaries within which humanity and nature live. Within these limits we are called to strive for growth in humaneness in sanctification, and in the quality of the common life with one another and with nature. This includes readiness to make sacrifices. Economic growth, to which there are limits, has to be regulated by this different type of growth. Justice, participation and ecological responsibility thus constitute an indissoluble unity:

Justice is indivisible: it embraces those who suffer today and those still to be born, as well as the non-human creation. Although our priority today is the defence of those who suffer now, this does not mean that we can reject our responsibility for the earth that is our common home. The life of both humanity and nature is jeopardized by the same basic attitude of oppressive exploitation.

But the converse is also true:

In the long run, only a just society can be a sustainable society. Efforts to preserve the ecosystem for the rich and the powerful at the expense of the poor and weak may cause the oppressed to resort to revolutionary means to bring about change. Violence and wars could annihilate our civilization far more quickly than any process of ecological destruction.

But justice and sustainability will only be achieved by *participation*. If restrictions on consumption and changes in life-style are imposed from above, the response may be evasion, a nihilistic attitude towards the future and an erosion of responsibility. The only answer is to develop participatory structures, capacities and motivations. In this the Christian Church must help show the way.

4. THE CHRISTIAN UNDERSTANDING OF GOD, HUMANITY AND NATURE IN RELATION TO NEIGHBOURS OF OTHER FAITHS

In the struggle for a just, participatory and sustainable society, we Christians should express our solidarity with human beings of other traditions. One way to do this is by sharing freely with them in discussion on humanity, nature and God. Thinking on these subjects reflects many influences, such as history, culture, economics and politics, and particularly religious faith. It is especially important for Christians to understand their neighbours and fellow workers as persons of faith.

Understanding our neighbours as persons of other faiths can help us to deepen and extend our own. It is out of our own faith that we turn to them for the sake of sharing with them and learning from them. We learn from them, not in order to substitute their ideas for the Christian faith, but so that our sharing can lead to mutual criticism and enrichment.

As Christians we realize that our encounter with the Bible, and the theology resulting therefrom, always occur in an interpreting cultural context. This interpreting context does not have to be that of the Occident, which is often remote from that of the Bible itself. The encounter with other religions sharpens our awareness that the dominant occidental view of the relationship of humanity, nature and God is not the only viable one. Some of the views of other religions may prove both closer to the Bible and more appropriate to the intellectual and social needs of our time. This means that learning from neighbours of other faiths can lead to a valuable enrichment of our understanding of the Bible and to a fruitful reformulation of our theology.

Among the achievements of some of our neighbours of other faiths to which we should attend are the following: a deep piety and obedience to a merciful God who is close to the faithful; the awareness of the interconnectedness of all things, the emphasis on the transient character of all existence, stressing continuities instead of discontinuities and eventuating in serenity, calmness and acceptance of suffering as part of life; the spirit of non-attachment, the ability to find oneself by letting go of material possessions; acting according to the principle of causing least harm and disturbance to all creation.

Though all these may be found in our Christian tradition, we do not gain credibility by asserting in a triumphalistic manner that we ourselves already possess everything. We can only be credible witnesses to our faith if we are on the "way" (Acts 18:24 ff.) towards God's future. If we listen, other religions may remind us of our blind spots and of insights we may have lost on our journey. We need this help in our efforts properly to understand humanity, nature and God in our shared struggle for a just, participatory and sustainable society.

We stand ready to witness to Christ to all of our neighbours of other faiths. This means that we would critically evaluate their achievements and limitations in the light of Christ and witness to the truth and salvation we find in him.

5. RECOMMENDATIONS

1. Further exploration of the relationship between humanity, nature and God

Within our section and in the conference generally the dialogue between theologians, scientists and social scientists has been carried a stage further. The discussions have revealed that the crisis of science and technology of the industrial nations stems from the present confusion about the right relationship between humanity, nature and God. The discussions also reveal that we are not yet in agreement about the proper relationship. We recommend that the WCC ensure that the debate continues, and urge a particular focus on the following questions:

How to ground and explain theologically the relationship between humanity, nature and God in the dialogue with contemporary science.

How to interpret the biblical mandate for humanity, with regard to a responsible dominion over the earth. Today this means worldwide ecological responsibility and stewardship in the face of the blatant misuse and exploitation of the world, its people and its resources.

How to express this responsibility through science and technology; the problem of developing ethical reflections in the different scientific disciplines; and the critique of the hidden ethos that technology expresses.

2. Dialogue with other faiths

The discussions of the conference and the sections have led to an encounter with the thinking of many religions, cultures and ideologies. We are grateful for this encounter and ask that the views of other faiths and ideologies be included in future conferences of this kind. We recommend that the WCC introduce the issues posed by science and technology into the work of its programme on Dialogue with People of Living Faiths and Ideologies (DFI). Today people of all religions are challenged by the desire for a just, participatory and sustainable society. We recommend that the DFI programme seek the contributions of different cultures and religions, in search for a cooperative approach to a just, participatory and sustainable society.

3. The Christian hope and the scientific understanding of the future

The papers and discussions of the conference have revealed that the future of our scientifically and technologically organized world is deeply threatened. What has the Christian message of hope to say about the future? This question was repeatedly asked at the conference but no single answer prevailed. We recommend that the Commission on Faith and Order, in cooperation with Church and Society, explore the meaning of Christian eschatology in relation to the human future of promise and threat arising from the rapid and seemingly uncontrollable developments in science and technology.

4. Relations with all creation

We call on the churches to re-examine their worship and liturgies to see whether these *(a)* sufficiently encourage respectful attention to the other creatures with which we human beings share the world, and *(b)* express repentence for the destructive consequences of our actions.

We call on the churches to rethink their ethics regarding creation in order that their teachings may reflect more fully our solidarity with all living creatures, as well as our special authority and responsibility for nature. We call for consideration of simpler styles of life and less violent relations both with other human beings and with all creatures.

We call on the churches in all countries to examine these issues of global justice and sustainability from the perspective of their own cultural, religious and socio-political setting.

5. Dialogue in churches and parishes

We recommend that the dialogue between science and technology at the level of the parish communities be strengthened; that the WCC initiate investigations into if, and how, the faith/science issue is considered by ordinary church people. There is also a need to examine how this issue is dealt with in popular literature, mass media and ideological propaganda. The parish communities should strive both theoretically and practically to understand science and technology in the light of Christian faith. They should be encouraged to take Christian responsibility for science and technology within their respective political and cultural context:

i)   We appeal to the member churches of the WCC to promote study and action on these problems by *(a)* encouraging scientists and technologists to consider the ethical implications of their work, and *(b)* training pastors to give theological and administrative leadership to their congregations in understanding these problems and implementing study and action on them.

ii)   There is need for a series of theological papers *(a)* to make theology understandable in scientific circles; and *(b)* to correct the superficial accounts of the enmity between science and faith which influences textbooks and popular understanding in many countries, and to display the more profound relations that actually exist between them.

III. Science and Education

1. SCIENCE EDUCATION AND ETHICS

The "industrialization of science"—to echo Prof. Brown's phrase—has radically changed its character. Since the Second World War, when powerful industrial nations pitted their entire military, industrial, technological and scientific resources against one another in a struggle to the death, governments have realized the huge power that science can give them. The multinational corporations, too, in their relentless pursuit of profit and growth, have harnessed science to their ends. It may always have been excessively idealistic to see science, in the words of the Book of Wisdom, as having "a spirit intelligent and holy, unique in its kind yet made up of many parts—subtle, free-moving, lucid, spotless, clear, invulnerable, loving what is good, eager, unhindered, beneficent, kindly towards men, steadfast, unerring, untouched by care, all-powerful, all-surveying, and permeating all intelligent, pure and delicate spirits", but the last few decades have moved it still further from the ivory tower to which the biblical writer consigned wisdom.

The "industrialization of science" means that the goals and directions of research are set largely by governments and industries, often with scant regard for the good of society as a whole. If they do not see this, scientists may in effect be allying themselves with oppression.

Even fundamental science is not, and never was, wholly objective, for even the most disinterested seeker after truth makes largely subjective decisions about which experiments he or she will perform. On the other hand, the element of objectivity is never wholly absent even in the most applied science. Science by its very nature imposes an obligation of an essentially ethical nature to accept the results of an experiment, however unwelcome or inconvenient these may be. There is thus a limit to the degree to which science may be prostituted, a limit beyond which it simply ceases to be science. A scientist commissioned by an industrial company to show that the pollution caused by the company's operations is harmless is obliged by this ethic of objectivity to present an honest report, even at the cost of his or her job. He or she may of course not do so, but this is to say only that individual scientists may fall short of the ethic, not that the ethic does not exist.

The obligation to be honest and objective is not of course confined to scientists, but the nature of science imposes this obligation upon the scientist in a very special way. The ethic is undeniably weakened by certain kinds of applied or "commissioned" science: it is at least plausible that some of the "scientific" tests carried out on certain consumer items are of highly dubious objectivity, and nobody seems to mind much. But deliberate falsification of results in fundamental science (as, for example, in the notorious "Piltdown Man" fraud) is still regarded with extreme seriousness. Our reaction is more than the ordinary reaction to dishonesty. A sacred trust has been broken. The ethic of truth, honesty and objectivity, however tarnished it may be by exposure to the air of the marketplace, does survive, and no scientific education is complete that does not imbue students with a strong sense of its importance.

A further ethical aspect of science arises from the way in which it changes and deepens our perceptions of the created universe. The humane scientist of today can surely find a depth of meaning in the verse from Psalm 139 that the psalmist could never have imagined. "I will praise thee; for I am fearfully and wonderfully made; marvellous are thy works; and that my soul knoweth right well." The science teacher who is a Christian can help to communicate some of that meaning and reverence for the creation.

So much for the way in which science creates and influences ethical attitudes. Turning now to the way in which ethical attitudes influence how scientists work, we consider first the *methods* of science. There are certainly ethical limits to the methods a scientist may use in discovering results—the experiments conducted on human subjects in the death camps of Nazi Germany are an obvious example—but at a less extreme level there are areas of disagreement about which all scientists and students of science should be aware. Experiments on animals are a common subject of controversy, and here we cannot separate our assessment of the morality of the methods from the purpose of the experiment. It is easier to justify pain-giving experiments on living animals to test new drugs or surgical procedures than new face powders or shampoos. Even in trying out justifiable surgical procedures and new drugs, the pernicious practice of using the people of the poorer nations as guinea pigs must be severely condemned.

The *uses* of science give rise to obvious ethical dilemmas. Many scientists do refrain on ethical grounds from researching into poison gas, biological warfare, or nuclear weapons; and some scientists have similar qualms about defence research in general, or about nuclear power. But this is an individual response rather than one by the scientific community as a whole: scientists are found in all these activities. The moral unease felt by scientists and non-scientists alike is revealed by the use of euphemisms: military research is called "defence" research, however offensive its goals may be.

This moral unease indicates that it is not sufficient to ask simply whether or not we approve of the *uses* of science and technology. The decision to ask a particular question in research or to design a particular artifact implies prior choices about social goals. We do certain types of research because we want to make better steel or because we want to cure cancer. The choice of these goals necessarily implies that certain other options are thereby foreclosed. The same applies to engineering: Why build this particular machine and not another? Scientists cannot simply pass judgment on the practical effects of science and technology, since these effects are determined in part by the way that research priorities are set. Whether they are aware of it or not, scientists are part of the process from the very beginning.

The ethical questions raised by fundamental science are a good deal less obvious. The scientist researching on nuclear bombs quite clearly does bear a major share of the moral responsibility if the bombs are used. But can the great pure scientists of the twentieth century be held to have a special share in the moral responsibility for Hiroshima and Nagasaki? We cannot give an unqualified answer. The uses of science are to a large extent ultimately unpredictable, though the lesson of recent history is that if a scientific discovery can be used for military purposes, it will be. On the other hand, science has good uses also: if controlled fusion turns out to be the answer to our energy needs in centuries to come, then that, to precisely the same extent as the hydrogen bomb, can be laid at the door of the scientists who unlocked the secrets of the atom.

Scientists in most countries are organized in associations which have traditionally tried to avoid overt political involvement. Yet, as we have seen, their results are often used for political ends, ends which the scientists themselves often find inimical. For this reason, scientists cannot evade the political responsibility which comes with their work. As a community they must ensure that the options for fundamental research and for the uses of scientific knowledge are taken in the light of the desire for a just, participatory and sustainable society. For this purpose they have to play a key role in informing all members of society about what is at stake in the scientific and technological options which are offered to it. For scientists, to act as an organized community is a must. The isolated decisions of individual scientists confronted with problems about the directions and uses of their scientific research may indeed be praiseworthy, but they do not solve the problem of the fundamental options. For these, the decisions to be taken are essentially of a collective nature.

The Christian community should find ways of helping scientists who depend on governments and industries for support to organize themselves within their own institutions so that an open debate about the dilemmas of science and technology can take place and policies can be revised.

Our section reached the consensus that science ought to be concerned with human values. By this, we generally mean that the expenditures of human and material resources that we make on scientific work have to be justified morally and that the opportunities for practical benefits which technology affords should not be wasted. Participants from the Third World made two important points:

i)   there is a need to connect science and science-based technology to specific and often fairly concrete social goals;

ii) there is a need for greater participation by the community at large in choosing the goals and in determining how a particular technology will be used to meet them.

The ethic of science directs the scientist to report the results of his or her experiment as objectively as possible, no matter what the paymaster might prefer to hear. But the scientist is also under obligation to ask whether or not he or she has done the right experiments, that is, whether or not the goals set by government or industry really coincide with the needs of the community. It is impossible for a scientist to be dissociated from political and economic interests. He or she is therefore responsible for trying to see that research is channelled in constructive directions. This requires a constantly critical and reflective attitude towards the paymasters.

Science and technology have helped to build a civilization that has achieved marvels of construction never before seen in the history of the world, but also of a greed and rapacity equally unprecedented. The snake is eating its own tail, and at an ever-increasing rate. It cannot continue.

It is futile to debate whether science and technology *in the abstract* are good, evil, or morally neutral. The only way to ask fruitful moral questions about technology is to consider particular technologies in their particular social contexts.

Students of science and engineering should certainly be aware of these ethical and social issues. But how should this awareness be imparted? It seems that if medical students are taught ethics in relation to their future profession and economic students are made aware of ethical aspects of their subject, then science students should consider the ethics of science. The goal of ethical teaching is to awaken critical reflection upon oneself and one's community. Although formal courses in ethics may be a necessary part of the effort, there is also a need for students to see working scientists publicly engaged in moral reflection, questioning established ways of doing things. Students themselves should be encouraged to enter the debate on social issues. This carries the implication that the curriculum should not be so heavily loaded as to make it impossible for students to engage in such reflections.

It is not possible to separate the question of education in "science ethics" from education in religious and moral values that must take place in all areas of social life. The extent to which this aspect of education has a specifically Christian content must depend upon the nature of the school and of the society within which it is operating. Christian education should in any event not be such as to alienate the Christian community from the rest of society. It should seek to reconcile, not to divide. In all societies, both individual Christians and the Church have the clear duty to make their message, both spiritual and moral, known among the people. In carrying out this duty, they should call upon all the resources of modern education, including the scientific understanding of moral development in children.

Science education, with its discipline, its mental challenge, and its insistence on honesty and objectivity, has great value in its own right. On the other hand, in our task as educators we must insist that science and technology, powerful though they may be, cannot define what it means to be fully human. Science and technology "with a human face" will seek to serve the good of humanity which, at least for the Christian, has been disclosed in Jesus Christ. Church-related colleges, in countries where these exist, have a particularly important role to play in this field.

2. SCIENCE EDUCATION AND THE THIRD WORLD

The present pattern of education in the Third World, especially education in science and technology, is open to severe criticism. Reports from third world representatives indicate that all too often the result of education is to create an alienated social and intellectual elite. While there can be advantages for students to undertake post-graduate study in a developed country, there is a danger that such students may adopt the values and customs of the countries where they have studied and feel estranged from their own people. Even if their entire education has been in their home country, the education system there is copied, for want of any better model, from that of the former colonial power, a model designed to serve a society at a totally different stage of development. Often, the only way in which a highly trained third world scientist can put his or her training to use is to emigrate. This pattern is, moreover, not confined to countries formerly in a colonial relationship. It applies also, for example, to developed Latin American countries and their relationship with the USA.

In some countries the situation is compounded by the fact that this educated elite comes almost exclusively from one race, sex, region, tribe or religion. This creates immense potential for conflict and can perpetuate a form of internal colonialism no more acceptable to the majority of the people than the external colonialism from which the country escaped.

The salient characteristics of an elite are social power, prestige and privilege, not simply expertise. The modern educational process, particularly science education, necessarily creates a category of people who retain part of the power in society because of their access to scientific knowledge. The question for these people, both as individuals and as a group, is to decide for whose benefit and for what purposes they will use the power they have. In many developing countries, for example, elites face at least two possible choices. They may link themselves with the aspirations of the suffering majority for self-determination and for controlled development, or they may act destructively by serving as a channel for alien cultural values and foreign domination. Some of us would argue that an intellectual elite will inevitably arise in every society. In any case, such an elite will be caught up in the tension between defence of its privileges and commitment to service. Scientists who are Christians and who are members of elites in their own societies need to pay particular attention to the guidance of the Christian faith: "Everyone to whom much is given, of him will much be required" (Luke 12:48).

Even in medical education, where the differing needs of societies are at their most obvious, there is a strong tendency for the western model to be followed. It is essential and urgent that medical education in the Third World should concentrate heavily on community health and preventive medicine, at the expense of more scientifically prestigious areas of medical research.

In many countries of the Third World, education is conducted in the colonial language. Where a single indigenous language exists, its use opens education to more people, but in many countries the colonial language remains the only practicable and acceptable medium for inter-regional educated discourse. In the higher reaches of scientific and technical education, there is the further difficulty that specialist textbooks are available only in European languages, the American/British market in English language books being especially dominant. Partly by their language, but even more by their content and emphasis, these books impose an inappropriate type of education on the developing nations.

The countries of the Third World must develop a style and goals drawn from their own needs for scientific and technological education. To a large extent they must do this on their own. The task will not be easy: it will require great imagination and effort on the part of all the people, and may take many years. It should take as one of its starting points the society's own indigenous technology. To quote Dr Odhiambo's plenary address: "The industrial world has profoundly influenced the advance of Africa primarily because the Africans themselves have not succeeded in countering this pattern of development with an alternative model of progress rooted in their own traditions." Special effort will be required to harness the expertise of those returning from post-graduate study abroad. The task will be not only to provide material incentives but also to inculcate a commitment to the society which will provide increased motivation for service.

3. SCIENCE EDUCATION AND NON-SCIENTISTS

The alienation from science and technology felt by many people is due at least in part to a huge failure by the experts to communicate with even the educated and literate section of the public. If decisions about investment in science and technology, which ultimately affect the whole community, are to be taken in a truly participatory way, then a well-informed public is essential. The secondary schools have a crucial role here, but since science changes so rapidly, the task cannot be theirs alone. Each nation in its own situation must take appropriate action to ensure the continuing lifelong education in "scientific literacy" of its adult population, not least of its clergy and theologians.

One important component of "scientific literacy" is an understanding by both scientists and others of the limitations of science. Statements beginning, "Science has proved", or "It has been shown scientifically" can be properly and critically judged only by a well-educated public.

In many countries television can play a crucial role. Its power as an instrument of public education has been amply demonstrated—for example an elementary education programme in the Manaus area of Brazil and the successful "Open University" experiment in Great Britain. At a less overtly educational level, it has been found in several East and West European countries that public taste can be educated to accept programmes of a high intellectual content. This being so, it is little short of tragic that so much television in, for example, Latin America consists of the alien, the trivial, the violent and the foolish. A triumph of technology with immense power for good is being squandered with mindless prodigality, or being used to deceive and control.

The kind of information disseminated to the public must of course be relevant to their concerns. A poor woman in Latin America may feel that information on nuclear bombs is remote from her life—let us pray that it remains so!—but a radio or television programme emphasizing the importance of tests for uterine cancer is clearly much closer to her concerns. Still on the theme of preventive medicine, but at a more general level, advice on hygiene, if effectively disseminated, can do much to control the spread of infectious disease.

There are of course countries whose resources cannot extend to television. In this situation the less powerful medium of radio can and must serve as an instrument of education of the people on all matters affecting public welfare, including science and technology. The role of radio is especially important in countries where a significant proportion of the population is illiterate.

Scientists need training and experience in the use of both radio and television if they are to be effective in contributing to a programme of public education. They must invest time and effort in improving their communication skills. Talking to a mass audience about science is exceedingly difficult, but the effort will be immensely worthwhile if it achieves simultaneously greater understanding of science and scientists among the public, and greater humility and humanity among scientists.

This programme cannot possibly be carried through without a high degree of participation in the control and administration of broadcasting. A government monopoly, deciding unilaterally what the people may know, is unacceptable, as is the control of radio and television by purely commercial interests.

It would be wrong to suggest that the broadcasting media provide the only way of educating the public in scientific matters. Much can be done at local levels through events such as "science fairs" and through the activities of teachers and other professional organizations.

4. SCIENCE EDUCATION AND SOCIETY

As has been said before, science education should become more conscious of and responsive to its social context than has traditionally been the case. A knowledge of the history and growth of scientific ideas can help to achieve this, as can an appreciation of the attitudes and concerns of the community as a whole. There is, for example, little point in developing a new grain crop with a high yield if the people for whom it is developed do not like the taste.

When engineers or scientists leave the classroom and laboratory, they must learn to work with people who are not technically skilled. Too often their training does not prepare them for this reality. Somehow, by means that would be hard to specify on an international basis, given the huge variety of styles and patterns of higher education, this training must be humanized and made more applicable to the realities they will face when they enter employment.

One valuable way of preparing students for life is to involve them in decision-making within the university or college. This happens to varying extents in different countries and, if wisely structured, is found beneficial both to the students and to the institutions.

The matter of public participation in decision-making has already been mentioned. Scientists should certainly be involved in decisions about public policy and expenditure on science, but the decisions cannot be theirs alone. Governments must endeavour to involve as many members as possible of a well-informed public in all important decisions in this field. In their relations with governments, scientists have a duty to encourage morally acceptable uses of science.

If a dictatorial government does not involve the public in decision-making and harnesses science to its own evil ends, many Christians would recognize revolution as the only solution.

5. SCIENCE EDUCATION AND RESEARCH

In science generally, but perhaps especially in the physical sciences, undergraduate students have so much "doctrine" to learn that the spirit of scientific investigation can all too easily be wholly absent from their training. Theory must be learned, and even laboratory sessions are a matter of acquiring standard laboratory skills. The "right" results must be obtained or the experiment must be repeated. The training has some value and does emphasize the importance of discipline in scientific work, but it is far removed from the open-ended questions of real scientific research.

The growth of scientific knowledge, unaccompanied by any increase in the length of the standard undergraduate course, puts still more pressure on the curriculum and makes it even harder to avoid over-formal training. For this reason, it is crucially important that the curriculum be continually subjected to examination and revision. There must be time, even at the undergraduate level, to introduce an element of open-ended investigation and of practical application. Students must be allowed and encouraged to take the initiative to learn on their own.

This approach carries the corollary that university teachers should devote time, thought and effort to the challenges of teaching. The "publish or perish" syndrome, whereby status and promotion prospects are determined largely, if not solely, by research output, does not exactly encourage this attitude. Responsible university teachers must, however, try to manage both research and teaching, however difficult this may be. The research, moreover, should be motivated by a desire to extend knowledge in a way relevant to society's needs and not merely to enhance the teacher's reputation.

"Good teachers", it is sometimes said, "are born, not made." While it is true that good teaching comes naturally to some and not at all to others, most of us are capable of improving our teaching with training and experience. Differing views were expressed on the degree to which there should be formal training of university teachers in teaching and assessment, but there was unqualified approval of the greater awareness in recent years of this important aspect of a university teacher's work. Student assessment of teachers by means of anonymous questionnaires was seen as a valuable way of increasing teachers' awareness of the reaction to their teaching and of encouraging self-criticism and self-improvement.

The opinion was expressed that the research activity of university teachers adversely affects the quality and emphasis of their teaching and imposes upon third world countries an over-specialized and inappropriate style of higher education. The majority opinion was, however, that participation in research imparts an awareness, freshness and open-endedness to teaching that cannot be achieved in any other way. By virtue of the courage and sacrifice involved in pursuing research, teachers can present their subject with authority. But at the same time, the doubts and uncertainties involved in research mean that an actively researching teacher can present a subject in an open-ended, participatory way. Authority without authoritarianism—surely an ideal to strive after.

6. RECOMMENDATIONS

To Christians who are teachers of science
i)   The teaching of science should reflect not only the ethical considerations intrinsic to science itself, but also the ethical aspects of the relationship of science to society.
ii)   The education of scientists should include discussions on ethical aspects of science, its methods and its uses.

To Christians who are scientists
iii) While basic research should certainly not be ignored, scientists who depend upon governments and industries for support must learn to ask whether or not the goals set by these institutions will serve the needs of the society as a whole.

To the WCC and its member churches
    We ask you to press the appropriate agencies to the following ends:

iv) The pernicious practice of testing pharmaceutical and other products on poor people in developing countries should be stopped forthwith.

v) In the developing countries science education, instead of following the western model, must find its own goals, appropriate to the needs of the society it serves.

vi) In order to achieve a high degree of public participation in decision-making, a major effort should be made to improve public understanding of scientific and technological matters. In particular, people should know about the limitations of science.

vii) Churches should take the initiative to provide opportunities for scientists, theologians and ethicists to study and discuss the relation of science and faith and the insights theology and ethics bring to the decisions scientists must make.

viii) We recommend that the WCC continue to explore and clarify areas of disagreement on experimental methods which are applied to gain new scientific insights.

ix) We urge the Christian community to find ways of helping scientists who depend on government and industries for support to organize themselves within their institutions so that an open debate about the dilemmas of science and technology can take place.

x) We call on the churches to exert their influence on curriculum planners to ensure that an adequate number of courses on the ethical implications of science and technology are included in the curriculum of each science and engineering student.

xi) We commend the WCC's involvement in health care issues particularly in the Third World and recommend that the Christian Medical Commission explore the ways in which its emphasis on community health care could have a greater bearing on the curricula of all medical educational facilities.

xii) We recommend that the WCC give more attention to appropriate forms of adult education in relation to 'science and technology. We recommend in particular that its Programme on Theological Education give attention to the need to incorporate at least minimal requirements regarding scientific and technological knowledge in the curricula of all clergy and theologians.

IV. Ethical Issues in the Biological Manipulation of Life

Recent advances in eugenics, genetic engineering, behaviour control and the problem of scarce medical resources raise urgent and new issues which command the attention of the Christian conscience.

In considering certain biological, genetic and medical manipulations of human beings, and also theories of the biological and genetic components of human nature, we must keep sharply in mind the tragic consequences suffered by many peoples as a result of past eugenic theories and practices. These have all too often been used by groups in power against exploited or disenfranchised minorities. We note the use of false biological theories to justify slavery in the United States, and the passing of eugenic laws in the US, Japan and Germany permitting or encouraging the sterilization of certain underprivileged groups of people, who were labelled "feeble-minded" or "degenerate". We must never forget that the massacres in the Nazi concentration camps evolved from an explicit eugenics policy of removing "inferior genes" from the Aryan population. Further development of human genetic analysis will not in itself prevent such misuses; the closest scrutiny of the social and economic conditions of its application will be continuously required to ensure that such technologies contribute to a just and participatory society.

1. EUGENICS

In the discussion of genetic counselling, prenatal diagnosis and abortion, as well as of artificial insemination by donors, the findings of the World Council of Churches' Church and Society report on *Genetics and the Quality of Life* (1975) provide certain important points of reference.

We realize that these topics are of immediate and practical concern in certain developed countries especially, but increasingly they must be viewed in a world perspective.

As Christians we believe that we are both creatures of God and co-creators with him in fulfilling the image He has given us. This belief informs our high estimate of human worth. We are also guided by the words of Jesus: "Inasmuch as you do it unto one of the least of these, you do it unto me..." (Matt. 25:40), which requires sensitivity to the life of each human being. This emphasis is a distinctive teaching of Christian ethics and it has universal validity.

Genetic counselling, prenatal diagnosis and abortion

The counselling of prospective parents and the diagnosis of the fetus *in utero* are intended to enhance the satisfaction of parenthood by assuring a genetically healthy child or early warning of one having certain defects. Due to the issues involved in such counselling, the question of abortion is often raised, and the parties involved are urged to consider a variety of criteria in making their decision (*Genetics and the Quality of Life*, p. 207). Their thinking is also influenced by concepts and words, currently and uncritically used in everyday speech, which tend towards a facile resolution of the abortion question.

We question the use of "meaningful life" as a criterion because of the uncertain definition of the phrase. It is clearly not of the same meaning as life of "value" and life of "dignity", which derive from God's creative act in the formation of each person. How can an undefined "meaningful life" be predicted for anyone? At the least we can say that, in Christian belief, a life is meaningful insofar as it permits the expression of faith, hope and love with the capacity to accept suffering. This expression may be in the life of the individual child in its effect upon others, or in both the child and others.

We strongly question the use of "cost-benefit" reckoning as a determining factor in the question of abortion of those diagnosed as abnormal. Wherever the resources and techniques of counselling and prenatal diagnosis are presently available, the economic implications of caring for affected children must not be decisive with regard to allowing them to be born.

It is very questionable whether prospective parents should be advised to consider the effects of a child's birth upon the total human gene pool, since the effect is marginal. Only in a very rigorous eugenic programme in which neither afflicted individuals nor carriers of the deleterious genes reproduce would there be any effect on the gene pool.

The distinguishing of "selective abortion" from other abortions is misleading for many people. It is better to avoid the adjective "selective" commonly used in reference to genetic problems, since it has been conveying the idea that abortion in such circumstances is always morally unobjectionable. Abortion for genetic defects requires decisions which are not exempt from the need to weigh the inherent value of life along with other personal, social and religious factors in every case.

Questions that need to be further explored are: the differences between abortion and infanticide, the ways in which the wider acceptance of abortion for genetic reasons may lead to other changes in the moral values of the community, how the churches in diverse societies can exercise a critical and constructive influence on the decisions that are made about abortion for genetic reasons, and the pastoral needs of Christians who seek abortion.

AFFIRMATIONS

i)   As humanizing communities in society, churches should lead in resisting any attempts to stigmatize parents having a genetically or other congenitally afflicted child. They should also support parents, who after careful consideration decide that it is in the interests of their family and society to induce the abortion of a defective fetus.

ii) Prospective parents who have access to prenatal diagnosis are entitled to have full information concerning its implications, including the possibility that they may have to face a decision on abortion.

iii) Counselling should always precede amniocentesis or other diagnostic methods and follow them when any problems are indicated.

iv) It is contrary to the integrity and freedom of the couple or woman involved to require an abortion should amniocentesis reveal abnormalities.

v)   Any compulsion by law or public pressure to have prenatal diagnosis is to be discouraged and opposed.

Artificial insemination

Discussion about artificial insemination by donors (AID) and embryo transfer with a donor egg for couples who are carriers of an inheritable deleterious condition involves a variety of issues.

The practice of artificial insemination of a woman with her husband's sperm is in a different category entirely. It is morally unobjectionable.

In deciding whether AID and donor egg transfer are morally acceptable, the churches need to explore together the Christian understanding of the nature and purpose of marriage, parenthood and the family. The one-flesh unity of marriage, the psychosomatic unity of human personality, and the blessing of children are all important considerations to be weighed.

The moral acceptability of these techniques is to be tested also by the criteria of the dignity and welfare of the whole person. In this regard a problem arises because of the separation of the donor's procreative powers from his personal responsibility for the life he has made possible, usually with monetary compensation.

Contraception permitting sexual union without the intent of procreation is now morally acceptable. However, many Christians believe that when new life is to be created, it should be by a loving couple in the personal intimacy of sexual union, for this is at once biologically normal and consistent with Christian morality. Donor insemination and the use of a donor egg in embryo transfer are disapproved and rejected by these Christians because they remove the processes of reproduction from sexual union. It may well be feared that the use of such techniques would lead further to the depersonalizing and dehumanizing of life. Some hold that faithfulness in the marital bond and the love and care of children rather than a biological contribution is of greatest importance in fatherhood. Hence, in the belief that children are a blessing enriching the couple's life, they accept AID as a legitimate and compassionate solution to human need.

There are two important unresolved legal issues related to AID. First, in a number of countries the AID child's legitimacy is not certain. Where AID is permitted, legislative action may be needed to ensure that the AID child has full legal standing as a lawful child of the husband and wife consenting to its conception. It is needed further, because the donor's rights and obligations in matters of maintenance, custody and inheritance are also at issue. Secondly, semen cryobanking, which accompanies the increased use of AID, is often not governed by law or administrative regulation. Therefore, private frozen semen banks with attendant risks may and do exist. Legal regulation and meticulous record-keeping are needed to control the collection, processing and distribution of frozen semen.

Standards governing AID practice have yet to be established. For example, how are donors and recipients for AID selected? What types of counselling should be required: psychiatric, medical, economic? Even now, although pressed by responsible professional organizations and others in the medical profession, there is still little long-term follow-up study. More research is clearly needed.

The issue of donor insemination for single women, of interest under the broader heading of eugenics, though not related to AID for genetic defect, is also being debated. In the traditional Christian understanding children are a blessing for a married couple, and awareness of the importance of a father for a child suggests that such insemination may be unethical.

Donor insemination from "superior" people as advocated in positive eugenics is unacceptable for at least two reasons. First, no consensus could ever be obtained as to what are "superior" human qualities, and second, it would require the manipulative power of some experts and raise insoluble problems of who would control the controllers. Programmes of "positive eugenics" attempted earlier in this century have invariably caused trauma and tragedy for people of certain ethnic identities.

2. GENETIC ENGINEERING

Promises and risks of genetic engineering of plants and micro-organisms

Genetic engineering, otherwise known as recombinant DNA technology, is a direct manipulation of the genes and therefore a determinant of what life may be. This awareness that it is life that is at issue must always be kept in the forefront of our thinking, otherwise we can too easily drift into the attitude that we are merely manipulating bits of matter, the genes. Such an attitude can readily lead to one of genetic determinism. Life, especially human life, is more than genes.

Selective breeding of cultivated plants and domesticated animals to produce new varieties has long been practised and has been of great value for human beings. This is a form of genetic manipulation which is acceptable and valuable. Selective breeding of humans (positive eugenics) has from time to time been proposed, but for the most part it has been rigorously opposed as an improper manipulation of human life.

Genetic engineering is a new form of genetic manipulation. It is one of the most powerful tools of biological research ever developed. It enables us to have a much clearer understanding of the life processes of growth and development than was ever possible before. Secondly, it puts into our hands a powerful tool for the direct and rapid alteration of the genetic constitution of individual organisms. It can be used to make new strains of bacteria that produce chemical compounds such as insulin which are normally only synthesized in the animal cell. Plants which cannot get their nitrogen requirements from the atmosphere may in the future be enabled to do so by appropriate genetic engineering. Similarly the efficiency of photosynthesis may in future be increased by these procedures. The possibility is also opened up of extending conventional methods of plant breeding to confer disease resistance. All these procedures have obvious benefits for human life.

However, there are grave hazards associated with recombinant DNA technology. They are:

i)   the inadvertent production and escape of micro-organisms pathogenic to humans;

ii) the inadvertent production and escape of micro-organisms that could disrupt the ecosystem;

iii) the deliberate production of pathogenic micro-organisms for biological warfare or terrorism;

iv) the move, especially on the part of commercial enterprises, to transfer their operations on genetic engineering to countries that impose few or no guidelines for this technology; this forms a special threat to developing countries;

v)   genetic engineering on humans and other vertebrates in ways that are ethically unacceptable (see below).

It is a fact of life that genetic engineering of micro-organisms, plants and animals, including humans, is under way. It is moving at a pace which far exceeds the expectations of even a year ago. The public must be informed of all that is now going on and planned so that it can anticipate the hazards and the unethical uses of this new technology before it is too late. Unless this is done, we may be confronted with a genetic holocaust. There is urgent need now to distinguish what is ethically acceptable and what is ethically unacceptable so that where constraints on the new technology are needed they can be imposed in time. The matter is of such urgency that it requires a much deeper analysis than is possible in this report.

Ethical issues in the genetic engineering on humans and other vertebrates

There are three sorts of areas of investigation to consider:

i)   For example, the attempt to remove the blood creating bone marrow cell, from a human suffering from sickle cell anemia and to insert into those cells the DNA segment for normal hemoglobin is no different in principle from other forms of curative medicine. It presents no additional ethical problems.

ii) The introduction of a DNA segment into a fertilized ovum for the purpose of replacing a gene that causes sickle-cell anemia by a gene producing normal hemoglobin could in principle be done *in vitro*. The ovum could then be reimplanted in the womb. This would introduce a gene for normal hemoglobin into the genetic inheritance. The offspring would have genes for normal hemoglobin as would children of subsequent generations.

iii) The introduction of foreign DNA by means of viral infection of human beings which could also result in change in the genetic inheritance.

These last two cases in which the germ line could be altered raise new issues of grave concern in the genetic engineering of humans and other vertebrates. They are:

i) The alteration of the genetic constitution of human beings represents a qualitative change in the biological or medical manipulation of human life. An individual may give informed consent to a change in his own body as in body cell alteration (see above) and that change is not transmitted to subsequent generations. The individual cannot give informed consent to the genetic alteration of subsequent generations. Because of the wider implications, such decisions should be taken in a much broader social context. They cannot be just the products of contracts between scientist and subject.

ii) Human genetic engineering focuses attention on individuals and their genes. As a consequence, the agents that cause the damage in the first place—mutagens, carcinogens, radiation, the causes of blocked fallopian tubes that lead a woman to seek *in vitro* fertilization and so on—are overlooked. Most medical and social problems are not genetic. Our attention should rather be directed to creating a society in which our genes are protected from unnecessary damage and full scope is provided for the development of our existing capabilities.

iii) The procedures of *in vitro* fertilization, with or without genetic engineering, are at present enormously expensive. They use scarce medical resources and skills that benefit relatively few people. These resources and skills might be better used in the relief of illnesses that affect many people. The procedures draw attention and resources away from preventive medicine.

iv) There is no certainty as yet that in gene replacement only the "desired" gene is transplanted into the fertilized ovum. If other segments of DNA happen to be inserted into the ovum along with the "desired" gene, we cannot know in advance what the side effects might be. This can only be ascertained by experimentation, first on animals over several generations but eventually on human subjects. Someone has to be the first human experimental subject.

v) *In vitro* fertilization and genetic engineering of the fertilized ovum make possible experimentation on human beings for purposes other than correction of genetic defects. Some of these purposes may be worthy aims, for example the desire to find out if certain drugs taken by pregnant mothers cause deformities in the fetus. At present, the only way of identifying side effects is through experiments on animals and the administration of drugs to pregnant women. The further development of *in vitro* fertilization may eventually mean a testing of such drugs directly on the embryo. Experimentation on live human embryos raises many questions of critical concern, such as the following: What are the limits of experimentation on human embryos? Is it legitimate to raise an embryo and then destroy it if it is deformed? If a deformed child is born, who is responsible? Is it moral to donate ova? Is it moral to use the services of a surrogate mother?

vi) Because of the difficulty of obtaining human ova for *in vitro* use, it is likely that the first efforts in human cloning will be to clone cells of the early stage embryo *in vitro*. Cloning results in the production of identical genetical replicas. If clones are brought to term in the womb we are faced with the production of cloned humans. This raises many ethical issues some of which are similar to the ethical objections to positive eugenics (see above). Central to these objections is the issue of power to decide what kinds of human beings are desired and what kinds are not. It puts the primary emphasis on the instrumental value of human life rather than its intrinsic value.

vii) The ethics of genetic engineering on humans and other animals. Animals and especially humans are more than collections of genes. Each individual has a subjective life, each feels, suffers and enjoys. This capacity for feeling makes available to human life a richness of experience which we believe to be unique in the whole living world. Recognition of this is one reason for our attribution of a special intrinsic value to all human life. Furthermore, the human is not only conscious but is aware of it. It is this knowledge which enables us to discover our responsibility to other humans, to the rest of creation and to God. This responsibility includes the marking out of the limits to which we may legitimately manipulate the human person. Christian faith derives its special evaluation of human life from many sources. One is the vision of human life as made in the image of God, and which recognizes the relationship of God to the rest of creation. We are not, however, individual replicas of God. Christians are that part of the whole humanity that strives with the help of one another to manifest God's image. We see an obligation not to jeopardize the consciousness and the sensitivity that make possible our relationship with God and with one another. Our understanding of the relationship of God to human life and non-human life requires much further development if we are to have a substantial ethical and theological base for evaluating genetic engineering in humans and other vertebrates. In our judgment, unfortunately, theology does not yet speak in a meaningful way to the problems raised by contemporary biology.

viii) We consider that a community which has to bear the potentially grave hazards of genetic engineering as well as receive the potential benefits of the new technology should itself be involved in decisions about its use. Furthermore, it has been demonstrated that lay participation provides a helpful challenge to the professional viewpoint. We need to derive further ways to increase participation in the discussion of such questions as the following: Who will benefit from these new discoveries? Is it meaningful to speak of "responsible" and "irresponsible" scientific inquiry? What are the criteria for dividing research into these categories? Is human nature such that the accessibility to some kinds of knowledge makes inevitable its destructive use? If so, does that indicate that such knowledge should not be developed? On the other hand, does the denial of the pursuit of knowledge constitute an even greater threat to the human spirit? Is it justifiable to hold present researchers responsible for the future abuse of their discoveries?

3. BEHAVIOUR CONTROL

Human beings influence one another's behaviour in countless conscious and unconscious ways. This is a necessary condition and consequence of life in society.

Control is a form of influence which removes from those subject to it the option or the ability to resist it. To be legitimate, any form of control must be publicly and/or mutually agreed upon: for example, the control of young children by their parents is publicly, but not mutually agreed upon; discipline within the armed forces is publicly and mutually agreed upon by those who voluntarily enlist.

Manipulation is the conscious exercise of influence on those who are not aware that they are being influenced, or at least are not conscious of the specific mode of influence; for example, indoctrination is a form of manipulation insofar as it is intended that those who have been indoctrinated should not know it.

The gravest misuses of behaviour control technologies occur with individuals or groups of people who are in a helpless situation; mental patients, prisoners, young children, poor people, military conscripts and prisoners-of-war. The dangers to such groups are greatest when they have been incarcerated in a prison, a mental hospital, or on a military base, and thus cut off from the larger community. When any of the technologies below are being applied in such settings, they must be examined with the closest scrutiny.

In general, manipulation is to be rejected since it implies a devaluation of the persons manipulated. Many kinds of control, on the other hand, are a normal part of social life, though the power behind such control can often be abused and thus needs to be subject continuously to checks and balances.

Advances in psycho-pharmacology and neuro-physiology have enlarged the possibilities of the control and manipulation of human behaviour in ways which call for special comment. We begin with problems which are already familiar and show the new possibilities as extensions of these.

Self-medication

People may try to influence or control their own behaviour in many different ways, both internally and externally, through, for example, self-improvement programmes, alcohol, and the control of anxiety or pain through drugs. Some methods are socially acceptable, others are not. Possible criteria for distinguishing them are:
— whether the method in some way enhances or builds up the personality;
— how far its effects are generally known, so that those who use it can reasonably be expected to understand what they are doing.

Tranquillizers

In many but not all countries, these are available only on prescription, the assumption being that their effects and the indications for their use are matters of specialized knowledge. Accountability for their use thus belongs to those who manufacture, prescribe, market and use them. Their use becomes manipulative when patients are not consulted about it and are kept in ignorance of its effects. This happens most frequently:
i)   in institutions, for example hospitals, prisons and military establishments;
ii)   as a quick alternative to more elaborate procedures, e.g. psychotherapy;
iii) as a means of avoiding mental pain.
There are particular pressures towards manipulating those whose behaviour is classed as deviant.

Accountability

On the basis of these familiar examples, it seems clear that the responsible control of behaviour must entail:
i)   the sharing of knowledge with those whose behaviour is being affected;
ii)   shared decision-making with those who are capable of making decisions for themselves, or in accordance with some public guidelines or special consultative procedure in the case of those who are not;
iii) the overall aim of enhancing personal freedom and responsibility within the context of respect for cultural differences.

Self-induced drug experience

Drugs of different kinds are widely used, legitimately and illegitimately, as devices for escaping from the pressures and anxieties of personal circumstances. In addition to being used in this way for medical purposes some drugs (e.g. LSD) may be taken with the sole purpose of enlarging or enhancing experience. Such use is commonly forbidden on one or more of the following grounds:

i)   the effects of the drug may not be fully understood or controllable;
ii) it may be addictive;
iii) it may have undesirable side effects.

Progress in psycho-pharmacology seems likely to lead in the very near future to the production of new pharmacological agents whose effects are much more specific. Current research on the "endorphins" and "encephalins", both of which occur normally in the brain, may open the way to a precise control of moods, feelings, experiences and even memories, with none of the disadvantages of the present relatively crude mood-changing drugs.

In addition, there are possibilities of using the electrical control of specific brain centres, notably the hypothalamus, for similar purposes.

The moral problem posed by such discoveries and techniques is whether, in the absence of the kind of disadvantages listed above, the ability to enlarge and control feelings and experiences artificially is to be welcomed or not.

Some would agree strongly that all experience is to be welcomed, that the frontiers of the mind are the last and most important still awaiting exploration and that it is wrong to try to prescribe norms in an area which has great potential creative value.

Others would point to the possibilities of abuse, the dangers of confusing fantasy with reality, and the threat which such methods might pose to the integrity of personality.

Christian tradition has on the whole put a question mark against experience for its own sake. For instance, two widely recognized tests of valid Christian mysticism have been its relationship to the corporate life of the Church and whether or not it bears fruit in works of love. Mysticism for the enjoyment of the experience itself has been regarded as a form of self-indulgence.

The need for the experience-seeker to belong within some cultural framework is illustrated by the American Indian use of peyote as part of a total cultural pattern. It seems likely, too, that the drug-taking sub-culture is an important element in the experience of others who defy social norms. It is as if the experience has to be given some meaning beyond itself, for example by being brought within a social context.

Personality and experience

A Christian understanding of personality, while allowing that experience has a physical basis and can therefore be influenced by physical means, must emphasize the higher levels of organization and meaning which are nonetheless inextricably linked with physical foundations. By analogy, a machine may consist of nothing but physical components, yet be inexplicable except in terms of the purpose for which it was made.

Likewise, human personality is ultimately to be understood in terms of God's purpose for human life. It has a genetic and cultural basis, whose potentialities are progressively drawn out and fulfilled, first within the world of human relationships and, secondly, with growing spiritual awareness in relationship with God. Only in God can it grow to its full stature and find its eventual and eternal fulfilment. Ideally, this is a growth in meaning, responsibility, freedom, sensitivity and love. It is emotional as well as rational, corporate as well as individual. In practice, however, all human development is precarious and ambiguous. People can suffer as much, if not more, through demanding perfection, security and certainty as by giving up the struggle to grow.

The integration of personality, therefore, is never a simple matter. Not all experiences can be brought within some scheme of progressive development or given a meaning within an individual's life history or that of his or her group. We are sinful human beings, all of whose lives contain chaotic elements. To recognize such elements is one thing, but deliberately to seek artificially induced experiences, which fall outside normal historical consciousness, is another. We foresee dangers to the development of personality in such experiences, sought for their own sake, if these:
— do not relate meaningfully to the rest of a person's consciousness;
— encourage an irresponsible and insensitive withdrawal into a private world of fantasy.

We therefore urge caution in the development and use of all such means of controlling fundamental aspects of the personality, call attention to the possibilities of abuse, not least in the manipulation of personalities, and advise that their use be limited to clearly defined therapeutic programmes.

Genetic determinants of human personality and the debate about sociobiology

It is commonly assumed that children will be like their parents, not only in physical characteristics, but also in some personality traits. But while it seems clear that there must be a genetic basis for at least some physical resemblances, there is no agreement about the part played by genetic factors in the inheritance of personality.

A number of students of animal behaviour have in recent years begun to apply to humans studies on the evolutionary origins of non-humans. This study is now usually known as sociobiology. It has aroused intense controversy, especially in the USA. The controversy has been partly scientific, in that it is presently impossible with any certainty to distinguish between any genetic component and the large and important role played by cultural conditioning in any given example of human behaviour. The arguments in favour of genetic conditioning are mainly based, firstly, on the inherent probability that brain function has evolved under normal selective pressures and, secondly, on the resemblances between human and primate behaviour. Further-more, theoretical analysis of the inheritance of altruism within families has removed some of the *a priori* obstacles to believing that genes can affect characteristics which do not at first sight seem to confer any evolutionary ad-vantage on their possessors. Critics point to the extreme complexity of human behaviour and its heavy dependence on its cultural context, as well as the difficulty of providing convincing and unequivocal examples of a genetic conditioning.

There are others who have criticized the whole approach on sociological grounds. They have tended to confuse genetic conditioning with genetic determinism, and on the basis of this misunderstanding they have drawn at-tention to the social dangers of sociobiology. They claim it encourages over-ready acceptance of the status quo, discrimination and moral irresponsibility on the grounds that what is genetically determined must simply be accepted and cannot be changed by moral or social efforts. It is true that any theory of this kind might be abused by reading into it more than is actually there. A theory is not to be dismissed, however, solely on the ground that people might misunderstand and misuse it. Social sensitivity is a reason for caution in presenting conclusions which might be treated in this way, but it would be quite wrong to suppress research which, if successful, could increase human self-understanding.

The complexity of the whole matter is apparent from even the most cur-sory study of the nature and origins of human aggression. Thus supposing, for example, it could be proved that human beings have innate aggressive tendencies, cultural conditioning might still play the major part in determin-ing whether they were expressed or not. A revolutionary and a pacifist com-mitted to non-violence might share the same genetic basis for aggressiveness, but the behavioural consequences of this would be totally different in the two cases.

The popular notion, therefore, that there are genetic determinants of human behaviour is seriously misleading, and it should be stressed that this is not what sociobiologists claim. There may, however, be capacities, tenden-cies and predispositions whose basis has a genetic component. This possibili-ty raises various moral issues:

i)   How far do human beings need to follow their natural tendencies in order to be themselves? The question might apply to individuals whose genetic inheritance sets them outside generally accepted social norms.

ii)   The question also applies to the natural tendencies of human beings as a whole. Are there, in fact, built-in characteristics of human nature whose exposure might form a basis for a new kind of natural law?

Both questions need to be asked in the context of the traditional Christian belief in the ambiguities of human nature. For example, Christian asceticism entails the sacrifice of natural tendencies for the sake of some greater good. Another tradition so emphasizes Christian freedom that natural tendencies fade into unimportance within the actual complexities of behaviour.

If some characteristics within the core of personality are fixed, are some changeable, and how? And what means are legitimate for changing them? For example, there are already proposals to inhibit certain patterns of sexual behaviour by surgical interference with the hypothalamus and to "cure" aggression by burning out sections of the amygdala. Quite apart from the dubious assumptions that both of these characteristics are "conditions" or "isolated components" of personality, such proposals raise enormous questions about the acceptable or normal range of human variation and the extent to which people become free by accepting or rejecting aspects of their personalities.

It may well be that there are extreme conditions in which gross interference with brain functioning can be justified as a last resort. In the present state of ignorance, however, there are good scientific grounds for moving only very cautiously. If at some future date a more precise understanding of human personality, its relationship to brain function and its genetic basis were to become possible, there would still be the need for a Christian reminder that what matters about people as moral agents is how they use their capacities, not how readily they can exchange them for "improved" versions. Indeed, the responsibility for moral choice would not be lessened even if a complete understanding of the causal connections in the brain and its relation to sensory input were to be achieved, since any behaviour has a meaning and function distinct from (and complementary to) the neuropsychological mechanisms involved.

The impaired personality

Those with impaired personalities are especially vulnerable to control or manipulation by others. Such labels as "sick", "bad", "mad", "stupid" and "possessed" may be legitimate, and often necessary for practical purposes, but it is important to remember that they are the product of particular theories and social assumptions which are themselves fallible. The question of who gives the label and how may be crucial in deciding the moral acceptability of some control procedure. For instance, the dividing line between crime and illness is notoriously difficult to draw, yet a person's whole future may depend on who draws it.

Continuing review of such labelling systems and of the procedures for changing and challenging labels ought to be a mark of a just society.

Other ways of manipulating the human mind

There are many other ways in which scientific and technological advances can be used or abused in the control or manipulation of human behaviour. We draw attention to only one—the new power conferred on some by the mass media of communication, including advertising—and urge that the WCC give further attention to the matter, as well as to the political dimensions of such power.

Some of the more invasive techniques, whether in medicine or surgery or the subtle manipulation of the human mind (from which even some church practices are not free) raise questions about the nature of human personality. Is there, in fact, an inviolable core of personality which cannot, or ought not to be touched by anything done in the name of science? Traditional concepts of the soul presuppose that there is. They refer to that part of a person which represents ultimate individuality, which is held in being by God, and which finds its significance in relationship with him.

A more scientific way of expressing the same belief might be to refer to the wholeness of human personality as it exists in a variety of contexts, the biological, the psychological and social, and the spiritual. Life is lived in all those contexts, and all of them affect what we are. All may change, but one thing remains constant: within the flux of human existence God's initiative in loving his creatures, calling them by name, and giving himself to them establishes their worth.

In summary then, the sacredness of a human life is ultimately based on God's love for us and on his call to all of us to serve and respond to him, free from fear, in justice and holiness, in the community of his covenant, and also on our destiny to be with him forever.

4. DISTRIBUTIVE JUSTICE IN THE USE OF SCARCE MEDICAL RESOURCES

The problems

The problems associated with the just use and distribution of medical and scientific resources can be illuminated by the following affirmations of the Christian Gospel. Firstly, all things are created by God and belong to him. This applies equally to the products of our minds and of our hands. Secondly, stewardship of these resources has been given to mankind, and their use should be unrestricted by sex, race, social or economic status, religious preference or other man-made conditions.

A major role of the Christian community is the reconciliation of human beings with one another and with God, following the command of Jesus to heal the sick and feed the hungry.

It was in this spirit of a worldwide community of healing that we considered distributive justice in the use of scarce medical resources. The definition of scarce medical resources differs from country to country and even within countries from locality to locality. The United States may be considered an example of a nation of highly sophisticated medical technology. Scarcity of resources in this context may present a rather dramatic scenario.

A.Z. was a healthy scholar-athlete when he first noted the easy bruisability and fatigue that heralded the onset of a rare blood disorder, which led to repeated hospitalization over a three-year period. In the summer of his eighteenth year, he expressed his weariness with a life that had become increasingly restricted and painful. He was admitted for the last time after a brief vacation with his family during which he began to complain of headache. This became increasingly severe and so alarmed his family that they rushed home. On arrival at the hospital, he was difficult to rouse, and emergency CAT scanning demonstrated a very large blood clot within the brain substance.

The attending physician, the hematologist, the neurosurgeon and parents all decided that every available means should be used to salvage the life of this young man suffering from a disease known to be incurable and ultimately fatal. The details of the surgical and medical care are irrelevant. However, the need over the next four or five days to utilize all blood products available along the eastern seabord is relevant. Their financial cost exceeded $80,000. The increased morbidity and potential mortality in those areas depleted of blood products was never estimated. It is ironic, but again probably irrelevant, that the young man died without ever regaining consciousness.

This brief narrative highlights several of the ethical problems faced by nations in which medical technology is widely available albeit not equitably distributed.

The questions

i)   In any given case, who shall make the decision concerning the appropriateness of expenditure of scarce or very expensive medical resources? Physicians? Patients? Families? Committees? If the latter, how shall such committees be structured to avoid the impasse which varying ethical and medical opinions often engender?

ii)   If guidelines are to be formulated for the use of scarce medical resources, how is "scarcity" to be defined? How is it to be decided which resources are to be distributed to all citizens as part of their "rights" to health as defined by WHO, and which technological advances or resources are, although feasible, inappropriate for development because of high cost or limited applicability? Equally relevant to the question of how is that of who: who gets and who decides who gets?

iii) Is quality of life to be taken into account in the judgment as to the appropriateness of expenditure of limited resources? What criteria can we use for evaluating life? Should socio-economic conditions ever be a factor?

In the illustrative story the scarcity of the needed blood products was, in large measure, responsible for their high cost. Such a "scarcity" is created by a continuing reluctance on the part of citizens to donate blood. Similar scarcities are created by the lack of cornea and kidney donors and more recently a lack of heart, bone marrow and liver donors. While there are valid religious, ethical and indeed medical reasons which prohibit some from becoming donors, in many cases the reason is apathy, an unconcern for one's neighbour. Medically appropriate, albeit expensive, care was available to this boy because he lived near a university centre in which a team of physicians had an ongoing research protocol which underwrote the cost. Availability of advanced medical technology is often limited by local geographic as well as socio-economic conditions. Specialists tend to concentrate in urban or university centres where good schools and cultural and artistic pursuits are available.

Gross impairments pose the question: "When does such a person cease to have any claim on the skills and attention of others?" An extreme example is the anencephalic child whose lifetime is brief and who, with the effective absence of a cerebral cortex, has no chance of developing even the most rudimentary personal relationships. Yet this child has been born by a human mother and has belonged, if only by anticipation, to a human family. It has therefore a certain social reality which is not to be treated with disrespect, even though the reality of its personal life is not strong enough to warrant any medical efforts to preserve it.

At the other end of the human scale similar problems are posed by the conditions in which some would advocated euthanasia. Their advocacy is likely to grow stronger as demographic trends make the pressures on old age, at least in western societies, more acute. The same principles surely apply. The social reality of individuals, even when they have ceased to enjoy or fully experience their own personal life, lays a claim on those who care for them not to destroy what God has given. The loving termination of intensive care when it can no longer achieve anything, and the avoidance of extraordinary measures which only prolong the agony, are a matter of good medicine, and it is better not to call them euthanasia at all.

Two issues for consideration

a) How is access to available health care to be ensured? If care (i.e. advanced technology) is regionalized more equitably, transportation to the medical centre, housing for at least one member of the immediate family, etc. must still be ensured.

b) How is the wide dispersal of information concerning available technology to be assured? If it is unrealistic to expect physicians to establish themselves in remote areas where their specialty training is under-utilized, would it be feasible to use paramedical personnel in these areas to treat minor illnesses, teach good health habits and direct patients to the appropriate medical centres? The increasing use of physician associates, nurse-practitioners and clinicians in closely supervised settings such as clinics and physicians' offices may be the first step in creating a more independent group of health personnel who could fulfil these needs.

In less technologically-advanced societies, and among disadvantaged groups within advanced societies, scarcity of resources and inequitable distribution create similar problems. But the primary problem there is the availability of and access to primary health care rather than scarce and expensive medical technology. The scarcity may be related to an absolute lack of equipment—e.g. a renal dialysis machine—or to inappropriate or mismatched equipment—e.g. syringes bought from country X not fitting needles bought from country Y. The harsh reality of resource scarcity can be illustrated by the following story. A cabinet minister of a developing country and his aide were injured in an automobile accident in their own country. There was little or no discussion concerning flying the minister and his aide to London for needed medical care. The driver remained behind to be treated with the locally available resources. He died.

As in the case of the technology associated with nuclear reactors and communications satellites, so in the field of health: the less developed nations must be encouraged to set their own priorities. Whether to allocate funds for sophisticated technology—e.g. a renal dialysis machine—in a nation beset by communicable disease, malnutrition and an unacceptably high infant death rate is a question too often decided by a political elite guided by profit-seeking corporations and self-seeking medical professionals.

Better methods must be found for solving these problems in both the technologically advanced nations and in those whose technology is just emerging. The responsibility for seeking joint answers should be accepted by individual Christians, by local Christian communities, by national Christian councils and by the World Council of Churches.

5. EXPERIMENTATION ON HUMAN AND OTHER VERTEBRATES

In the western world in order for results of research involving humans to be published in a recognized scientific or medical journal, the author must attest that the research was carried out under rigorous national guidelines. Papers on human experimentation must carry the annotation that such research has been approved by a Human Investigations Committee (HIC). Such committees consider not only the safety of the experimental method but whether or not the knowledge to be gained justifies the perceived risk to the subject. Nevertheless there is great need for the Christian community to ensure that these constraints are observed (see recommendations). The scientific community is also becoming more aware of its responsibility to non-human vertebrates used in experimentations. Even so animals suffer, and sometimes unnecessarily. The Christian community has a responsibility to ensure that such suffering is reduced to a minimum (see recommendations).

6. RECOMMENDATIONS

Genetic counselling, prenatal diagnosis and abortion

We recommend that the WCC sub-unit on Church and Society establish a continuing body to deal with ethical, theological, social and legal problems arising from *(a)* abortion of genetically defective fetuses, and *(b)* AID, donor egg and embryo transfer. The group should consist of persons from different disciplines, of different theological views, and should contain at least 40% women, preferably more.

Genetic engineering
We recommend:

i)   That the WCC constitute a working group to consult with UNESCO, WHO, UNEP, ILO and other appropriate international organizations to encourage the establishing and implementing of international guidelines for all recombinant DNA technology and related technologies throughout the world. Since the potential hazards of such technology are threats to both humans and the ecosystem, these guidelines should be developed and implemented with the broadest social participation as exemplified by the Recombinant DNA Guidelines Committee of the Canadian Ministry of Supply and Services. The working group should recognize that any efforts in these directions are likely to be strongly resisted by commercial enterprises interested in the new technology.

ii) That the WCC group on transnational corporations be asked to include in its investigations the prospect that transnationals will move the site of their genetic engineering operations to countries where there are few, if any, restrictions on such technology, especially the developing countries.

iii) That in consultation with UNESCO, ILO, UNEP and other UN agencies the WCC initiate a discussion of the grave ethical issues involved in human genetic engineering as indicated in the conference report. In the meantime, we register opposition to the use of genetic engineering on the human fertilized ovum for purposes other than the correction of genetic defects, and even here we recommend that the research not proceed without full participation of the public in decisions of what is and what is not ethically acceptable in these procedures.

Behaviour control
We recommend that the WCC call a consultation on "Behaviour Control and the Quality of Life" with special reference to the following considerations:

i)   the extent to which invasive techniques for the control of behaviour have developed and are likely to develop further;

ii) the extent, if any, to which these techniques build up personal life and enhance personal worth;

iii) participation in decision-making and consultation procedures;

iv) the effects of the mass media of communication and advertising;

v)   the rights of people who are exploited by technologies of behaviour modification; those in prison, hospitals, mental and military institutions.

Distributive justice in the use of scarce medical resources
    We recommend:
i)   *To individuals:* Individuals should, when confronted with the need for limited resources for themselves or for members of their family, carefully and prayerfully examine their claim to these resources in light of the need of other individuals, especially those whose economic and social condition is not as advantageous as their own.
ii)   *To local Christian communities:* Local Christian communities should, through study and through social action groups, seek to be as fully informed as possible about the needs of the whole community so that they can be influential in setting priorities—both local and national—for the just allocation of medical and health services.
iii) *To national church councils:* Such councils with the support of local Christian communities should work with other concerned groups to influence national policies with respect to:
    a) establishing national guidelines for obtaining and maintaining adequate levels of health care for all its citizens; this includes prenatal and postnatal care and good nutrition through education and adequate distribution of food;
    b) the setting of national health priorities;
    c) the fair distribution of health resources to rural areas, low income communities and racial and ethnic minorities;
    d) influencing the direction of needed resources; they should seek to achieve greater participation by their national governments in bilateral and multilateral programmes for developing health services in third world countries, with priority being given to preventive medicine and the meeting of primary health care needs.
iv)   *To the WCC:*
    a) that the sub-unit on Church and Society and the Christian Medical Commission of the WCC continue their excellent work on justice in the distribution of scarce medical resources and on other health care problems created by advances in science and technology, particularly the artificial prolongation of life;
    b) that the WCC group on transnational corporations be asked to investigate the deleterious effects on health of the activities of pharmaceutical transnationals.

Experimentation on human and other vertebrates
    We recommend that individual Christians, local Christian communities, national Christian councils and the WCC:
i)   be actively engaged in local, national and international efforts to establish and enforce guidelines such as the Helsinki Convention which safeguard the rights of all peoples and prevent their exploitation in the pursuit of scientific or technological advancement; reaffirm the necessity of scrupulous adherence to the basic principles of informed consent

and of the avoidance of any form of compulsion, however subtle, in experimental procedures on humans;

ii)   oppose in every possible way the testing of pharmaceutical products on poor peoples in developing countries;

iii)   encourage the formation of animal care committees to ensure that animals are not used heedlessly, regardless of how humanely, and recognize the intrinsic value of each individual animal life in addition to the instrumental value of these lives to humans.

V. Technology, Resources, Environment and Population

INTRODUCTION

The relation between human beings, their religious convictions, and their impact on their environment is too complex to be reduced to simple formulae. Historical evidence indicates that people in different cultures, in different epochs (indeed from prehistoric times), and with different religious values have all been guilty of destructive practices on their natural surroundings. As the dominant species, *homo sapiens* has always had—and exercised—an enormous capacity for destroying other life, a capacity which has increased many times over since the advent of industrial society. The acquisitive actions of many people are often plainly in excess of what is necessary to satisfy their basic needs for survival. Our drive to experiment with the world, and through our science and technology to change it, while surely part of our glory, is also part of our tragedy. We need to take our predicament seriously, and to marshal all our skills, including our religious resources, to salvage the situation.

It is important first of all to be realistic about the human situation. A return to a pre-technological age is not possible either for those large areas of the world already highly populated and developed, or for areas of high population density in the process of developing in order to be able to feed themselves better. A pre-technological culture of low population density may be able to sustain itself comfortably with wise traditional methods of cultivation, but for most of the world's people, the accomplishments of science and technology in some form are essential to life. If we were to follow such counsel as "return to harmony with nature", meaning let "nature" take its course, great numbers of people would simply die. It seems better, therefore, to avoid such imprecise and ambiguous terms and to adopt one of the theme words of this conference, "sustainability". How should we treat our natural environment so that the life of our species may be indefinitely sustained?

In phrasing the goal thus, this report obviously focuses on *human* need. To that extent its approach is anthropocentric, reflecting the biblical doctrine that humanity, the image of God, is the height of creation. But this does not mean we may treat non-human nature as of no value except for its usefulness to us. All of God's creation has value and is to be treated with reverence for the sake of its Maker, who accounted it good. We are commanded, as several speakers at this conference have reminded us, to be good stewards of God's world. We are held responsible for it. It is not ours to do with as we please. Rather, we are to care for it and maintain it for its Lord.

What happens, then, when human needs appear to require some "destruction" of the natural world, e.g. in the turning of wildlife preserves into farmland to feed a growing human population? We think that the ethical issue here is not the inviolable "rights" of the non-human world. "Nature" is not divine with a superior wisdom of its own that we must obey. That would be fatalism on our part. The ethical issue is, rather, the order of priorities. Human needs—ours and those of future generations—must come first. *But* they must be genuine basic needs, related to our survival, not merely frivolous desires. The dividing line between these two will often be indistinct, but it is important to establish the principle: it is our *necessities* and not our boundless appetite for pleasure which should come first when dealing with non-human nature. The integrity of the natural world is to be preserved, not only so that we and our descendants may live in it, but because it is God's world.

Thus we state an attitude, or a general direction for policy, we do not dictate specifics. We do not think we can say, on the basis of Christian faith, what the particular purposes of God are for non-human nature, i.e. what the future of the natural world or of any species within it should be. Neither can we specify which among non-human creatures are of greater value in God's sight than others. No criterion, whether it be complexity, or capacity for feeling, or rarity, or anything else at once commends itself as specifically Christian; and there is always the danger that the concept of a hierarchy of values may be applied to human beings also, with the temptation to assign a lower value to people who seem lacking in the chosen criterion, e.g. children who are born handicapped.

We *can* say, however, that God values *all* of his creation—the natural world with all its creatures—and that human redemption involves the redemption of the whole cosmos from its "bondage to decay" (Rom. 8:18-24). If it is true that human sin has brought evil to the natural world, so then our acceptance of the salvation from sin wrought for us in Christ should show itself in our respectful treatment of that natural world.

Even if such a general attitude cannot yield a table of preferences in the natural world, it is nevertheless quite useful as a guide in our relation to our environment. The following discussion illustrates the operation of this attitude in concrete situations.

1. AGRICULTURE, FORESTRY, WATER AND FISHERIES

The physical reality

Long before King Solomon cut the cedars of Lebanon for his palaces and temples, the human race had not been able to meet its needs for food and fibre while maintaining the essential soil, water, vegetative and marine resources. Since the beginning of recorded history, more than half of the earth's arable soil resources have been lost. Annually, one half a ton of top soil is irrevocably lost for every man, woman and child now living. It is predicted that 30% of the remaining half of our soil deposits will be lost by the end of this century... during a time when human populations will increase by this same percentage. Desert encroachment as a consequence of the abuses of the land takes place on every continent: more than 70,000 square kilometers of agricultural land is lost in this way every year. Fresh water resources are diminishing at approximately the same rate as soil. Only 1% of the earth's fresh water resources is usable for agriculture. When the vegetation is gone, the ability to recharge lakes, rivers, and aquafers is impeded. Abusive agriculture and forestry by the clearing of land of forests and grasses have contributed greatly to the build-up of atmospheric carbon dioxide, to the destruction of normal patterns of atmospheric oxygen generation, and to changing the global albedo.

"In short, the two worlds of man—the biosphere of his inheritance and the technosphere of his creation—are out of balance, indeed potentially in deep conflict. And humanity is in the middle. This is the hinge of history at which we stand, the door of the future opening on to a crisis more sudden, more global, more inescapable, and more bewildering than any before encountered by the human species and one which will take decisive shape within the life span of children who are already born."

The technological reality

i) COMMODITIES, RESOURCES AND TECHNOLOGIES

It is necessary first to distinguish between the concepts of commodities, resources and technologies.

Timber and water can be looked at as commodities or as resources. Forests are resources which provide timber, pulp for the paper industry and firewood. But more importantly, forests are regulators of water resources through their role in maintaining water tables by the retention of water in the soil. Forests are a habitat for many species of plants and animals and they are vitally important in converting atmospheric carbon dioxide to oxygen and biomass through photosynthesis.

The water of lakes, rivers and ponds is a resource used for fisheries and aquaculture, generating hydro-electricity and transport. Water is a commodity used in irrigating and draining land. Clean water is an essential commodity for healthy domestic life.

The management of forests is closely related to the management of water. Both forests and water are basic resources for soil formation and conservation. The most important input for optimizing and sustaining agricultural yields is the control of water resources.

Agriculture and inland fresh water fisheries are technological methods used by rural people to obtain commodities from resources. These commodities may be food commodities (plant and animal), animal fodder, or commodities used in textile, pharmaceutical, leather and food industries by rural and urban people.

ii)   APPROPRIATE AND INAPPROPRIATE TECHNOLOGIES

The appropriateness of some existing technologies for food production is being brought into question. In some parts of the USA, for example, two bushels of top soil are lost during the production of one bushel of wheat. The processing and delivery of food to the dinner table in the industrialized nations require many more calories of fossil fuel energy than are represented in the caloric value of the food itself. Soil, water and atmospheric agri-chemical residues threaten the health of all forms of life. Widespread mono-cropping systems leave the whole agricultural enterprise vulnerable to widespread pathogenic and insect pest infestation. The worldwide fish catch, like per unit crop yields, peaked in the mid 1970's.

The social reality

i)   RURAL PEOPLE

In the world as a whole the vast majority of people live rurally, although in the industrialized countries the majority are town-dwellers. The land is *the* resource of the rural people. They have the first right to the land, as it has been their home for centuries. The relentless spreading of urban centres over the land is increasing the exploitation of rural people and placing ever greater pressure on rural resources. This exploitation causes suffering to peasant peoples worldwide; it is an oppression which subtly but brutally deprives them of their rights to the resources of their land.

Rural development is normally linked to the healthy development of all sectors of the economy, including the urban sector. But all too often the real needs of rural people are not adequately considered in total development schemes. In many countries, the help which has been given them in the form of education has perpetuated a system that undermines traditional rural values, technologies and cultures. This system has forced rural peoples to cultivate on their best land cash crops for the cities and transnational enterprises rather than food for their own use. They have been forced to sell at prices set by buyers in the cities. Modern technologies imposed upon rural peoples have increased the immediate yield of these cash crops but have led to an agriculture which is less sustainable than their traditional form.

In many places rural people have been dispossessed of their land and either forced to work for new masters or condemned to a life of unemployment in urban slums. Some have been forced on to marginal land which the new landowners did not want and which often should not have been cultivated. And many of them exiled from their country to become migrant workers.

The history of relationships between forests and human beings is different from that between agriculture and people. Examples of symbiosis are few (e.g. pygmies in Africa and the indigenous people of the Amazon). Too often people have exploited and destroyed forests and then suffered the consequences. Spain and Turkey are unfortunate examples. Current trends in deforestation are disturbing in many countries, particularly in the tropics where the land may be unable to support sustainable food production after clearance. Governments and the people must participate in managing forests in a sustainable manner. This is essential for the common good of the national and international community.

ii)   PRESERVATION OF LAND

Land may be "preserved" by being set aside as a wilderness reserve, as well as "conserved" by being worked so that its productive capacity is maintained. It may be preserved for a variety of motives: because we need it, now or in the future, to nourish us (wild land also contributes positively to the ecosystem); or because it gives us esthetic enjoyment; or because non-human creatures need it to live on; or because in preserving it we are honouring the design of the Creator.

These motives overlap, but they are also distinct from one another and often in conflict. The direction of the resolution of the problem is indicated above: priority goes to genuine human need, but God has given the non-human world value also. Preservation honours that value, and must yield only where human need is clear. Even this conflict can be reduced by limiting population growth and defining "need" more narrowly.

Real need is notoriously hard to define, of course, in relation to land as well as to other things. Changes in land status are usually the result of economic pressures, serving the needs (or greed) of some people, but hurting others. Farm land may yield to urban growth when sound ecology and care for the needs of future generations indicate that housing could be built on less productive land. Development of tourist facilities may bring economic relief to poor areas, or may simply enrich distant promoters; it may allow urban people to regain contact with nature and educate them to its value, or it may overcrowd and destroy places of natural beauty and alienate their rural people. Preservation of wild places may save valuable land, or merely reserve access and use for the few at the expense of the spiritual and material growth of the many. It may do both.

The dilemma of what constitutes the use of land pits people with different interests against each other and challenges all of us to rethink what we really need. We have to consider who really needs what, and who are simply advancing their own interests while pleading for a change in the land's status.

Conditions of sustainability

Current judgment is that virtually all land that can support agriculture is now in such use; modern agricultural technology is not sustainable and this must be corrected. This will be possible on condition that agricultural experts and decision-makers engage in dialogue with the peasants. These are the people, whether in Africa, India, Europe or elsewhere, who continue to practise established traditional agricultural methods. It is in the adapting and refining of these that the best hope lies for developing sustainability.

It is not possible to be optimistic or complacent in the face of the evidence which indicates that there are probably more hungry and malnourished people in 1979 than the 450 million to whom the United Nations World Food Conference directed its attention in Rome in 1974:

"The number of people who do not have sufficient food will vary according to one's definition of sufficiency—between 450 million and 1.3 billion. What is not in dispute is that a vast number of people do not get enough to eat, that the number is increasing and that efforts to reduce it have so far been woefully inadequate."

The number of farms is diminishing in the aftermath of soil, water, forest and grassland exhaustion and new forms of land occupation. Rural leadership for community enhancement and agricultural development services continues to decline in proportion to growing needs. Citizen participation in the determination of the destiny of soil, water, vegetative and animal resources is almost non-existent in most nations of the world. There is little justice in land distribution, tenure and use.

Not enough progress has been made in the area of food security and agricultural research for the building of the rural infrastructures essential for the emergence of sustainable (resource renewing) agriculture, forestry and fishing systems. The primary task that lies ahead is to strengthen the millions of small farms and rural communities of people so they can develop and maintain mixed and sustainable cropping systems.

Summary

To summarize the problem and set forth the challenge, it can be said that agricultural technologies of the several bio-zones of the world, in general, are not sustainable. The achievement of a just, participatory and sustainable agriculture (fishing and forests) is of critical importance. Time is running out. By the end of the century, only 2% of the earth's surface will be useful for the support of more than 6,000 million people.

"The responsibility that now confronts humanity is to make a deliberate transition to a sustainable global society in which science and technology will be mobilized to meet the basic physical and spiritual needs of people, to minimize human suffering and to create an environment which can sustain a decent quality of life for all people. This will involve a radical transformation of civilization, new technologies, new uses for technology and new global economic and political systems. The new situation in which humanity now finds itself has been created in less than a generation. There is even less time to create the transition to a sustainable global society if humanity is to survive" (from the report of the WCC assembly, Nairobi).

Without a radical departure from the historical and contemporary record there will be little of all life forms for future generations to inherit. *Unlike the energy crisis, there are no alternative possibilities if the soil, water, grass, fish and forest resources become exhausted.*

"The times call for a new land ethic, a new reverence for land, and for a better understanding of our dependence on a resource that is too often taken for granted."

The concepts of *justice*, community *participation* in deciding the ways the land (soil, water, forest, grass resources) shall be used, and *sustainability* into the foreseeable future of agricultural and fishing industries, provide the content for this new ethic. These concepts provide hope for the future.

Recommendations (agriculture, forestry, water and fisheries)

We call upon the member churches of the World Council of Churches:

i)   to foster and give priority to sustainable agriculture in both developed and developing nations, and to strive for policies of land use and management which give maximum sustainable yields without depleting soil fertility;

ii) to encourage storage of crops at local level, for the sake of self-sufficiency and to counteract excessive profiteering; since in developing countries the greatest loss occurs in the larger storage centres, the most effective preservation and maintenance techniques should be enforced;

iii) to examine the sustainability of mixed farming versus monoculture;

iv) to acknowledge the value of indigenous technologies; when technology is transferred three considerations are of critical importance: the appropriateness has to be determined by the recipient; it should be "grafted" upon the indigenous technology wherever possible; the relationship of the imported technology should be compatible with the local ecosystem;

v)   in the face of diminishing natural resources and energy supplies, to promote research on the ways of adapting agriculture to these limitations;

vi) to promote reappraisal of land ownership and the priority given to investment in agriculture development; such a reappraisal will often entail reordering entire political, economic, and social systems;

vii) to set as a primary goal of local and national agriculture policies self-sufficiency in food production, as far as possible;

viii) to encourage each country to have forestry programmes to regulate the amount of land use for forests, and urgently introduce reforestation where necessary to ensure soil conservation and water regulation;

ix) to call a halt to the destructive exploitation of the tropical forest.

2. NON-RENEWABLE RESOURCES

As Christians involved in science and technology, we address these comments to the ethical rather than the technical issues related to non-renewable resources.

We are in a situation unique in the history of humankind and of technology. We can clearly foresee the steady decline of the world's non-renewable resources. It should be noted that if all countries were to use non-renewable resources at rates similar to the OECD countries, most of the world's non-renewable resources (e.g. heavy metal ores, oil, etc.) would be depleted in a few years. At the present rate of growth, oil reserves are not expected to last longer than 20-35 years. Such consumption rates would frustrate the legitimate hopes of the poorer countries for development.

Resources: availability, limits and future technologies

It is agreed that we should act as though the world's present known reserves of non-renewable resources—which are very limited—are all that are available. Yet, with hope for the future, we should not hesitate to search for alternatives, such as new appropriate technologies, greater efficiency, recycling, substitutes, etc. and strongly increase research into new sources of energy.

But we now realize that we should not be so optimistic as to assume that more of the type of revolutionary technology which appeared during the last half century will rescue us. We do not know that it will emerge and we cannot rely on it.

Problems

The basic reasons for the rapid depletion of non-renewable resources are greed, the material demands of world economic growth, and the struggle for power. In this connection, the biblical view of humanity as steward rather than lord of creation must be emphasized. Some of the greatest problems are a direct result of the actions of large corporations irresponsibly exploiting the world's non-renewable resources. Foreign capital-investors, particularly those investing in developing countries, drain the resources of the area and leave behind them a sad trail of "ghost towns" unfit for decent human life. These corporations control the whole economy of many developing countries, dictating terms to governments which are literally at their mercy because of the countries' great need for foreign exchange. In most circumstances, these transnational corporations recover the non-renewable resources in a developing country, partly refine them there and then export them. The refining is completed abroad and the finished products are sold sometimes at enormous profit. In fact, some of the refined products are sold back to the country of origin at an even higher price (e.g. copper from Zambia). In the absence of a just international economic order, there is a scramble by powerful countries for non-renewable resources in which the developing countries are trodden upon. Contributing to the problem is the economic structure of most countries, which is consumer-oriented. This orientation is encouraged by the subtle but powerful methods of advertising, which promote increased consumption. Very often government and public regulations encourage waste (e.g. decreasing electricity rates for higher levels of consumption). The questions that arose time and time again are: What is the Christian's responsibility in such situations? What is the responsibility of the churches?

Christian response: "Care for your neighbour"

Modern technology has created for the first time a truly global society, even though it is not always apparent. For example, actions which seem purely local may in fact have an impact on people thousands of miles away, and similarly on present choices.

Christians and churches alike should *not only* address themselves to the work of charity, but *also* be more constructively involved in the life of society. They should avoid being hypocritical and genuinely begin to practise alternative life-styles, especially in developed countries (e.g. often families own a city and a country house which they only occasionally use, they have several cars, more than one TV set and other luxuries).

Church leaders should take greater responsibility for seeing that their congregations are enlightened on specific social problems and possible courses of action.

As representatives of the people, governments should engage appropriate technical expertise comparable to that employed by transnational corporations to enable them to exercise better control over their own non-renewable resources. Waste is a growing problem, especially in the consumer society, and every effort should be made to minimize it. A very practical starting point would be the conscious reduction of the use of energy and consumer goods in developed countries. Governments and other authorities should be encouraged to provide greater incentive for decreased consumption. They should also be encouraged to limit advertising through the media.

Recommendations

Christians as individuals, through their churches and their communities, can act responsibly in the conservation of the earth's non-renewable resources. We recommend that the churches:

i)   support educational efforts which increase awareness of our neighbours around the world and develop such educational programmes where they do not now exist;

ii) encourage and support corporate and individual participation in the social, economic and political life of society with the goal of promoting both charity and justice;

iii) foster the exploration of less consumptive and wasteful styles of life;

iv) promote legislative and private programmes which restrain governments and private enterprises from depleting non-renewable resources and encourage the development of technologies which are efficient, participatory and sustainable.

3. WORLD COMMONS

The world commons refers here to the atmosphere, the ocean, the sea-bed, the Antarctic and space. These are parts of the world not yet completely divided up among nations. Consideration of the commons represents a new emphasis on the commonality of resources, a change from the tradition of claims by each nation for its own benefit. However, use of even these areas is divided according to the technological and economic ability of various nations to exploit the resources.

The theological foundations of the common heritage may be found in the biblical doctrine of creation. In the biblical view of the natural world, the earth belongs to no individual, group or nation; it is a gift to all. The Old Testament reminds us that in fact *the earth belongs to God alone*. It is to be used for the common good. No one can lay claim to any resources for solely private or national use if the exercise of that claim places the lives of others in jeopardy. The common resources of the earth must be shared justly by all humanity.

The multitudinous claims on land, sea and air space are evidence that humanity has forgotten or ignored the biblical teaching. We must remind ourselves of our obligation to protect our common areas. We must examine these commons, as Christians, in terms of justice, sustainability and participation.

The atmosphere

Long-term natural climatic changes do occur, and the World Meteorological Organization has organized important international cooperative programmes to gain a better understanding of the workings of the atmosphere. This section notes with growing alarm the long-term and, in some cases, irreversible damage being done to the atmosphere by humanity. Scientific opinion is not unanimous as to the sources or the extent of this damage. Yet in our view, it is both prudent and ethically necessary to monitor carefully the effects of discharging large amounts of gaseous, solid and radio-active materials into the atmosphere. Whether the pollution is from industrial plants, power stations, automobiles, agriculture, aircraft or other sources, it threatens the protective ozone layer, the global thermal balance, and affects all forms of life on earth.

This section questions the ethics of valuing industrialization more than human health, and rejects decisions made without the participation of peoples directly affected. We support particularly the current ban on atmospheric testing of nuclear devices and urge all nations to accept it.

The ocean and the sea-bed

The ocean is a great source of relatively unexplored and unutilized resources. A just and equitable legal framework for their use is needed if serious problems of mismanagement and conflict are to be avoided. The

United Nations Conference on the Law of the Sea is hammering out a system by which all nations, coastal and landlocked, developing and developed, will participate in decision-making concerning ocean use and the management of the sea-bed resources. Composed of more than 150 countries, and writing international law for most aspects of the ocean, it is the largest and most complicated participatory conference on law ever held.

It is crucial to remember that the ocean is the final sink: all pollution leached from the land or washed from the atmosphere accumulates there. International law in this regard is ineffectual unless subscribed to by all nations, since pollution spreads freely in the ocean. One nation's failure to abide by rules and regulations can affect many others. For example, pollution's effects are far-reaching: it threatens the life and beauty as well as the capacity of the ocean to produce oxygen and thus it may also affect the climate.

Stewardship of the ocean and its resources, in addition to requiring utilization of wealth for the sake of today's poor, also implies the conservation of resources for future generations and the preservation of the marine environment and salt water species. These are also elements of humanity's common heritage.

Another aspect of the total concept of the common heritage deals with the distribution of benefits secured from that part of the sea-bed which is beyond national jurisdiction. Today, the technology for utilizing these resources is confined to a very small minority, such as some governments and transnational enterprises. The Law of the Sea will provide the first concrete example of the transfer of technology, in a manner freely arrived at, which balances the interests of the technology holders, suppliers and recipients. As such, it is the first major product of its kind resulting from international deliberations, replacing negotiations between supplier and recipient nations, where the former's power usually prevails.

Never before have there been negotiations concerning the international management of a resource of commercial value. If this attempt is successful, it could serve as a blueprint for action on a global scale in the utilization and management of other world commons and resources.

The Antarctic

The Antarctic refers to the Antarctic continent and all islands and ice shelves bounded by the latitude 60° south. Many scientists feel that this area is integral to the world's climate and ocean circulation, although its exact role is still under investigation. The Antarctic is considered to be rich in mineral resources. Also, the ocean around the continent is fertile in living resources. Krill, at the bottom of the food chain for many marine creatures, abounds in this area. The thirteen nations party to the current Antarctic Treaty are discussing the utilization of both mineral and living resources in the near future. The vast distances and sparse information about the area will make exploitation difficult. However, many scientists and technologists are concerned about potential environmental damage from such exploitation.

The current Antarctic Treaty provides for both cooperation in and freedom of scientific research and stipulates that the Antarctic be used only for peaceful purposes. Since only nations with superior technological and economic power can participate in the exploration and utilization of mineral and living resources, it is clear that they are likely to be the ones to benefit from any development of the Antarctic.

To what extent will the international community be able to (1) have a say in the conservation and management of resources in the Antarctic continent and the Southern Ocean, and (2) participate in and benefit in their exploitation? The latter will depend to a large extent on whether or not claimant nations exercise offshore jurisdiction, both over the continental shelf and margin and over the living resources in their economic zone of 200 miles. A truly international solution would find a way to accommodate some interests of the majority of the world's nations in both living and non-living resources in the area. And before any resource exploitation accelerates, careful consideration must be given to protecting the unique environment and ecosystem.

Space

It is less than 25 years since the first satellite was launched. The rapid increase in the number, size and complexity of these tools of humanity's penetration into space boggles the imagination. Practically all activity in this field so far has been the monopoly of the two super-powers, and most of it has been prompted by the arms race. Space technology for military purposes is fast becoming a real danger to humanity and to our very existence on earth.

Yet space technology has also offered humanity numerous new benefits: an increased understanding of the origin and character of the universe, of the complex natural processes of our tiny planet, and even of the location and amount of earth's natural resources. It has made global communication possible and given support to the possibility of drawing on energy from outer space.

To maintain these benefits we must seek to limit, decrease and eventually end the use of space for military activity. We support the existing international prohibition on orbiting armaments. We must work together to see that the peaceful uses of space are not diverted to serve the short-term advantages of the rich, the mighty and the technologically advanced. We call for a truly international cooperative effort in space science and technology—an effort in which scientists and technologists from all over the world would contribute and the benefits of which would be the common heritage of humanity.

Shared natural resources

The concept of common resources can be extended to those areas where only a limited group of nations are involved. This is the situation where two or more nations have in common such natural resources as regional seas, river basins, watersheds, aquafers or even petroleum deposits. In such cases, it must be recognized that the resources are common to the peoples of the nations concerned, and arrangements should be worked out to ensure the just and sustainable sharing of such finite resources. The environmental implications of the utilization of the resources, which are not always clearly defined, should be given appropriate attention and be continually monitored. International efforts are already establishing a basis for the sharing of common resources of river basins such as the Nile and the Rhine and for joint action in regional seas, like the Mediterranean. We support these efforts and hope they will be emulated. The technological or economic advantage should not be used for the unjust exploitation of common resources by one or more countries of the group involved.

Recommendations

This section sees the idea of world commons—the oceans, the Antarctic, atmosphere and space—as valid, and supports not only the concept, but its codification in the international community through such efforts as the United Nations Conference on the Law of the Sea.

Member churches of the World Council should educate themselves on the issues of the commons, most immediately the exploitation of the sea-bed, and support the international endeavours. They should also educate their members for action on these issues.

The scientific and technological community in the North and the South involved in activities relating to world commons must abide by and implement the principles of justice, sustainability and participation as enunciated above.

4. ENVIRONMENTAL DETERIORATION

The nature of environmental deterioration

The types of pollution which damage the earth's natural life-support system can be classified into:
i)   land (persistent insecticides and heavy metal);
ii) water (sewage and oil spillage in rivers, lakes and oceans);
iii) air (atmospheric dust and excessive carbon dioxide).
The resulting environmental damage can be further classified into:
i)   soil erosion;
ii) degradation of soil fertility;
iii) thermal pollution (e.g. waste heat from power stations);
iv) noise pollution;
v)   destruction of beauty.

Social consequences

Pollution contributes to social *injustice:*
i)   the polluter does not carry the proper share of the financial or social costs;

ii) the harm done may not be just local, but may be regional and global (a good example is the occurrence of DDT poisoning in Antarctic regions);
iii) it is the weaker and poorer members of the community who are least able to counter effects of pollution (e.g. the poor and elderly who cannot escape air pollution and who can least afford medical care to counter the respiratory damage which follows);
iv) pollution can affect generations yet to come, for example by its long-term effects on the ecosystem and on human genetic mutation;
v) polluting processes are exported with technology from developed to developing countries.

Although the environment has some capacity to absorb pollution, its ability to do so varies with the pollutant and the locality (e.g. the environmental toxicity of mercury is greater in polar and tropical zones than in temperate ones). Again, some life-support systems are fragile, while others are more robust: clearance in a tropical rain forest leads to rapid deterioration of the residual soil, whereas in temperate regions where the underlying soil is of good quality, an ecosystem can be sustained. In other locations, e.g. the Rhine, levels of pollution have reached such heights that the life-support system has been destroyed.

The degree to which members of a community can participate in countering pollution will depend upon the political system of the country. In many democratic countries, the most effective means is that of coordinated and organized protest. Local environmental exercises have the advantage of making a visible impact on the surrounding community, creating a sense of identification with the project, and the satisfaction of attempting to find a solution by local participation. Concentration solely on the global aspect of pollution diverts attention from visible injustice close by.

A prerequisite for effective participation is the dissemination of scientific information and technical know-how. For example, it is not possible for people to take action against the supply to less-developed countries of inferior foodstuffs which do not meet the standards set by the developed countries unless they have some accurate means of analysing the products concerned.

Goals

While recognizing that some deterioration of the environment is inevitable simply because of human existence and activity, we should seek:

i) non-polluting industrial processes, even if they are more costly;
ii) stricter control of pollution, including the coding of each activity according to pollutant risk;
iii) alternative industrial technology and agricultural methods which are less damaging to the environment;
iv) a reduction in the rate of growth of consumption of resources in the developed countries.

Moving towards solutions

Even if solutions to environmental problems are possible, they are often complex. They involve an inter-relation of industry, individuals, and the political system. Sometimes there appears as yet to be no solution. In the German Democratic Republic, for example, there seems little alternative to the burning of lignite as a source of energy, with its high level of atmospheric pollution. Sometimes there is a conflict of interests. In the Caribbean, the exploitation of potential oil reserves would reduce unemployment and generate wealth, but it might involve some degree of pollution of the seas. The shortage of housing in many countries is being met by a programme which involves the construction of cement works with concomitant pollution of the atmosphere.

Solutions will involve:

i)   a strong emphasis on education of all levels of the community to awaken their awareness of pollution;
ii)   training of those utilizing resources in ecological principles;
iii) the realization that pressure can be brought most effectively at local and neighbourhood levels where concern for people is primary;
iv)   the encouragement of policies of conservation, the limitation of economic growth and a change of direction and priorities in planning for the future of our communities;
v)   pressure on polluters through public opinion, the press, mass media, protest organizations, boycotts and legislation where politically possible;
vi)   increased dialogue between churches and government;
vii) laws and regulations for the independent inspection, control, and limitation of pollution.

In relation to these, we feel that our greatest responsibility is in *education*, without which informed action will not take place. In this our churches can play their part: as *institutions* churches in some countries can speak directly to governments and have effective means of communicating throughout the country, often where alternative means are lacking (e.g. the Roman Catholic Church in Brazil); as *individuals* we church members show our neighbourliness and Christian witness by being involved on all levels of social life.

Recommendations

As the churches have a special transnational and transgovernmental position in the world, we urge them to promote education and awareness of the nature and injustices of environmental damage, thus facilitating participation in the necessary action for change.

5. POPULATION AND SUSTAINABILITY

People matter; not just their numbers, but their individuality, as each bears God's image. We are not concerned with a mere ecological approach to the population issue: to be human is to be more than a member of a species that must be kept in an ecological balance. We are interested in *social sustainability*—a moral criterion which includes the quality, dignity and purpose of human life of every individual and every society. This criterion requires that concern for population policy be set in the context of the concern for the totality of social and cultural life in all its global diversity and richness. Thus our questions of population policy imply recognition that different cultures, societies, and traditions and even individuals draw upon different sources of meaning and have different outlooks and different hopes. Therefore, in population policy-making and family decision-making it is imperative that all have free choice and free access to all relevant information.

Goals of population policy

In responding to the problem of rapid population growth and the social, environmental and resource problems that accompany it, nations have become increasingly aware of the need to set policy goals which will enable them to deal efficiently with such inter-related issues in ways that are just and responsible.

Christians, likewise, are compelled to respond to this cluster of issues, given the Christian view of humanity as created in the image of God, the Christian view of nature as God's creation, and the implications of the incarnation for life in the world.

Christians therefore find themselves in a joint venture with the nations in seeking policies which deal effectively with the population issue. In doing so, however, Christians have a somewhat different set of criteria by which to develop and judge specific policies. Consequently, they always have that difficult task of recognizing the constraints of reality while pressing for policies that conform to the demands of a "just, participatory and sustainable society".

A primary goal to be sought by both nations and churches is the harmonization of population numbers and growth rates with the life-supporting and life-sustaining capacities of the earth. Along with ecological sustainability, the goal of social sustainability must be sought with equal fervour if the desired population levels are to be achieved within the framework of a just, participatory and sustainable society. This would include sustaining a life of dignity, meaning and human worth, achieving a participatory consensus and cultural reinforcement for new policies, and encouraging to the fullest extent possible the participation of society's "mediating structures" (e.g. family, church, neighbourhood, voluntary associations) in policy determination and execution.

In seeking to achieve these goals, nations have before them a range of options. The choices made will depend in part on the population situation in a given nation, its own needs and its own cultural traditions. There are, however, needs of the international community and of regional communities which cannot be responsibly ignored and which require national attention to the common good of the wider regional and international community. These policy options (not mutually exclusive) apply both to the quantitative aspects of population policy (e.g. a policy of zero population growth, immigration limitation, education and provision of a range of both positive and negative incentive programmes for population limitation) and the qualitative aspects of population policy (e.g. the humanization of work and the workplace, greater work opportunities for women, low cost family health care and family planning services, conservation of resources).

Population variables

As nations choose their policies for dealing with the population question and the issues related to it, they face a variety of issues which must be taken into account. In some cases, there may be serious barriers or constraints to effective population policies. In others, these variables may even be used to facilitate such policies. But seldom can they be ignored. As churches and other concerned groups seek adoption of public policy on population-related issues, both political realism and human compassion require attention to such variables as the following:

i)   religious variables, such as taboos, diet restrictions, attitudes to family planning, religious sanctions for polygamy and large families, the expected role of the Church in the public arena, interpretations of natural law;

ii) economic variables, such as the cost of technology, the conflict between national goals and many of the goals of the transnational enterprises, lack of economic resources, economic priorities of prevailing power elites, the economic realities which are perceived to necessitate large families;

iii) political variables, such as existing immigration policies and the national sentiments behind them, interest group activities, different structures of political systems which are influenced in differing ways;

iv) cultural variables, such as the equation of marriage with having children, differing views of decision-making (consensus vs. majority vote), resistance to change, the degree to which consumerism is a dominant cultural value, the degree of authority given to the Church by the culture;

v)   structural variables, such as an inflexible stratification of society, the nature of Church-state relationships, labour union activities, and the existence of an infrastructure of professional and participatory agencies to inform, instruct, encourage, and enable action on matters related to population limitation.

Both the options and the strategies chosen for implementation will have to deal with at least some of these variables, though these should not of course be the final determinants. But they will all have an impact on what issues are debated and how they are handled (e.g. is population control a form of "genocide"?). They also have an impact on the manner of participation in the debate by organized churches (e.g. as lobbyist, critic, advocate, community mobilizer, interpreter, quiet encourager, centre of support). The churches, however, should seek to unite to the greatest extent possible on common policies and develop unified strategies.

Priorities in policy

In light of the foregoing analysis and the tripartite theme of this conference, we recommend as priorities the following broadly stated actions related to population issues, actions which are commended both to governments and to churches, and which are aimed at both ecological and social sustainability. Specific programmes of implementation will vary according to circumstances:

i)   immediate action to relieve hunger and malnutrition, factors which among other things contribute to high birth rates;

ii)   the fostering of integrated public preventive health programmes which include family planning as one aspect, and research into reliable and appropriate contraception technology;

iii)   development of education programmes designed to increase the understanding of the inter-relationship between population growth and other world problems, of family planning and responsible parenthood, and of the impact of wasteful patterns of consumption on the world and its people;

iv)   greater freedom of movement for populations;

v)   accelerated rural development programmes and fostering of traditional agricultural methods;

vi)   screening of technology imports for better labour/capital appropriateness;

vii)   subordination of profits, necessary though they may be, to the human values implicit in the just, participatory and sustainable society;

viii) encouragement of and provision for incentives to both self-responsibility and social responsibility in family planning decisions, use of resources, and demands for goods; discouragement of and disincentives to irresponsibility in these areas could gradually be built into the social fabric by appropriate government policies as well as by appropriate Christian example.

Recommendations

This report has been cast in a series of decision choices which might be made in different national contexts. But the following *ethical principles* can be identified, implicitly or explicitly, within the analysis. These might have some more generalized validity for those seeking to develop population policy in their own circumstances, recognizing that all nations contribute to the population-resource crisis and all share responsibility for its amelioration and correction.

i)   No solution to the population crisis which would adopt a policy of the "lifeboat ethic" or "triage" is acceptable in the light of Christian faith.

ii) Justice in population policy lies in the equitable distribution of risks, benefits, and costs among and between groups in the population, male/female, rich/poor, parent/child.

iii) Participation in population policy requires that there be no single-sector decision-making (ethnic groups, power groups, men only, women only) and also no single-sector solutions (population limits for the poor only, rich only, one cultural group).

iv) Sustainability in population policy requires both ecological sustainability and social sustainability. This means, among other things that population policy must allow for the realization of human expectations within the constraints of social justice, i.e. population policies have an ecological "anchor" while seeking a just social outcome.

v) Improving the status of women, necessary in and of itself, is believed to be also a crucial factor in lowering fertility and population growth rates. This means working for economic and legal equality as well as working to change male attitudes which traditionally have been marked by a sense of male superiority and domination over women and an association of male virility with numbers of children.

vi) In making decisions on family size and consumption parents must take into account not only their own personal needs, but also the wider needs and concerns of the community at large.

vii) Equality of access to information, services, and community support in family planning and other programmes of responsible population control should not be compromised by sexual, marital, socio-cultural, religious or economic status.

viii) Responsible and equitable population policies which seek to bring population growth into harmony with the earth's capacity to sustain life, far from being a veiled policy of "genocide", is a means of preventing a form of "self-genocide" by the peoples of the earth.

ix) National policies which provide incentives to regulate population growth are generally to be commended, especially those which offer positive incentives. However, such policies that might prejudice the basic human rights of the innocent child born beyond a statutory per family quota, or which carry risks to the health of the persons involved, or which tend in practice to penalize the poor disproportionately, are unjust.

x) While Christians differ profoundly on the question of abortion, it may sometimes be the lesser of two evils, to be chosen only for the most compelling reasons, and is not to be commended simply as a means of birth control.

xi) There is no one "blanket" response to the population question, either globally, nationally, or locally, because of the situational diversity. A plurality of responsible policies is thus preferred to uniformity.

VI. Energy for the Future

During recent years there have been many discussions of the problem of energy, including some under the auspices of the World Council of Churches. Several reports have been produced, particularly on the problem of nuclear energy. The most recent WCC meeting dealing with this theme was held at the Ecumenical Institute, near Geneva, May 1978 (see *Anticipation*, No. 26, June 1979, pp. 32-80). It produced a detailed statement dealing with the following main themes:
— the prospects of non-nuclear energy sources;
— social costs and risks of nuclear energy;
— the debate about the breeder reactor;
— nuclear power and non-proliferation;
— ethical issues in relation to nuclear energy.

The meeting of the Central Committee of the WCC (Kingston, Jamaica, January 1979) voted to receive a four-point statement on nuclear power. Summarized, it stated that:

i) the nuclear debate cannot be addressed in an absolutist sense but must be seen in the context of other energy options;

ii) energy consumption and more rational utilization deserve much more attention;

iii) most of the nuclear debate is but symptomatic of much deeper societal debates: more versus less, centralized technologies versus decentralized, etc.;

iv) nuclear power can be neither rejected nor accepted categorically; it is a conditional good.

Given the amount of ecumenical discussion that has already taken place on this subject, it is not unreasonable to wonder whether a further report is necessary. The present text makes no claim to replace any of the previous reports. But it can take into account more recent studies which throw light on a constantly developing problem.

A conference such as this, moreover, allows us to set the energy issue in a broader context, because:

i) the problem of energy is only one element in a complex of problems being studied at this conference;

ii) here the energy issue can be looked at in a truly worldwide perspective;

iii) the global perspective on energy helps to put the nuclear issue into its proper context.

1. THE ENERGY PROBLEM AND THE SEARCH FOR A JUST, PARTICIPATORY AND SUSTAINABLE SOCIETY

The energy supply problem

The critical nature of the energy problem is now recognized worldwide. It arouses profound questions about the future prospects of societies. It is firstly a problem of fuel supplies. Because of declining reserves of oil, the main fuel for many societies, there will have to be a transition to a post-oil era. Furthermore, in many developing countries there is a critical shortage of firewood for basic cooking and heating. At the same time grave questions are being raised about the use of nuclear power and the environmental effects of further increases in the combustion of fossil fuels much beyond present levels. A second problem arises because more energy is required to help meet the basic needs of the majority of the world's people; other people are using energy so intensively that serious social and environmental stresses are resulting.

Obviously, then, a global perspective is necessary in the search for solutions. A vision of the long-term desirable social goals is also essential. In this report "short term" is defined as the period in which decisions and investments already made will predominate (the next 5-10 years); "medium term", the period in which decisions about to be made will predominate (the next 10-25 years) and "long term", the period beyond the turn of the century.

In this connection it is also necessary to distinguish between renewable and non-renewable energy sources. Non-renewable fuels represent capital stock obtained from the earth; those available at present are the fossil fuels (coal, oil, gas) and uranium. The non-renewable sources with long-term potential are coal, uranium (if fast-breeder reactors or converters with near-breeder characteristics are used) and nuclear fusion which has yet to be proved practicable.

Renewable energy sources are a continuous energy income from natural energy flows and material cycles. These include direct solar, wind, biomass, ocean and geothermal energy, hydropower and energy obtained from urban and rural wastes. The rate of inflow and the requirements of the ecosystem set limits to the amount of energy obtainable from these sources.

Ethical issues and the churches

Our report and recommendations on energy are addressed to the churches, and through them and their members to the public, scientific groups, governments, and other advocacy groups.

Discussion of the energy problem cannot be limited to its scientific, technical, economic and political aspects. It raises the question of the whole nature of the society in which we live and to which we aspire.

In the matter of energy, our societies are not models of justice, participation and sustainability. Indeed it would be truer to say that the present energy situation highlights the inequalities between rich and poor both within and among countries; it encourages the depletion of resources at the cost of serious damage to the environment and pursues the choice of options without adequate information.

This conference calls the churches to give particular attention to this situation. They must speak out in condemnation of it and, though starting from present realities, must be prophetic in their witness for a new society. Obviously, the churches are not alone in seeking a future of greater justice. Moreover, they confess that human beings, though created in the image of God, are inclined to pride and excess. They know that history does not move in a straight line towards the Kingdom. Yet they must bear witness to their faith in a God who requires them to seek justice not only as a future hope but also as a present obligation.

There is in the churches a sense of concern and a range of human and material resources which could contribute to the continuing debate on energy policies and choices. We recommend that the churches:

i)   encourage their members to continue to strive for unity in the midst of tensions and uncertainty;

ii) encourage Christians to listen to one another in a worldwide fellowship, and to bring different perspectives to bear upon local and national problems;

iii) work for an understanding of creation which informs decisions about resources, renewable and non-renewable;

iv) develop among their members a sense of vocation which seeks to ensure that decisions reached find expression both in personal life-styles and, through their work and civic responsibilities, in changing structures of corporations, governments, etc.;

v)   make available the range of informed judgment and data accumulated by the WCC and national church groups on this issue.

We suggest that, whatever method or style of ethical reflection and decision is used by Christians, it should enable us at least to:

i)   exercise a critical capacity in two ways: (a) by identifying our prior commitments and loyalties, as affluent or poor, as male or female, as citizens of nations, etc., and (b) by asking questions concerning facts, policies, and conclusions which expose underlying and determining assumptions;

ii) clarify the commitments and values which should inform decisions;

iii) examine carefully the options and risks (there are greater or lesser risks in every energy policy), and the foreseeable consequences;

iv) encourage continuing reflection and critical study, so that we become aware of wrong choices, have the humility to acknowledge error, and seek to change direction.

We are wary of forecasts of what "the energy situation will be" over long ranges of time. "Who decides" will influence both the present and the future directions in policy. We detect a bias towards technocratic decisions, towards decisions by national elites, towards developed countries making decisions which affect developing countries, and towards an over-emphasis on economic factors over against political and moral considerations.

All countries are beginning to ask profound questions about the consequences of their present energy choices for the nature of their society in the future, and the acceptability of risks involved in alternative choices. We suggest the following ethical considerations in the evaluation of the options:

i) the extent to which fuel resources may be shared in order that the essential needs of the poor may be met;
ii) the extent of risk to the health of the existing population;
iii) the extent to which the health of future generations may be endangered;
iv) the extent to which present consumption may deprive posterity of its birthright;
v) the extent of ecological damage;
vi) the extent to which the freedom of the individual may be imperilled;
vii) the extent to which social stability may be endangered.

Additional guidelines arise when we consider energy choices in the context of justice, sustainability and participation.

Energy choices in the search for justice, participation and sustainability

Justice: In a just society everyone would have access to the energy necessary to meet their basic needs. People must learn to limit their demands rather than endlessly extend them. Energy needs are studied in greater detail below (Part 2).

Justice would also require fairer distribution of energy between rich and poor, within countries as well as between countries. This applies not only to the main energy resources, but also to the technologies related to energy use; it is necessary to find "inequality-reducing technologies".

We believe that justice requires the development of more self-reliant national policies which place emphasis on the needs of local areas. This means finding patterns of energy use and modes of supply designed to overcome economic and technological dependence, and avoid the creation of further exploitative dependencies.

Participation: Both ends and means are important in the move towards a just, participatory and sustainable society. We consider participation as both an end and a means, in the search for energy decisions informed by the norms of justice and sustainability.

The focus on participation could be strengthened by recalling the historic ecumenical concept of the responsible society, in which those who exercise power are held accountable to God and to those who are affected by it. (The first assembly of the World Council of Churches, Amsterdam, August 1948, stated that churches should work for "the responsible society where freedom is the freedom of men who acknowledge responsibility to justice and public order, and where those who hold political authority or economic power are responsible for its exercise to God and the people whose welfare is affected by it".)

In a society based on participation the basic choices cannot be made by a small body of experts, planners or entrepreneurs alone. Despite the complicated nature of some of the problems to be solved, democracy must not yield its place to technocracy.

This means in particular that access to essential information must not be restricted, nor evaluation and control procedures be kept secret. It also means that total energy use patterns and supply sources must be discussed as widely and frankly as possible, with particular attention to the full range of risks and benefits of each option.

Sustainability: A society which is sustainable and considerate of the future must resolutely combat the wastage of the earth's riches and make the development of renewable energy a top priority. This will mean a search for higher levels of efficiency and sober, careful use of non-renewable fuels. A sustainable society must attach prime importance to all the risks and injuries caused to both human beings and to nature by its activities and consumption of energy. Energy choices should be carefully evaluated in terms of their implications for the world's long-term ecological sustainability and for the existence of other species on the earth. Energy politics must be designed to reduce international tensions and contribute towards the solution of other global problems, including the establishment of a new international economic order.

Dilemmas in formulating energy policy

Changes in the basic directions of a society are difficult to accomplish. There are technical and social pressures which make abrupt changes difficult, dangerous and even contribute to social or political destabilization. Moreover, to impose overly rapid changes without the consent of those concerned is to run the risk of contradicting the ideal of participation already described. Simple economic and political pressures push towards short-term solutions, but the underlying social, ethical, technological and resource problems require long-term strategies, and many of these different approaches conflict. There is therefore a narrow way to be sought, one which calls for a more informed, alert and properly motivated people.

In order to carry out a meaningful and effective programme of participation in energy decisions, it will be necessary to develop appropriate education programmes among all elements of society. This applies especially to the training of scientists and technologists. It must be emphasized that education and participation alone may not provide the justice we seek or assure the choice of sustainable sources of energy with appropriate balancing of benefits and risks. The proper choice can evolve only following independent study and research. Unfortunately, the majority of education and training programmes in the advanced countries are financed and directed by government agencies and in many cases the primary objective of these agencies is to support preconceived notions and decisions, to perpetuate their existence, to devalue research data that are contrary to their official position and forever expand (in size and political stature) by artificially maintaining an unblemished public record. Thus a major responsibility of this conference is to oppose this bias and assure free and more unfettered education, training and research programmes in all countries so that people may better understand and judge the issues.

While any national energy policy will require centralized decision-making, the choice of complex capital-intensive technology, such as nuclear power, brings the prospect of an even more centralized society which makes participation difficult and could adversely affect human liberties.

On the other hand, it is possible to envisage a more decentralized society using renewable energy technologies, which places greater responsibility on individuals and local communities. Such a society would tend to be more labour-intensive and participatory.

Are these two types of society mutually exclusive? Or are they complementary? Can they co-exist? These questions call for a deeper study, which leads to the greater detail given below (Part 3).

2. ENERGY NEEDS

In order to establish the main outlines of an energy strategy for the future with a view to achieving a just, participatory and sustainable society, it would seem appropriate to start by assessing the basic needs and demands of such a society.

Basic needs include material needs of food, shelter, clothing, resources, and services, and non-material needs relating to human fulfilment, the sense of meaning and the quality of community life. Happily the human being is not a machine whose needs can be entirely quantified. It is important that basic material needs be met in ways appropriate to the non-material needs of the whole person. We can speak of a vital minimum of biophysical needs necessary for a dignified survival. It is important to distinguish also what is needed for survival in any society with its specific social and economic system and culture. The perception of these needs may change with transformation of the social system. In addition there are wants which do not fall in either of the above categories and which derive from adopted life-styles; these are not basic.

We must try to assess basic needs within the social, cultural and human contexts, and then look for a set of energy strategies which will help to satisfy basic needs first, both material and non-material. One particular need must not be overlooked: to be able to take part in rewarding, constructive and dignified work.

In the following sections, we consider basic needs of food, housing, transport and industrial activity in more detail, pointing out some aspects of the different human and social contexts in the industrialized and developing countries.

Energy for food

Food is a basic human need. The existence of "hunger zones" in so many places in the world despite the availability of excess food in other parts of the world is evidence that deep international changes must be made.

Agriculture makes use of solar energy but, particularly in the developed countries, it also uses large amounts of fossil fuels. This is especially true in areas of intensive monoculture based on a high degree of mechanization and massive use of chemicals. The protein output per unit of direct energy input is lower in such cases than in less mechanized agriculture, but such methods evolved historically at a time when energy was unrealistically cheap. The rising cost of energy will necessarily reduce its current levels of use in agricultural production. In addition, the adverse environmental impact of many energy intensive agricultural processes, such as pesticide and fertilizer application, mechanization and intensive livestock methods, suggests the adoption of alternative methods which would also be energy conserving.

In developing countries a basic conflict arises between demands for energy for food and non-food export cash crops, and energy for domestic food production. This conflict is intensified by the current economic development strategies pursued by many developing countries.

It should also be recognized that large-scale utilization of biomass conversion as a long-term energy supply strategy would undoubtedly lower food production in the world because it would make for additional demand on the limited arable land available. This problem will be intensified as the world's population and its nutritional needs increase.

Much energy is also used for processing, storing, selling and transporting food within and between countries. Reconsideration should be given to the unnecessary transport of luxury goods or off-season products for the consumption of privileged groups, and to the over-processing and over-packaging of food.

Cooking is another major use of energy in the food chain. Industrialized countries could use more efficient cooking practices and appliances. In less industrialized countries, where wood and agricultural wastes are generally the main fuels, more efficient stoves coupled with major reforestation efforts are needed.

Energy for housing

In the industrialized countries heating and air-conditioning systems in offices, homes, factories, schools and other public buildings consume a great deal of energy. Employing electricity for low-grade heat is not always a good matching of end use and energy source. Furthermore, many buildings were not constructed with energy-saving in mind, and the efficiency of their heating and cooling systems is poor. It is essential to improve the insulation of old and new buildings, as well as building codes and designs. More efficient heating systems are needed. Much of the present housing was constructed at a time when the problem of finite fossil fuel reserves was not fully recognized and substantial change in the existing building stock will take time. This means that a medium-term strategy is required. Such a building improvement programme will also create new jobs.

Energy for transport

The automobile is the symbol of the industrial society. It seems to embody and fulfil the longing for human freedom; yet it also imprisons us in the urban culture which it has helped to create. There is a mythology of the automobile which would bear examination in greater depth.

Considerable changes will be needed in the field of transport if energy, and in particular energy from fossil fuels, is to be used more efficiently.

Yet here again, the weight of infra-structures and habits developed in the past will act as a powerful brake. In the highly industrialized countries, large investments have been made in suburbanization, land utilization and roads on the basis of an automotive civilization. The automotive industry, a cornerstone of present industrialized societies, has been very closely linked with political authorities in creating the present situation. However, a too brusque change of strategy could have a destabilizing effect on the economy and lead to widespread unemployment. During the time of transition, attention must be given to increasing the energy efficiency of the car and of its use (for example, by imposing speed limits), to providing for public transport, walking and cycling, and to urban planning for lower energy-use cities.

Transport is one of the basic needs in all countries. Many forms of mass transportation are highly energy-efficient and this has important multiplier effects on the economic use of energy in other sectors. Mass transit, except in highly dense urban clusters, has been neglected in many industrialized societies. Increased investment in these transit modes can provide important long-term and short-term energy savings and can help society to restructure its "consumerist" life-style. In the future, improved telecommunications may aid in reducing the energy demands of transport.

Energy for industrial activity

Industrial activity is necessary to supply basic material needs and otherwise support populations, especially in cities. The considerable energy needs of industrial activity also depend on infra-structures developed at a time when fuels were cheap and supply seemed unlimited.

Drastic changes in the industrial systems are inevitable both in industrialized and in less industrialized countries, and are already underway. As these changes are being planned, the quest for a just and sustainable society requires that human beings should not be sacrificed to the industrial imperatives of profit and productivity. (The report of Section VII deals with these matters in detail.)

3. ENERGY STRATEGIES

There are three fundamental energy paths or strategies for the future:

i) *The "hard path":* This involves large-scale, capital-intensive, centralized technologies depending on large amounts of nuclear fuels and coal for the middle-term; in the long-term fossil fuels would be phased out entirely in favour of breeders, and possibly fusion.

ii) *The "soft path":* The technology is small-scale, less capital-intensive, decentralized (e.g. solar heating, biomass), emphasizing conservation technologies (e.g. co-generation, passive solar heating). In the middle-term the transitional use of coal is anticipated, while in the long-term solar and other renewable energy sources will be used.

iii) *The "hard-soft path":* Most government planners and energy specialists claim that all options need to be pursued. This constitutes a third strategy, which results in a mixture of policies and technologies depending on the availability of regional, natural, financial and industrial resources.

Until 1973 energy policies in industrial countries mainly followed the "hard path"; now most countries are pursuing policies that emphasize the combined path. In most developing countries the 1973-74 oil crisis also initiated a drive to replace oil and to search for indigenous resources and more appropriate technologies (e.g. solar, wind, hydro, etc.).

For the long term we believe that no options should be excluded per se, but for the short and medium terms we make a strong plea for a major shift towards the development of an effective implementation of the huge, as yet untapped, potential of the soft option.

These shifts will require certain changes in life-styles and consumption patterns. However these need not reduce economic growth. In order to achieve these changes it is essential to provide full and honest information through public education and social dialogue to counter values presently conveyed by the media (e.g. energy demand forecasts put out by large energy companies).

A just and sustainable society requires more growth of energy use in poor countries, the curtailment of its use in rich countries, and a major shift over time from non-renewable sources (coal, oil, gas and uranium) to renewable ones (direct solar, biomass, hydro, geothermal, tidal and wind) for all nations. A participatory society implies the fuller participation of individuals and groups in decision-making processes concerning energy.

It was generally agreed that for some purposes the present widespread use of electrical energy is inefficient. But some energy systems (e.g. nuclear, photovoltaic and hydro) can only produce electricity. It was also noted that the electrical sector may need to be enlarged in order to reduce dependency on oil.

Options and risks

i) SHORT TERM

The section agreed that energy conservation is of primary importance both in developed and developing societies. There are many possibilities for conservation in industrialized societies. However, these should be pursued in such a way that economic disparities within these societies are not increased. The section defined conservation as the *just, rational, efficient matching of energy systems to energy needs.* If such conservation programmes are implemented, present energy sources will be adequate. No additional capacity such as nuclear will be required.

There are, however, barriers to the implementation of conservation programmes. Future benefits from conservation tend to be heavily discounted when decisions are based primarily on political and economic considerations. Furthermore, conservation affects various sectors of the population in different ways. Without strong government intervention conservation programmes are unlikely to be fair, effective and to get off the ground on time.

The continued burning of coal is essential in the short-term, with the possibility of increased use in some areas—especially in certain less-industrialized societies. ˙

Further dependence on the burning of coal may result in serious environmental problems which have hitherto gone relatively unrecognized, for example, air pollution and the long-term disposal of wastes. Some of these, such as air pollution due to coal burning, can be substantially reduced by the more widespread use of fluidized-bed combustion and coal gassification. The production of atmospheric carbon dioxide and other pollutants may result in climatic changes which would alter agricultural and living patterns with benefits to some regions but with harm to many more. This would lead to international disagreements over what should be the global energy strategy. In the long-run irreversible changes could occur such as the melting of the polar ice caps. However, climatologists do not agree on the consequences of a large-scale build-up of atmospheric contaminants, especially carbon dioxide. The importance of this issue calls urgently for further research.

Do these dangers strengthen the case for nuclear energy? The majority of the section argues as follows: Nuclear power, as such, cannot have a significant impact on reducing carbon dioxide build-up for a very long time. On the other hand, conservation measures which would double the efficiency of automobile engines and/or building insulation could dramatically reduce the rate of CO_2 accumulation by the turn of the century. Thus the CO_2 problem cannot be a decisive factor in deciding one way or the other on nuclear power for the short and medium terms.

A limited moratorium on nuclear power for the short and perhaps the medium term would have the following positive aspects:

a) A temporary moratorium would give our nuclear technologists breathing space to enable them to resolve serious technical questions associated with reactor safety, appropriate standards for radiation protection, effective international safeguards, and the disposal of radio-active wastes—both low-level (i.e. uranium mill tailings) and high-level (i.e. spent nuclear fuel and high-level liquid wastes). It would also permit further research on the Thorium/Uranium 233 cycle and the feasibility of fusion. This stand is in agreement with recent official statements from a number of political jurisdictions (e.g. the West German "Gorleben" decision, the California Energy Commission's moratorium decision, and the Ontario Royal Commission on Electric Power Planning which concludes that a moratorium may become compulsory if the waste disposal problem is not solved by 1985).

b) A temporary moratorium will allow investment capital to be rechannelled from nuclear expansion to energy conservation, and the further exploration of the soft path approach.

c) The nuclear industry is facing serious financial difficulties worldwide because of unforeseen costs, strong political opposition, a sharp decline in new orders and, in many quarters, a significant over-capacity in electrical generating facilities. It must be recognized that even if the nuclear industry is eventually phased out for economic or political reasons, we will still be faced with difficult and expensive decontamination problems for at least a hundred years after the last reactor is shut down. This will impose an unjust burden on future generations. It is therefore an opportune time to declare an official moratorium which could allow for a rationalization of the industry, a more realistic appraisal of the future prospects for nuclear power, and appropriate financial arrangements to cover the costs of decontamination.

d) It has been recognized in a number of studies around the world that the continued spread of nuclear power facilities will measurably increase the threat of nuclear warfare (e.g. the Flowers Report from the UK, the Fox Report from Australia, the Burns Report from New Zealand, the Ford/Mitre Report from the USA, and the Porter Report from Ontario, Canada). Yet the nuclear industry has to find new orders to stay in business. In view of the dangers of proliferation and the inadequacies of current safeguards, a temporary halt to such sales could be of great assistance in bringing the entire question of disarmament, proliferation and safeguards into much sharper focus.

ii)   MEDIUM TERM
As oil supplies diminish and in order to limit the burning of coal, further conservation of these fuels will be needed. We advocate greater use of renewable energy which includes direct (e.g. solar heat and photovoltaics) and indirect (e.g. biomass, wind and hydro) uses of solar energy. These offer a way out of dependence and opportunities for more participation, and their environmental impact is smaller, though not negligible. For developing countries in particular they offer possibilities for decentralized, labour-intensive methods which can be appropriated by the rural poor.

But it was recognized that there are limits to the rate at which these energy sources can be introduced. There are already major problems including deforestation in the tropics, monocultures with all their ecological dangers, and large hydro-power chopping rivers into separate sections that destroy ecologically integrated systems. It is therefore essential in these regions that major reforestation programmes are started and that other renewable technologies such as biogas are promoted.

The section considered whether or not further nuclear plants would be needed in the medium term and the claim that nuclear power could be necessary to achieve energy independence.

A distinction must be made between "burners" and "breeders". Burners are already in operation, are not sustainable for more than a few decades, and do not require reprocessing facilities. (It is debatable whether or not reprocessing is desirable prior to the ultimate disposal of nuclear wastes.) Breeders can extend this period considerably, but introduce much larger environmental and social risks. Both systems could lead to the establishment of highly centralized authoritarian governments and levels of surveillance of civilians, both of which militate against the ideal of a participatory society. The production of plutonium in the breeder cycle would also increase the danger of the proliferation in nuclear weapons.

Objections were raised to the idea of achieving energy independence through nuclear power on the ground that this could only be made possible by controlling the entire fuel cycle at enormous cost—an expensive programme even for an industrialized society. (The cost of ultimate waste disposal and final plant decommissioning would increase this cost even more.) In addition nuclear power requires an industrial effort out of scale with the technological base of most developing countries. To replace approximately 10% of the present total world energy consumption (now almost entirely being met by fossil fuels), one thousand nuclear reactors (1 TW capacity) would be required. In other words such a huge investment in nuclear plants would make only very little impact on the consumption of fossil fuels.

Nuclear reactors produce heat which is converted into electricity. This heat could also be used directly for heating homes. However, it is difficult to distribute heat from a large nuclear plant for cogeneration purposes unless the plant is situated in the vicinity of a large centre of demand. This limits their value as a replacement for portable liquid fuels.

Considerable attention has already been given to the risks of nuclear energy in previous WCC and secular discussions. The risks arising from the different methods of energy generation are of varying kinds. Some are technical and relate to the possibility of loss of life: for example, mining accidents, liquid fuel explosions, and exposure to radio-activity. Others are social: for example, the consequences of introducing surveillance measures designed to counter terrorist activity geared to, say, possible thefts of plutonium.

Discussion of the political risks associated with energy generation in the medium term has tended to focus on the question of nuclear proliferation. Dissatisfaction with the discriminatory nature of the nuclear Non-Proliferation Treaty (NPT) has long been expressed by third world governments who see it as a fundamentally unjust attempt by members of the Nuclear Club to protect their own political and military interests. However, in recent years a number of third world governments have begun to have doubts about the feasibility and cost of acquiring nuclear hardware, and the virtually inescapable patterns of political dependence involved in acquiring nuclear fuels in the early stages of setting up a nuclear weapons programme. This poses the ultimate political dilemma of third world countries: to be dominated by the military power of the nuclear states or to be dependent on them for developing nuclear capability.

iii) LONG TERM

In the long term both industrialized and less industrialized countries could use considerably diminished quantities of coal, more renewables, and, possibly, nuclear burners and breeders. Nuclear fusion may also begin to contribute energy. Insofar as the fusion process does not utilize fissionable materials such as uranium and plutonium, its commercial implementation will avoid some of the technical, social and political problems associated with nuclear fission. But it needs to be stressed that fusion reactors have their own distinctive kinds of risk. So, for that matter, do the relatively benign renewables!

Socio-ethical considerations

In the choice of energy options various criteria need to be taken into account: technical, economic, social, political and ethical. These are not always easily reconciled because in differing situations different weights may be given to each of these criteria and there may be no universally applicable choice.

It is difficult for governments to make political decisions about choices which will have effects far beyond their normal life. There are no precedents for deciding how to weigh the short-term welfare of contemporaries against the long-term health of future generations. Heavy reliance on nuclear reactors would produce radio-active waste which would need to be safely contained for hundreds—many say even millions—of years, if a satisfactory method of nuclear incineration is not commercially developed. At present such a technology is technically feasible but economically forbidding. Accidental release of radio-active materials into the environment also entails future health risks. Moreover, heavy reliance on coal and oil would deprive future generations of useful industrial resources, and involve a risk of climatic change if the pollution of the atmosphere is not controlled.

The process of weighing such major risks and benefits, and the resolution of conflicts between them, is one that can be undertaken only by societies as a whole. Churches do not, any more than governments and other concerned groups, have a monopoly of insight into such matters. But they must nevertheless play a role in the decision-making process, insisting on the seriousness and magnitude of the issues, the urgency of facing them squarely and offering, where possible, to provide a forum in which the ethical factors can be elucidated and debated.

Planners have invariably extrapolated from historic patterns of gross fuel consumption. The resulting forecasts are used to argue the case for the continued expansion of energy supply. These fail to take account of real needs of the different sectors of energy use: space heating, transport, industry, agriculture, etc.

It is important to distinguish between short-, medium- and long-term planning. Short-term economic and/or political gains should not over-ride the requirement of a just, participatory and sustainable energy supply which would be designed to meet the basic needs of the present generation and its successors.

4. RECOMMENDATIONS

A. We recommend to the churches that they:
i) give high priority to the development of strategies for full participation in discussions and decisions regarding the energy issues within their membership, in ecumenical councils and in public;
ii) insist that such participation include all classes and groups of the population with full access to relevant information and real involvement in the discussions and decisions through fair and open procedures;
iii) arouse concern and conscience regarding energy decisions with specific consideration for the responsibility people bear as citizens, consumers and workers in all aspects of the energy sector;
iv) identify ethical criteria by which the social impacts of energy technologies must be assessed and insist that in setting energy policy such criteria be given equal weight alongside technical and economic factors;
v) identify and utilize members with special knowledge and responsibility in the energy field who can help one another and others to be equipped for informed participation;
vi) involve such experts, along with those who have insight in the theological and ethical issues, in equipping church members for participation in critical and informed deliberations and decisions;
vii) develop a climate of trust and critical self-awareness in which biases can be acknowledged and corrected, differences of opinion and conviction can be faced and conflicts be dealt with, thus facilitating a continuing programme of education, participation and choice;

viii) develop education materials about the energy issue for different levels of church life which give people a chance to acquaint themselves with the discussion thus far, enter a process of honest and open dialogue and so make up their own minds about opinions to be chosen and decisions to be made;

ix) engage in a constructive and critical analysis of the national and international energy policies of their own countries, engage wherever possible in open discussion with their governments about these policies and keep each other informed of both progress and problems in these efforts;

x) engage with people at the local level in projects which enable them personally and together to experiment with a life-style which makes appropriate use of the available energy sources;

xi) endorse, promote, and support the use of the WCC "Energy For My Neighbour" programme through their agencies and congregations.

B. We recommend to all national governments that they:

i) study the actual use of all forms of energy in their countries and not only the consumption of commercially traded fuels;

ii) base the forecasts of future energy demand on the real needs for different forms of energy in the different sectors, rather than on extrapolation from aggregates of past fuel consumption;

iii) provide incentives for the most rapid possible transition to the just, rational and efficient matching of energy sources to energy needs;

iv) ensure that scarce resources of capital and skills are allocated in the first instance to the development of systems that will, as soon as possible, efficiently provide energy in the forms really needed from renewable sources;

v) mitigate any severe injustices between different sections of the population which may develop during the transition to efficient and renewable energy systems;

vi) limit the growth in combustion of fossil fuels as much as possible, using these fuels, especially coal, as bridging fuels in the transition to renewable energy sources over the medium and long term;

vii) meanwhile, use existing nuclear power plants only to the extent, for the purposes, and for the time, that there is no better alternative;

viii) immediately introduce a moratorium on the construction of all new nuclear power plants for a period of five years; the purpose of this moratorium is to encourage and enable wide participation in a public debate on the risks, costs and benefits of nuclear energy in all countries directly concerned;

ix) not reprocess spent nuclear fuel to extract fissile material such as plutonium—except for separation of small quantities for research and medical applications—and not construct plutonium-fuelled reactors;

x) devise short-, medium- and long-term national energy strategies designed to achieve these objectives and which are mutually compatible;

xi) at all stages of the devising and carrying out of such strategies, keep people fully and honestly informed, and encourage the widest possible public participation through fair and open procedures;

xii) cooperate with other governments in order to ensure that:

    a) rates of consumption of the world's remaining non-renewable fuels are reduced as quickly as possible;

    b) injustices between countries caused by the unequal distribution of the fuels over the earth's surface and by market mechanisms are mitigated through international agreement;

    c) pollution of the environment by excess carbon dioxide, radio-activity and other by-products of the consumption of fuel is substantially researched and kept to the minimum that is technically feasible and ecologically sustainable;

    d) all countries move, with all possible speed, towards the efficient use of energy from renewable sources;

    e) the trend to destruction of the earth's forests be reversed;

    f) there is international support to aid the autonomous capacity of developing countries for energy research and development and for self-reliant energy projects in the poorer areas of the world.

C. INTERNATIONAL ENERGY SAVING PLEDGE

In order to encourage individual efforts for energy saving in addition to governmental and institutional action, we recommend the introduction internationally of a "Fuel Pledge", written in simple terms. We recommend that churches throughout the world, acting in concert or through national councils of churches, should cooperate where possible with governments and non-governmental organizations in publicizing the pledge and promoting signature among all people of good will. We hope that suitable publicity and simple explanatory leaflets will be forthcoming in each country.

We propose the following wording: "I pledge myself to save fuel and electricity at home, at work and at leisure and to help to make available more for those whose basic needs are not being met."

The WCC, through its programme "Energy For My Neighbour", is asked to coordinate the implementation of such individual and communal efforts (for a description of the programme see the WCC booklet *Energy For My Neighbour: an Action Programme of the WCC*, Geneva, 1978).

Editor's note: the minority opinion on the issue of the moratorium

The Section report as first presented to the plenary proposed an indefinite moratorium on the construction of nuclear plants. However, the Section had not been unanimous on this and appended to the report was a minority opinion arguing against such an indefinite moratorium on the following grounds:

i) The production of nuclear-generated electricity is to date the safest energy industry throughout the world; there are some uses of energy for which electricity is most efficient and there are some parts of the world that do not have an over-capacity in electrical generation.

ii) An indefinite moratorium without a precise method of determining its conclusion is tantamount to a veto; it would result in the dispersal of scientists and engineers, and prevent the recruiting of new ones, thus making it difficult to develop the nuclear industry if such a decision should be taken during the moratorium.

Later, in the conference plenary, a five-year moratorium was proposed instead of an indefinite one and was accepted by the majority, thus making the original minority report inapplicable. However, a minority of the plenary opposed a moratorium in any form.

VII. Restructuring the Industrial and Urban Environment

1. A BIBLICAL PERSPECTIVE

The views of the Bible on the city, expressed chiefly through the image of both an ideal and a historical Jerusalem, continue to offer insight into the nature and purpose of city life. "Jerusalem is built like a city that is bound together in fellowship in itself" (Ps. 122). The reference is to the actual physical structures of the city, whose houses and palaces, standing close over narrow streets and lanes, seem to belong together as friends. The lay-out of the city actualized a social ideal where people could know their fellow-citizens and be aware of belonging to the city as a whole.

But Jerusalem's vocation was a special one—a home for the Temple of God. The Temple assured the citizens of two things: God's presence and his personal concern. Another psalmist wrote: "As the mountains are round about Jerusalem, so is the Lord round about his people." If nature is one of our most enduring contacts with our divine "Ground of Being", then we have a spiritual criterion for the optimum size of a city: that it should never be so big that it insulates the inhabitants from awareness of the environment in which it is set. If that limit is passed, the city becomes a subliminal voice telling its people: "You are controllers of your own destiny; you are as God." Great cities foster megalomania.

But scale is not the only consideration. There is beauty. The heavenly Jerusalem in Revelation is pictured as radiantly beautiful. In so many of our cities today the hideous and derelict overwhelm us. Most of the people live amid hoardings, junkyards, factories, tenements, featureless housing estates. How can human beings believe in their own dignity when this is thought a fit setting for them?

Jerusalem's function was not to provide homes and workplaces for as many people as possible, but to be a focus of their pilgrim hopes, faith and values. So, too, God's Jerusalem in Revelation is perpetually open to all nations, but not as their dwelling-place.

It is a common error of Christians to imagine that the Bible says work was laid on humankind as a curse. Not at all. Even in Eden, before the Fall, God "put Adam into the garden to work it and keep it safe" (Gen. 2:15). Human transgression meant that we were now fighting nature instead of evoking its cooperation. *The importance of work lies in the fact that the worker is need-*

ed. The relevant quotation here is from Paul's picture of the Body of Christ, where the honour and equality of the members rest on the fact that "the eye cannot say to the hand, 'I have no need of you'".

Biblical wisdom suggests that the right use of technology is not to replace *human* work but to replace *dehumanizing* work. Any other programme destroys both the individual and the possibility of the participatory community.

2. THE PRESENT STATE OF URBANIZATION IN INDUSTRIALIZED AND DEVELOPING COUNTRIES

Industrialized countries

In the western industrialized countries the growth of urban society has reached a relatively "acceptable" level. In fact, some claim that the historical migration from the rural areas to the cities is now being reversed in certain parts of the highly industrialized countries (e.g. Denmark, Netherlands, Israel, Japan and the United States), but our Section was not able to substantiate this claim during the conference. If it is the case that the direction of population movements is changing, as it is clear that many industries are indeed moving into rural areas, it may be possible to see a type of rural-urban equilibrium in the future. To what degree energy shortages and higher energy costs will affect this shift remains to be seen.

But we must not draw too cheery a picture. Serious urban problems in the industrialized countries remain. For example, a hundred years ago urban industries could absorb millions of unskilled semi-educated labourers, but this is no longer the case. Nonetheless, rural youth seeking a better life "vote with their feet" and migrate to the cities and become part of an unemployed, underemployed, and underpaid class. They are often foreign workers driven from their own countries by economic problems (some 25 million in Europe and the United States). In this vulnerable position they are special prey to the rich and powerful who can easily exploit their desire for employment, education and entertainment available only in the cities.

Furthermore, there are other, newer problems created by the changing composition of the labour force and the new patterns of community and family life which large urban complexes foster. In industrialized countries only about 5-10% of the labour force now work in agriculture, about 30% in industry and over half in service functions. In some countries women now make up as much as 50% of the labour force. Family life has changed profoundly, and under these pressures conventional social norms soon lose their validity.

As one author says, we have become a nation of strangers—an atomized mass society of rapidly moving individuals. Many communities, including Christian congregations, become transient. And the whole of this modern society is dependent on high-level science and technology, using enormous quantities of material resources and energy, much of it wastefully.

Developing countries

The cities in third world countries, with very few exceptions, started as administrative centres or colonial outposts whose primary purpose was to facilitate operation of the colonial government. Like feudal centres, they sought resources from their periphery and used their power to maintain the colonial, social, cultural and political structure.

While it is true that many third world countries, particularly those in Asia and Africa, are not at present heavily urbanized, the trend in most of them is towards increased and very rapid urbanization. In recent times, huge metropolitan areas have developed, many with more than 10 million inhabitants. It is in these cities that the accelerating pace of modern life threatens to exceed the limits of human adaptability and endurance. There is a lack of space, air and water; public services (housing, sewerage, clean water, schools and public transport) cannot be organized to keep up with increasing demand; industry offers only limited employment opportunities, often at low wages and unsafe working conditions. The (often remarkable) ability of families to adjust is overstretched; local neighbourhoods cannot manage to crystallize into communities. In short, patterns of suffering and exploitation predominate.

Urban planning

Urban planning is a social activity which reflects the various interests and ideologies of the planners and is not merely a neutral technical profession. Even something like the physical character of a city mirrors the social history of its people with their interests and biases. For example, the wealthy with their style of housing and manicured neighbourhoods live separately from the poor who dwell in slums and squatter housing. Often urban planners look past the social character of the city and its structure, seeing only external aspects like townscapes, facades, boulevards and so on, and ignore the importance of features like old and poor schools and decaying buildings in the slums which affect large numbers of lower-income people.

In some developing countries, city plans do not even show squatter communities as part of residential areas; as far as the planners are concerned, squatters are non-people. "Squatting", a common occurrence in the cities of developing countries, is the practical expression of an ideology: "We have a right to exist and share in the benefits of urban life." But squatters are vulnerable because the legal systems are usually biased against them. Urban planning and government regulations can combine to make life impossible for the squatters, forcing them back to an equally untenable rural life. Already in urban renewal programmes which relocate industry, clear slums, and "reclaim" the decaying central cities, low-income people are dislodged and forgotten. This consequence of many urban plans, depriving the poor of shelter, is a denial of a fundamental human right and is to be condemned.

The city and its environment

Generally, it is the national urban-industrial centre which has the greatest contact with the world economy and cultures. At the same time, these centres often maintain an exploitative relationship with their respective provincial peripheries. The provincial commercial centres in their turn act as exploiting metropolitan centres in relation to their respective rural hinterlands.

In this process, we see the role of the city as "pulling" the country's resources and funnelling them to the urban-industrial centres. Part of the resources pulled are human resources which move in what is commonly referred to as rural-urban migration. All sorts of theories have been formulated to explain this process. The "push-pull" theory is acceptable to many. The "two-sector internal trade-model with employment" is becoming increasingly popular. But these theories do not go deep enough. They do not explain the socio-economic relationships between the migrants and the state organization representing the dominant classes. Migrants and squatters are a displaced rural labour force produced by either the expanded use in the rural areas of inappropriate technology which provokes unemployment, or the lack of sufficient suitable land for a growing rural population. But at the same time, these people could and should be seen as a revitalizing and enriching source of meaningful urban life.

The key issues

Science and technology, including planning and administration, have not succeeded in creating urban societies which are just, sustainable and participatory. Can religious faith, not only Christian but others as well, again contribute to the search for a new, just and healthy urban life as it has at times in the past?

We note with admiration that in fact this contribution is being made in certain places and takes the form of suffering with those who suffer, solidarity with the oppressed, and unbounded care for the weak and wounded. Even where—as too often is the case—public authority is unwilling to see and acknowledge the real situation, and labels concern and action as subversive conspiracy, there is evidence of steadfast faith in the face of persecution and martyrdom. Voices from the developing countries at this conference have been compelling witness to this.

It is against this background that the more detailed considerations of the section were undertaken.

i)   In both industrialized and developing countries science and technology in the form of mechanical, electrical or chemical processes constitute the basis of production. The forces guiding these processes determine the nature of work and of the working environment for millions. "Work" is an intrinsic part of the socio-economic structure and any structural remodelling of patterns of work should directly involve those who contribute most to the means of production: the labourers themselves. In modern society, technological transformation creates displacement of workers, technological unemployment and redeployment. In the longer term, the choice of more appropriate technology would lead to radical changes in the established patterns of political, economic and social planning in every society.

ii) The section went on to consider the criteria for "appropriateness", and subsequently, the concept of ownership. The widespread impact of transnational corporations was examined since these companies are instrumental in standardizing both the scale and the method of production across national boundaries. This results in many negative features which could inhibit and even prevent the transition to a just, participatory and sustainable society if they are not recognized, challenged and overcome in each particular locality.

iii) The dissemination of information concerning the nature of these activities is of critical importance. Private and state corporations should be made publicly accountable for their investment decisions, and this will demand close scrutiny of the corporate planning process. Labour unions should become much more closely involved in strategic planning decisions, as it is these decisions which will ultimately determine patterns of social organization and the nature of the urban and industrial environment. Information is therefore one key to true participation in such decisions.

Finally, the section considered the potential for changes in living patterns for individuals, groups and whole communities in order to reflect new thinking about quality of life in different parts of the world. Such changes almost defy description, but we have attempted to provide some guidelines for the churches' thinking and action on this subject.

3. WORK ORGANIZATION AND LABOUR PRACTICES

The concept of work

According to the Bible, God created the world and called it good. The creation includes human beings who have been given certain powers over the rest of creation and certain tasks to accomplish. Both involve creative acts; in fact, humanity is called to participate in the on-going creation of the world. It is this creative aspect of work which must be emphasized.

Throughout history work has been seen by Christians from many different perspectives. These have included work as a curse, work as the means to salvation, etc. It has also been viewed as a contribution to society, to our sisters and brothers. Such a concept recognizes that people are inter-related, that we define ourselves in social terms, in relation to other people and to our culture and world. It sees work as participation in creative activity which benefits other people.

It is easier for the worker to see the purpose and importance of work if society needs the job to be done. It is true that people often work in noncreative jobs which are more a curse than a blessing. They work in order to eat. It is in this circumstance that technology in a just society can make a contribution: a just society allocates goods according to basic needs and uses technology to liberate people from dehumanizing labour.

The development of technology has created a continual evolution in the methods of work, the conditions of workers, the work environment, and the ethical values connected with work. In ancient societies workers needed physical strength. In the middle ages the refinement of "crafts" required more complex skills. In the industrial revolution production became "machine-based", and people had to cope with that part of the process which was assigned to them.

People's lives were affected in many ways. The new technological society evoked many varied responses from the Luddite rejection of all machines to sociological analysis and the rise of the socialist movement. It is important to remember that the labour unions were not only involved in "defensive" issues such as the protection of workers' rights, but also developed a more general strategy and contributed to profound changes in society. Their actions followed different patterns in the industrialized countries (e.g. involvement in designing laws, reforms, political action and the early revolutionary movements).

The demands made by the workers and their organizations were commonly accepted only after a long struggle and much suffering (e.g. the eight-hour day, the abolition of child labour, the emancipation of women and the right to social securities). While the Church did not generally initiate these measures, it did often struggle to make them culturally acceptable. However, it has by no means been united—some elements in the Church have opposed measures ensuring justice for workers, while others have supported them.

Some issues are still being debated today. For example: *(a)* Health was defined in the past as the absence of detectable illness. The World Health Organization now defines health as "physical, psychological and social well-being". Yet workers continue to suffer and to die from occupational diseases. Little research is being done on this and compensation is denied. Workers with little political consciousness or weak labour organizations (the immigrant, those without a contract, etc.) are particularly vulnerable to accidents and health hazards. A company official recently admitted that his corporation freely exports technology which does not conform to US safety and health laws. *(b)* A person must be able to see the purpose of his/her work. This is a primary requirement for humanizing work. Among workers there is a growing demand for participation in planning, decision-making and priority setting. While many models are being experimented with, even among the socialist nations this right to participation is still not generally accepted. *(c)* The laws concerning work and workers' rights still differ widely from one country to another; for example, the right to organize and the right to strike are still challenged or denied by many governments.

The churches can play an active role in supporting these and other ideas about the nature of work in a just, participatory and sustainable society. We would especially emphasize the need for further discussion on the issues of participation. For example, the working of a single factory is best understood by the workers themselves, and if they bring together their individual experiences, they may find clues to the possible solution of some problems.

The impact of production technology on the organization of work

Throughout history people's lives have been organized around the dominant economic form of their society. This is still true today, when technological developments are having an increasing impact upon both rural and industrial areas.

Any analysis of the impact of a particular technology must go beyond such usual questions as: Is this more efficient? Will it produce cheaper goods? Its impact on the whole social process must be evaluated. Who owns the technology? Who designs and develops it? Who has the power to introduce it and for what purpose is it being introduced? What are its effects in human terms? Who pays for it? On what basis are such decisions made? An investigation of these questions will unmask the power relationships at work and lead to a more accurate determining of whether such technological impact is just, participatory and sustainable in human terms.

In rural areas, the growing use of technology has contributed to the increased capitalization of agriculture, leading to consolidation into larger farming units. Small farms, whether privately or communally owned, are threatened, and production is viewed in terms of yield per acre rather than yield per person. This process has resulted in severe disruption of social structures and culture in many places.

In industry, production technology has had several kinds of impact. Some technology increases productivity and efficiency and makes products more readily available to society, but often at the profound social cost of loss of jobs. It may also introduce new hazards (e.g. the use of radiation to cure dyed yarn), or have problematic consequences (e.g. heavy capital investments push towards increased operating time of machines resulting in seven-day, three-shift operations). Other technology has made possible the elimination of hazardous or physically debilitating work. Both types of impacts may be desirable, depending upon how and by whom decisions to introduce the technology were made, and whether the society can handle the resulting social dislocation.

However, concern must be expressed about the use of some newer forms of production technology which reduce worker involvement in production (elimination of skilled jobs) or which involve increased monitoring of workers and production (control of people). In free-market economies, such technology profoundly affects power relationships in the work place.

While this subject is clearly too complex to be explored fully here, the examples given of how production technology affects not merely the production process but also the people involved suggest some tentative criteria for evaluating the impact of such technology: (1) What worker participation was involved in the decision to introduce it? (2) How does it affect the power relationships in the work place? (3) What kinds of alternatives are available for the workers? (4) Does it eliminate skilled work and result in the downgrading of the worker? (5) Does it promote more control of the production process by those who work in it? (6) What kind of work is available in other sectors of the economy? Other criteria can certainly be added which are appropriate for capitalist, socialist and third world economies.

The response of the churches: the persons, the organization and the culture of urban-industrial society

Called by God to be "the salt of the earth" and "the light of the world", the disciples of Jesus are to participate in the building of society. Such participation will vary from country to country. It may be characterized by:

i)   *A ministry to persons* displaced or hurt by the impact of new technologies. This must never be neglected. Such suffering often falls on those least able to defend themselves. To be effective, the Church must develop a concept of pastoral ministry which considers the intimate relationship between work life and life outside the work place.

ii) *The reorganization of urban-industrial structures:* The Church has a role to play in the struggle for a just society. It should support collective bargaining and other forms of worker participation, pressure governments to enact laws which protect worker interests, promote the eradication of poverty, seek to keep before people the global perspective, and long-range strategies.

iii) *The shaping of the urban-industrial culture:* The Church must seek to influence the values, legitimations and symbols of society that form its culture. The changes needed will often be brought about by organizations other than, or in addition to, the Church. But such movement depends upon community consciousness. The contributions of the Church to this cultural consciousness in urban-industrial society may include:

— Promoting global understanding particularly among workers.
— Providing "counter-information" about the results of particular social policies upon people all over the world. Governments, corporations and other institutions often seek to prevent people from becoming informed. The Church can help give the voiceless a way to speak, and those shut off from information a way to hear.
— Standing for the concept of work as the service of people who are collectively building a just, participatory and sustainable society.

Finally, we recognize that the Church's traditional theology of human work is inadequate as a basis for shaping work in the context of today's world. We have *theological work* to do. It is essential to draw upon the experience of worker-priests, industrial missions, and workers themselves in this task of furthering the interpretation of the Gospel in relation to unprecedented economic struggles.

4. CRITERIA FOR APPROPRIATE TECHNOLOGY

Appropriate technology is understood as technology which is dynamic, adaptable and supportive of the needs of people living in community. It is our understanding that the term "technology" is not value-free. We recognize that there may sometimes be a clash of values or even a merging of values when a particular line of action or inquiry is pursued. The choices may appear to be either technical or political, but closer examination may reveal them to be matters of ethical decision. Hence the need for ethical criteria to guide our assessment of appropriate technology for both industrialized and developing countries.

Our provisional criteria are based upon the recognition that persons are simultaneously "originators" and "resource" coupled to a "goal" (reward, satisfaction, health, even survival). The total production process involves expectation, suffering, dignity, happiness and grief. The choice of technology has much to do with these human experiences. Society cannot be evaluated simply from the standpoint of physical contributions required to meet social goals. The factors of production (materials, energy and capital) are frequently exploited solely for "profit". Appropriate technology, on the other hand, is nature-related and people-oriented.

Time plays a crucial role in the rhythm of work and rest. In a rural society, time is measured by the interaction of sun, moon and earth. But in the city and in industry it is the clock which dictates this rhythm. The transition to urban and industrial life therefore requires profound personal and societal adaptation.

i) One criterion for appropriate technology is that the unit of human cooperative effort should not be larger than needed to reach the desired goal without loss of effort, energy and time.

ii) Appropriate technology should make available products and services which enrich the whole society.

iii) It should avoid the waste of material resources through the unnecessary destruction of natural systems and their related carrying capacity (e.g. by recycling materials and reducing pollution).

iv) It should use energy as judiciously as possible and consider its availability, if not its ultimate base, as a scarce resource.

v) It should have a positive impact on work productivity and welfare distribution among people and among nations by incorporating the work of as many people as feasible.

vi) Appropriate technology should be conceived and implemented with due regard to the given or desired social context.

As a body of knowledge, appropriate technology should recognize and serve the need to redesign systems, means of production, products and even industrial goals according to the above criteria and those expressed in intergovernmental agreements on non-waste technology and the global concern for the environment.

From the vantage point of various socio-economic systems, it was agreed that these six basic criteria are valid, but the degree to which they are (or could be) applied in any community is influenced by the social context and values, as illustrated by the following three situations:

i)   In developed, affluent societies the criteria are frequently over-ridden by economic considerations, greed or indifference.

ii) In socialist (Marxist) societies, there may be a strong ideological influence on policies and the prevailing scale of values.

iii) In developing societies people who have long been deprived of an adequate standard of living demand rapid material development as soon as this appears possible. In some such cases, they see rapid exploitation of a particular resource as the only way to this goal, while lacking an understanding of its real value or the dangers of its waste.

We recognize that there are historical examples of the application of technology which, while not meeting our stated criteria at the time, have radically changed and improved social conditions and possibilities for people. Two examples are:

i)   the building of railways and, at a later stage, lateral roads into undeveloped arable areas has facilitated the development of local agriculture and improved socio-economic life for large numbers of people;

ii) the massive use of insecticides has eradicated malaria and other endemic diseases in some areas.

Nevertheless, we believe that as individuals in a community we should set these criteria as goals for our society, and that the role of the Church should be to develop a strong social conscience which deepens concern for all human beings. We cite in this connection the declaration of the National Council of Churches in the USA on appropriate energy technology.

In a changing world, technology must change. The advocacy of appropriate technology does not imply that old or traditional technology was necessarily good or that all new technology is bad. We cannot escape the vast body of human artefacts (techno-systems) which we have inherited. But there is an urgent need for much more local, national and global effort to correct mistakes, to redesign, to invent, create, promote and develop new technologies that will serve better the interests of people and nations. We find that in many situations there is a severe shortage of initiative and ideas, and where these do exist, supportive efforts and funds are invariably limited. We recommend that Christians and non-Christians alike share their concerns for advances in this field and help to mobilize more comprehensive action for these purposes.

5. THE CONCEPT OF OWNERSHIP AND MANAGEMENT

Ownership and management determine to a large degree the type of technology that is selected for a particular purpose. As noted above, large-scale production often results from dynamic management which moves to meet an expanding market demand in the short term through the introduction of inappropriate technology. It is recognized that these structures have a long history.

In many traditional societies, the land belongs to the community—it can be neither bought nor sold, but used only for the benefit of the community. This often follows a feudal pattern with a rich overlord and poor peasants, who where in some sense bound together by the prevailing circumstances. Feudalism in one form or another still exists today.

In western Europe the concept of private ownership developed and, with the advance of the Industrial Revolution, it became a cornerstone of an ostensibly free society, embracing the ownership of land, factories, stores and banks. The British classical school of economic theory (Adam Smith) lent it substance, although in the USA the Founding Fathers did not subscribe to this comprehensive approach as appropriate to their needs at that time. Karl Marx formulated the idea that industrial workers should control the means of production and that the industrial state should act as custodian for the industrial proletariat, in other words, should fulfil the role of "owner". For a long time these two views were diametrically opposed to one another.

However, in this century, especially since the depression of the thirties and World War II, nations have sought ways of managing their economies that fall somewhere between the polarized extremes of Adam Smith and Karl Marx. Over this period, we have therefore witnessed the emergence in some western countries of the "mixed" economy with the balance of investment more or less evenly divided between the demands of the public and private sectors. In the West, substantial changes are already under way as literally thousands of small-scale family-based enterprises are being acquired by larger economic units (firms, corporations and conglomerates). Under socialism, a great variety of multi-family enterprises have developed (state firms, communes, public factories) and also various forms of cooperative structure have been devised and implemented. Thus, at present, a considerable diversity of forms of ownership and management coexist.

There is some evidence that both the so-called "western" and "socialist" groups are searching for new forms, that each has acquired its own dynamic—but not always moving in the direction of justice and participation. The worker, as well as the consumer, may find himself alienated. Participation in decision-making and operational direction is only possible through processes of identification and education—making more people aware of their situation and their continuing predicament. Everywhere absentee ownership is a problem and is often exploitative.

In the smaller, developing nations all of this is true, and the movements for change are faster and often more erratic. They are the battleground for ideologies and economic theories. At the same time, certain movements in these nations have proved to be dynamic and often participatory in the midst of poverty and exploitation. In some countries, the churches were until very recently still participants in the feudal structure; in some cases their property has been taken away from them in revolutions. But in the West, churches own land, factories, stocks and bonds; they are co-owners with others and therefore co-responsible for the evils of society. They should be in the forefront in demanding justice and participatory structures and in assisting those who suffer by being good stewards of their wealth.

Transnational corporations

The role of transnational corporations (TNCs) is one of the most controversial matters before this conference. We have limited our examination to features which make a TNC different from non-transnational corporations.

The first consideration was to define clearly what TNCs are and set out certain facts about them. The second problem was more fundamental: do we start with the assumption that the TNC is totally unacceptable and then proceed to consider how to terminate and replace it? Alternatively, do we start from facts of today's economy and then try to reduce systematically the worst features of TNC organization?

i)   WHAT ARE TNCS?

There are about 10,000 TNCs in the world, 4% of which have more than twenty branches in other countries. Nearly half of the total number are based in European countries, one quarter in America. Important state-owned companies with the character of a TNC operate from the USSR into Finland and from other socialist countries into Africa and other areas.

When TNCs are cited in connection with the use or abuse of power, as a rule only the 4% or large ones, and not the other 96%, are meant.

The overwhelming number of TNCs started as manufacturing companies in one country, then sold also in other countries, and then opened their own subsidiaries there. It is at this point that they became TNCs. Since European countries are much smaller than the USA, the expansion into markets of neighbouring countries came about much earlier. This explains the far greater number of TNCs based in Europe than in the USA.

The subsidiaries concentrate on selling rather than producing because, contrary to general opinion, production costs in the host country are usually higher. A striking exception is the case of Swiss subsidiaries in the United States which both produce and sell in the highly industrialized US market at costs which are lower than in Switzerland.

While this larger group of TNCs developed through the transnational expansion of their *sales*, a much smaller number of TNCs, but individually of great importance, were created through the transnational expansion of their *production*, e.g. oil companies, companies with plantations, companies using natural resources. Their resources come often but not always from developing countries. It is mainly—but not exclusively—in this group that the greatest abuse of power has occurred.

Most references to TNCs during this conference have been unfavourable. Why is this so? Many people feel that every function they perform could be better carried out by other means. However, the alternatives are not clear. The following observations are noted:

— There seem to be technological tasks reaching beyond national borders for which TNCs are particularly suitable.
— In some cases TNCs, as international organizations, contribute positively to international cooperation.
— Subsidiaries of TNCs must obviously act under and in the spirit of the laws of the country where they operate. Problems arise when there is a genuine conflict between these laws and those of the home country.
— The leading persons in subsidiaries should as far as possible be citizens of the country where these operate or should at least live there for a considerable time. In other words, if coming from abroad they should learn not only to work there but to live there.
— Subsidiaries of TNCs must refrain from any participation in politics.
— There is a tendency towards generalization in all matters concerning TNCs and because of the immoral acts by some.

ii)   HOW THEY ARE PERCEIVED BY THE DEVELOPING COUNTRIES

The United Nations document on *Multinational Companies and World Development* (1973) implies that it is no longer the capitalist state, acting as conqueror, protector, or trustee which is the major agent of imperialist aggression against the nations in the so-called developing world, which determines the relationship of dependence imposed upon them and the strategies of exploitation to which they are subjected. It is rather the transnational corporations. Today the capitalist TNCs in many national situations have become monopolies. According to economic theory monopolies have a natural tendency to expand and are based on maximization of profit and on continuous growth. Through this process of expansion the TNCs are conquering and dominating the world. As agents of imperialism the TNCs are actively participating in the preservation of that part of the world dominated by capitalism, sometimes even at the expense of immediate profit or commercial operations. That is why their operations have far-reaching implications for the economic, social and political development of the underdeveloped countries.

Because of their monopoly of capital and their ownership and control of science-based technology, the TNCs dominate the economies of many underdeveloped countries. They are in a position either to sustain or to strangle those national economies which depend on them for their economic growth and stability. The TNCs tend to sustain the economies of those countries willing to develop a capitalist economic system. In countries which have decided to pursue alternative economic systems, TNCs are known to have sabotaged such efforts, sometimes to the extent of cooperating in the overthrow of regimes committed to the development of such alternatives. The fall of the Allende regime in Chile provides an example.

Another level of TNC involvement in maintaining the power of capitalism in the world is their facilitating the development of sub-imperialist states seeking hegemony in the Third World, e.g. South Africa and Brazil. Such states are strengthened both economically and militarily by TNC investment of capital and technology, including nuclear technology. They are expected to dominate the economies of neighbouring countries and when necessary to intervene militarily to deal with any revolts or popular uprisings in those countries. Moreover, such states use the military and economic strength gained through the TNCs to perpetuate internal repression and oppression of the poor.

It is not possible in this conference to go into details concerning the implications of TNCs' operations for the economic, political and military development of the less developed countries. We are aware that studies have been made of the negative and positive impacts of foreign investment on the economies of underdeveloped countries. But as far as we know, less research has been done on the involvement of TNCs in investment in and transfer of military technology with a view to creating hegemonic states in Asia, Africa and Latin America. Similarly, little research has been done on the influence of TNCs on structuring the urban and industrial environment through the location of their industries and their participation in providing goods such as housing and entertainment.

6. INFORMATION, KNOWLEDGE, POWER

Social control over urban populations is generally exercised by power elites of interconnected political and social institutions. They maintain their control by choosing patterns of development which benefit them and which require control of the general populace and especially the poor. Control is exerted through the processes of information-gathering and public education, the use of print and broadcasting media and skillful appeals to national security.

The nature and degree of the use and abuse of information, knowledge and power vary according to the type of society (capitalist, socialist, "third world"). Political and corporate executive power is increasing in many countries aided by more sophisticated technology which enables greater centralization. Granting access to information by the public at large is usually only a token procedure.

Therefore greater and improved possibilities for citizen participation seem absolutely necessary. The assumptions, provisions and effects of decisions with such far-reaching consequences as those in energy and related environmental fields must be adequately discussed; their consequences for the individual must be made clear. Moreover, if such decisions threaten to encroach upon the living patterns of the population, particularly in matters of planning cities and transport networks, they will in the long run probably be carried out successfully only through intensive citizen participation.

Generally speaking, a difference can be made between spontaneous and structured participation. Spontaneous forms of participation such as sit-ins, demonstrations and other means used by citizen action groups are very important for mobilizing people to engage in political life. But it must be recognized that the effectiveness of citizen participation depends on:

— the formation of a durable structure providing for a good degree of continuity of participation; as some interviews with citizen action groups show, the longer they exist, the more successful they are;
— institutionalized cooperation with the political and economic leadership; where constructive cooperation has existed between citizen action groups and administration, citizen action groups were likely to gain their end;
— improving the conditions of participation; on the one hand this excludes the claim of planners to more complete and earlier information about the planning process and government, urban and industrial policies, and on the other, it includes a minimum of financial support for those who wish to participate in an appropriate manner.

Within the process of participation scientists, engineers and technologists fulfil the role of "gate-keepers": they provide the public with information and proposals and shape scientific research. The WCC should support methods and systems that will assist in:

— making scientists aware of the potential social impact of their work; special attention should be given to scientists embarking on their careers and to students;
— increasing public participation in shaping the objectives of scientific research and technological development to meet social needs;
— the monitoring of all activities that are of potential consequence to the general public and will bring out the issues involved;
— encouraging scientists/developers to air their differences about the consequences of their work, and ensuring their possibility of doing research on problems considered to be of importance by minority groups of concerned scientists within the scientific community;
— making companies, administrators, scientific researchers, engineers and technologists more aware of societal concerns and even more accessible to the concerned public;
— interpreting scientific development, objectives and issues so that everyone concerned can understand the issues;

— making it possible for all to participate effectively in the decision-making process, for concerned citizens to have access to the planning process;
— helping its member churches to gather information on the various methods, structures and models of participation in different countries and different social contexts in order to enable an extensive exchange of experiences, not with the aim of transferring a given method, structure or model from one setting to another, but of learning from each other;
— helping its member churches to organize their own lives *(a)* to care for individuals of all economic, political, social and cultural groupings, and *(b)* to encourage all to participate in public life for the pursuit of justice in society as a whole.

We wish to make some specific observations regarding the role of technical experts in choosing "appropriate" technology. We have noted three main forms or patterns whereby technical information, or "know-how", is transferred from one community to another in an urbanized society. These are:

— by direct employment of individual experts or teams of experts;
— by arrangement with corporations or other commercial organizations to operate a particular industrial factory or process (the so-called export companies);
— through reciprocal learning operations involving the exchange of technical people between two communities.

It is recognized that all cases involve a relationship between technical people and government officials or politicians. The principal decisions are made by the latter who have to show results to the electorate. This necessity provides fertile ground for graft and corruption.

Finally, we have considered the personal attributes and attitudes required by those involved if they are to be successful in these situations. First and foremost they must have personal integrity and individual morality, together with willingness and an ability to identify with the community. This requires patience, humility and spiritual renewal. Finally, they must develop effective communication in the host community. Also, they must limit their influence to the field of their real competence.

7. QUALITY OF LIFE: LIVING PATTERNS FOR A JUST, PARTICIPATORY AND SUSTAINABLE SOCIETY

The living patterns of increasing numbers of people have been adversely affected by an economic/materialistic orientation of societies. The churches must intervene in this situation through their affirmation of faith, human dignity, responsibility and community. It is illusory to think that a just, participatory and sustainable society will emerge through structural or legislative changes alone.

Therefore, one element in our ecumenical discussion should be the spiritual renewal of the churches.

i) The Christian faith can assist people to reaffirm and develop a spiritual dimension in their lives, a sense of meaning and purpose.

ii) Together with such a strengthened faith, the churches should work for a more balanced and appropriate use of resources and a greater awareness of the needs of their neighbours.

iii) The Church should provide leadership in the search for an understanding and appreciation of values which are both God-centred and human-centred. In the past, the Church may have contributed to the destruction of culture. Now it must work to enable people to identify and articulate their cultural heritage. The Christian faith can contribute to such values as dignity, self-determination, justice, truth, and a personal and group identity.

iv) Life-styles change is an important part of spiritual renewal. The Church, by actively advocating the Gospel message, is a major force in changing life patterns. As changes in life patterns are implemented it is important not to look to a single model but to recognize the need for variety rather than uniformity. Life-patterns must reflect the unique situation and culture in which they exist. In working towards alternative life-styles, more equal distribution of wealth and/or reduction of consumption, we are not advocating self-imposed poverty but rather responsibility, concern for others and self-discipline.

v) Christians should be prepared to take initiatives in the development of communities to which they belong. "Community" can be an antidote to too much individualism and a source of recognition, self-esteem, dignity, belonging and participation for its members. Participation in turn enables people to take responsibility for their own lives (rather than being shaped by paternalistic or authoritarian forces).

vi) The churches can share responsibility with other organizations involved in community-building. To that end, they can provide resources, leadership, information, support (or appropriate opposition) for a wide variety of organizations—unions, legislative bodies, and *ad hoc* groups —when these are working towards a just, sustainable and participatory society.

Some examples of ways through which we see these changes in life-styles being implemented:

i) *house churches:* small groups, formed spontaneously or specially structured, can be helpful in community building within the Church;

ii) *consciousness-raising:* providing information and education on significant social and public issues, so people may be informed for appropriate decision-making; emphasizing education in social and ethical values (for example, technologists have developed tools but need more understanding of the human values they are to serve);

iii) *self-reliance:* providing appropriate forms of self-help assistance, e.g. leadership development, financial assistance, knowledge and skills;

iv)   *education:* promoting forms of education in which the learner is viewed as a responsible, self-directed person on a "need-to-know" basis; these would value the potential contribution to learning of every participant in the group rather than relying solely on experts;

v)   *dialogue:* fostering responsible sharing and dialogue between a variety of people, e.g. intergenerational, intercultural and international;

vi)   *communication:* making appropriate use of the technologies we have for communication, e.g. radio, TV, newspaper, telephone (the churches must also note the role of TV and films in advocating a consumer-oriented life-style and in promoting violence);

vii)   *judicatories:* central church organizations need to develop resources (information, personnel, materials) which can be used by local churches, groups and individuals for consciousness-raising, education and community-building; to assist pastors in education for an understanding of technology, for moving towards voluntary simplicity in life-style, and for being good stewards of our resources.

The church community needs to recognize the reality of stress related to change and loss. We need to assist people in "mourning" such changes and in bringing such realities into the sacramental experience of the Christian faith. In this way they will also be enabled to move forward to the new reality—and a new pattern for living.

8. RECOMMENDATIONS

A. The WCC Conference on Faith, Science and the Future, considering the life of people and nations in an increasingly urbanized world, notes that:

i)   it has become impossible to separate the city and industrial activity from rural areas and rural people; they must be seen together;

ii)   industrial-urban expansion is a dynamic process, bringing a heavy responsibility for providing adequate, just and participatory services in housing, transport, health, education and other fields, including communication; in this context, we affirm our conviction that hope for the cities is largely vested in the resident communities made up of people from all walks of life; they are required to portray a vision of victory through suffering, sacrifice and courage;

iii)   young people in particular have a significant part to play in the continuing process of rehabilitation and enrichment which will determine the future of the cities.

B. The conference expresses solidarity with those in need and calls upon the WCC and the national and local churches to:

i)   continue to study the various urban situations and find possible ways of support and action, in a participatory way, wherever possible and including non-members in their activities;

ii)   where appropriate, continue and strengthen ecumenical protest and ac-
      tion against negligent, oppressive and authoritarian public and private
      centres of power;
iii) support, in imaginative ways, efforts for self-help by people in their own
      location;
iv)   promote the development of a vastly intensified network of action on a
      national and world scale for these purposes;
v)   support urban ministries, especially among those who are required to
      adjust to changing circumstances.

As it is important to move from study to action, we wish to endorse the
programme of the sub-unit on Urban Industrial Mission which seeks to
develop patterns of ministry relating to and affecting the work place and
those problems which spill over from the work place into the rest of society,
and to break down the rural/urban contradictions and promote the rights of
working people. This can be done, for example, through the worker-priests,
industrial missions, tent ministries, organizing working people, etc. all of
which not only affirm humanity but contribute to a self-critical analysis of
the Church's role in society and the possibilities for moving towards a just,
participatory and sustainable society.

C. The conference also wishes to bring forward the following proposals as
these relate to particular sections of the foregoing report:

i)   WORK ORGANIZATION AND LABOUR PRACTICES
      That the WCC promote further meetings between scientists and
      engineers, economists and other social scientists together with
      theologians and ethicists, to explore the contemporary understanding of
      the terms "employment", "unemployment" and "the nature of work"
      in different regions. If possible, these groups should address themselves
      collectively to the task of developing a theology of work which is consis-
      tent with the prospects of diminishing levels of paid employment for
      large sections of the community in both industrialized and developing
      countries.
ii)   CRITERIA FOR APPROPRIATE TECHNOLOGY
      That the WCC actively promote the development of people-oriented
      technology which uses human resources in a creative and rewarding way
      in contrast to machine-oriented technology which is capital-intensive
      and leads to higher levels of unemployment in all countries. Whenever
      possible, this advocacy should be carried forward to other international
      organizations, particularly the UN agencies, in order to ensure that the
      criteria for appropriate technology can be explored, refined and upheld
      by national governments.
iii) THE CONCEPT OF OWNERSHIP AND MANAGEMENT
      That the WCC examine the following subjects in detail as part of the
      continuing dialogue on the role of transnational corporations:

— the need to select production technologies which fulfil social objectives, including an acceptable balance of costs and benefits in terms of employment opportunities, worker participation and environmental control of the process;

— the need to develop new forms of ownership and control of these production technologies which are consistent with a longer time-scale of planning than that of most commercial organizations operating on a worldwide basis.

iv)   INFORMATION, KNOWLEDGE AND POWER

That the WCC establish a working group to study and report on the specific issues identified and listed as a necessary step towards enhancing and extending widespread public participation in decisions over the introduction of new science and technology. We further propose that this group should also consider and report on the increasing use of computers in various forms, their impact on society and the ways in which the management and control of data banks may be used to influence decision-making in the future.

VIII. Economics of a Just, Participatory and Sustainable Society

1. INTRODUCTION

The striving of women and men for a just society is part of their struggle for survival in dignity. The Bible reveals to us, through the liberation of the children of Israel, through the prophets, and ultimately through Jesus Christ, that God wills human justice in a society where people find their identity and wholeness by living for one another in faith. Our hope for the Kingdom of God must be reflected in part through the quest for social justice, but we require a firm theological foundation for appraising the existing socio-economic order and for transforming it, and we look to other sections of this conference for guidance and directions on that theological foundation. However, a link must be established between theology and political economy as a means for action.

2. THE DEBATE THUS FAR

Our starting point in this discussion is the report of the consultation on Political Economy, Ethics and Theology (Zürich, June 1978). It proposed, among other things, a new paradigm in political economy, one that should correspond to the operational requirements of a just, participatory and sustainable society, and also enable a new understanding of:
— the dimensions of poverty in the world (not merely in the developing countries);
— the non-participatory nature of much of the present social order; and
— the present malfunctioning economic systems.

The current paradigm of political economy prevailing in western industrialized societies, and influential in many others, was criticized by the Zürich consultation on several counts:
— its partial perception of the humanity-nature relationship;
— its bias towards the interests of a minority of the world's people;
— its emphasis on accumulation and growth as the primary answer to unemployment;
— its undue reliance on market mechanisms for solving the problems of the world economy and thus for achieving the greatest good for the greatest number;

— its assumption that consumer demand depends on consumer sovereignty;
— its insufficient attention to the critical and real adjustment problems arising in the world economy;
— its absence of moral judgment about what is produced and who consumes how much; and finally
— its self-imposed limitations: it resists controlling the economic effects on society of certain institutional arrangements which concentrate power according to class structures.

With the world economy in the grip of inflation, unemployment, slow or no-growth and a reckless spiralling of defence spending, this critique constitutes an indictment on the prevailing paradigm.

The Zürich report proceeded to suggest an enlarged frame of reference for a new economics for a just, participatory and sustainable society. This meant reinstating in economic analysis the historical and spatial dimensions, an integrated and inter-disciplinary approach to social problems, and a shift from self-interest to common social concern for the wellbeing of all as the basic motivation for economic activity. In other words, economics must again become political economy, before it can assist in the struggle for a just society, consistent with the demands of the Gospel.

We endorse this Zürich approach and seek to explore further the direction in which Christians and churches may move in thought and action. We attempt no blueprint but only to understand the economic requirements for a just society which is participatory and sustainable.

3. POLITICAL ECONOMY OF A JUST SOCIETY

The distinction between positive economics and political economy deserves to be clearly understood and accepted. Positive economics is narrowly founded on economic considerations such as revealed choice by individual consumers, free markets in which these choices can be satisfied, and the maximization of profit as the primary tool for allocating resources efficiently. While positive economics recognizes that goals are required for the system, it either assumes that these are externally given or that they are embodied in the choices of individuals in the market place.

The wider view of economics, for which political economy is an appropriate term (this was its use in the nineteenth century in Europe), links economic analysis with wider social goals. It admits the need for, and exercise of, value judgments and is concerned with social classes as well as with individuals.

In our view, political economy is to be preferred to positive economics. Not only does the latter adopt too narrow an analytical frame, but its focus on the "individual" is not adequate from a Christian point of view which would rather emphasize the concept of "person", the difference being the recognition by the latter of one's social responsibilities to the community and the rest of the world. Moreover, although positive economics theoretically allows for the setting of varying social and individual goals, in practice the development of economies based on positive economics seems to be inevitably channelled towards continuous growth, increased production and capital accumulation. Political economy, on the other hand, offers a better chance of changing the direction and speed of growth and of achieving social goals like justice and sustainability which are related to the use of resources.

Poverty is the world's foremost economic problem. Learned opinions differ on whether or not the next century will see the worldwide abolition of absolute poverty. But the present evidence is clear: the disparity in incomes, even in per capita terms, between nations, and between the rich and the poor in most countries, is huge and growing; full employment is difficult in the West, achieved at a certain human cost in the East, and almost impossible in the South. The majority in the world (not only in the developing countries) have less food, less health care, less meaningful work and less protection—per capita—today than at the end of the last World War. There is certainly more privilege but for fewer people.

This reality has less to do with the availability of resources than with the way they are used. It is a reflection not so much of the relevance of technology as of the reigning concept of development as a linear advance in ability to sustain present levels of economic activity, or for that matter the desirability of doing so—and the theoretical universality of the problem is understandably not shared by the majority of people in the world. What does matter, however, is that the problem of poverty worldwide is growing worse both relatively and absolutely. The situation obliges us all to state that the community of nations will continue to stand under judgment until the blasphemy of world hunger is removed. Against such a background, the West must be reminded of where the priorities lie between the present and the future. To paraphrase St John: "In so far as you claim to be concerned about the unborn humanity that you cannot see, but show no regard for the humanity you can see all around you, you are a liar."

4. POLITICS OF PARTICIPATION

Our central concern is with justice. Nothing must detract from the scandal of massive poverty and growing inequality in the world and from the necessity for change that this demands, both of ourselves and of the structures under which we live. But in seeking to speak a word of truth about this fact, we found it necessary to explore further the relevance of both *participation* and *sustainability* as they have been defined in recent ecumenical thinking. In clarifying the meaning of a just society we have found that, if justice is the goal, then sustainability should best be seen as a necessary, though not sufficient condition for the existence of justice, while we found participation to be a necessary condition without which neither sustainability nor justice will be achieved.

Spelling out the meaning of justice is important. Even more urgent, in our view, is the need to understand what is happening in the world so that people may find ways of transforming and humanizing the structures (the principalities and powers). Such transformation is not possible without participation at the appropriate level from local communities all the way through to the whole world. Participation is, however, not possible without power. Thus a necessary condition for ensuring participation is the dispersal of power, both political and economic, and avoiding its concentration in the hands of a few who are not fully accountable to those affected by its exercise. Participation is necessary also to ensure a due sense of priorities both within and between nations and to release the energies of people in such a way that the existing resources (which are already sufficient to fulfil the basic needs of all in every country of the world) meet the needs of all. God has given to all people the right and power of decision-making. The deprival of that power (as a consequence of existing political and economic structures, not least of modern technology) is a major cause of the distortions of production and distribution in the world economy of today. The need to transform and evolve the political systems existing in the different countries to a higher level in the hierarchy of values is an urgent precondition for a just society. What kind of a value system would be suitable to a more human social organization, conforming to the Christian ethic?

The long and mixed experience of mankind, acquired by trial and error, is perhaps adequate to enable us to define the political framework for social justice. Indeed this is crystallized, in substantial measure, in the Universal Declaration of Human Rights, adopted by the General Assembly of the United Nations on 10 December 1948.

It would not be far wrong to say that it was forgotten on 11 December 1948! True, an effort was made in 1966 to translate these principles into treaty provisions creating legal obligations for the ratifying states. And by 1976, two international covenants had come into force, one on Economic, Social and Cultural Rights and the other on Civil and Political Rights. With what results? There are some countries that have not yet subscribed to them; and not all those which have ratified seem sufficiently committed to their implementation. Food and freedom are both to be ensured; they are not mutual trade-offs.

Whatever label one may give to the political frame for a just society, it must be seen as the institutionalization of solidarity among human beings and as the recognition that the community is responsible for the welfare of its members. It is the opposite of individualism in the sense of each individual being solely responsible for his or her own welfare. It is the task of society to maximize the welfare of *all* its members, the free development of *each* of them. This is possible only in a society where the people *control* the production of goods, the maintenance of order and the development of culture. It is not possible if national elites, including the military, foreign governments or transnational corporations make or influence national decisions. In the latter case, political power is exercised in a highly centralized way irrespective of whether the system is formally democratic or openly dictatorial. Ownership can and must be socialized step by step to the extent necessary to achieve social goals.

Society is pluralist and must be accepted in its rich diversity. This implies that only when all the people participate in a decision does it become morally binding on all. Is this practicable? The answer is *yes*. With the increased complexity of technology and of products, more decision-making power must be laid at lower levels, both in enterprises and in administration. This is the actual experience in big enterprises everywhere as well as in centrally planned economies. And the lesson must be learned in the political sphere as well. Decision-making must be deliberately dispersed at different levels, for nothing enhances democracy and increases efficiency more than the release of local initiative by decentralizing effective power. New and higher forms of local government and industrial democracy will have to be introduced and nurtured as political inputs for a participatory society. Social cohesiveness and justice cannot be ensured except through the participation of all members in the decision-making as well as the production processes. If politics is to outgrow its attributes of uncertainty and short-term orientation, the forums for decision-making must widen to transcend disciplinary boundaries.

Can illiterate people, ignorant of the implications of public policies, participate in determining them? This question has often been asked by oppressive regimes and complacent individuals. There have been cases, even lately, where the poor and the unlettered have answered, at the first opportunity, by making unerring judgments with an unsuspected ethical insight into politics that touch their lives. Authoritarian regimes have come to grief in the process. We wish to emphasize that lack of education must not be used as an excuse for preventing participation.

An obvious condition for a participatory society is the uninhibited flow not only of scientific and technological knowledge but also of information on current affairs. A new global information order must come before open governments can function in free societies which is what participation is ultimately about. Reforming or restructuring the internal political structures of individual nations makes sense only if the respective peoples decide the shape of things to come. A just society cannot be raised by remote control or by passing resolutions any more than revolutions can be exported. By the same token, a nation-state may be too large and too heterogeneous to permit meaningful participation of the whole population in various areas of decision-making. The scope of participation is to be determined by the extent of shared interest. The dual trend towards increasing autonomy for regions within nations and widening cooperation between nations must be consciously promoted as a supportive measure for a participatory world society. Both tendencies are evident in contemporary societies and must be understood as pointing to the operational insufficiency of the concept of national sovereignty.

The roots of injustice lie embedded in the inequalities of wealth and incomes. They are nourished by the non-participatory nature of social organizations.

5. ECONOMICS OF SUSTAINABILITY

Sustainability is a condition of social justice. The massive squandering of the world's resources by the industrialized countries itself prevents the substantial reduction of global inequality and poverty. Waste by some is not unrelated to the want of others. In the industrialized countries, the concept of sustainability provides a basis with which to judge wasteful consumption of non-renewable resources, heavy reliance on material growth at the expense of spirit and of justice, and the increasing trend towards large, non-participatory, complex organizations. However, the developing countries cannot be expected to be as concerned as the West about problems of sustainability that are not of their own making. And our concern for the unborn generations must square with a thought for the millions who are hungry today. A sense of proportion should therefore inform our perception of the undoubted relevance of sustainability to social justice. Problems which are essentially western both in scope and responsibility must not be turned into global issues with a certain consequence for the struggle against poverty and for justice. The norms of sustainability must encompass the concerns of the developing societies as well as the problems of the developed ones.

We note that unsustainability arises not just from increasing consumerism and the rate of economic growth, but especially from competitive commercialism over which a non-participatory community has little control. In a situation where the people cannot define, much less promote, the goals of society, science and technology are harnessed to meet artificial rather than real needs in both the civil and military sectors. If this point is accepted, the link between sustainability and participation is easily seen.

6. SOME KEY ISSUES

Let us now take some questions relevant to a sustainable society.

Consumerism
Concern has been expressed about the adverse ethical and ecological consequences of economic growth, as well as the ever-rising levels of consumption in western societies due to the sales promotion of trivialities. The elites of the poorer countries closely follow this trend. This problem has three inter-related aspects:

— the individual's desire for material goods, a human characteristic which the developed socialist countries also find difficult to counter;
— the manipulation of demand through advertising and marketing;
— the market orientation of an economic system that can be maintained only by continuous increase in production.

It has thus to be tackled simultaneously at these three levels: education for restraining consumption of material goods in favour of expenditure on social and cultural services; curbing the artificial creation of demand; and pursuing the possibility of regulating society's use of resources in the aggregate.

Militarism

Resources are today being used up on a massive and increasing scale in the name of "national security" in the West, the East and the South. Apart from the obvious threat to peace and survival which this diabolical build-up implies, there are also economic implications: a protected source of profit is maintained and financial resources leak into channels unrelated to defence and which are unlikely to be put to productive purposes, thereby promoting continued concentration of economic power. The global defence expenditure today equals the total income of the poorer half of the world population. In fact, the developing countries themselves spend about a fifth of their exchange earnings for military purposes. Here again exposure, education, and public pressure at the domestic and international levels on *all* governments concurrently are urgently necessary.

Power

Another problem in developed and developing countries alike is the concentration of economic power arising from:
— unequal distribution of resources;
— higher technologies decreasing the possibility of participation in decision-making;
— the growing complexity of knowledge and the exclusiveness of saleable expertise.

This concentration of economic power manifests itself in the political sphere as an authoritarian tendency. Even in socialist countries where disparities in wealth have been considerably reduced, the problem of dispersing decision-making power has not been solved. Suggestions for correcting this systemic defect are:
— assured minimum income for all (where this does not already obtain);
— upper limits to personal incomes and wealth;
— equitable distribution of resources;
— greater public participation in and control of the use of technology;
— wider dissemination of knowledge and information;
— higher public expenditure on social needs.

New International Order

A major question in the context of sustainability is the basis of distribution of resources among nations. Although much goodwill for the poor countries was expressed by the rich countries over the past two decades or so, along with their promise of voluntary transfer of resources to the poor countries, the performance bears little relation to the promise. The socialist countries, for their part, must also increase support to the developing countries. Furthermore, the persistent demand of the developing countries for fairer trade practices and terms of technology transfer has not received any significant response. More recently, proposals for a new international economic order and for reshaping the world economy have been put forward by the United Nations agencies as well as by private groups, but these again have not met with success. Two main reasons for this stalemate are:

— national possession of resources that are the "common heritage of humanity";
— the legal obstacles preventing national governments in market economies from intervening in the economic decisions of corporate entities, including transnational corporations, as well as of individuals.

Could these not be overcome?

Natural resources

As nature's resources are used up by the growing number of people and the rising level of consumption of the few, a set of questions are sharply raised about:

— the rapid depletion of non-renewable resources;
— the degradation of the environment;
— the destruction of the base of renewable resources (air, water, land).

The concept of sustainability, as now used, grew out of this perception. Apart from a host of down-to-earth ecological problems that need immediate attention, certain issues for economic analysis arise in this context.

Social costs

One of the more important issues is the concept of "cost". In an economic theory based on individual decisions about the use of common resources, the costs to one individual register as the earnings of another. The depletion of resources and the pollution of the environment entail a cost to society as a whole, but such "social costs", though recognized, go unreckoned or are often treated as external elements which do not and cannot enter into the calculations of the individual decision-maker. Considering the magnitude of this problem, how far can it be solved through public measures such as taxation and subsidy? Do we not need to develop new concepts to measure and incorporate "social costs" and try to apply such techniques as may have already been developed?

Future generations

The growing awareness of the exhaustion of resources makes it necessary to apportion their use between the present and the future. Here several complex technical issues arise such as the principle of pricing of resources for present and future use. Assuming that an answer can be found, is it enough to have expert advice and government decision without effective participation of the society or its concerned segments?

Population growth

A human perspective needs to be maintained on the unquestionable need to contain the exponential growth of population in many poor countries. Actual experience shows that as living standards increase, the population growth rate slows down. In other words, where the poor can expect to see some regular income, they themselves limit the number of their children who, in a situation of absolute poverty, are the only asset they have. This is not to underestimate the need for education, persuasion and technical facilities, but only to emphasize that family planning must be part of a socio-economic programme concerned as much with the aging and the elderly as with the unborn and the young. It must be seen not as a crude intervention to limit, almost mechanically, the size of the population, but a legitimate, non-coercive means to improve the quality of young life. Society must be sustained, but population is not just the economist's "resource".

The economics of sustainability is riddled with many complex questions. We feel it would be optimistic to expect that answers can be found without transforming the existing economic systems and social organizations in line with the principles in this report.

7. CONCLUSION

In conclusion, we would strongly argue the need to see the struggle for a just, participatory and sustainable society in coherent terms which will *not* allow us to dismember the concept and the goal into, for example, justice for the Third World, participation for the Second World and sustainability for the First World.

We of the human race are all members of one another. We must together struggle to extend participation, develop sustainability, and to let "justice roll down like waters and righteousness like an ever-flowing stream" (Amos 5:24).

8. RECOMMENDATIONS

As initial steps towards the desired society:

i)   We plead for a new scheme of international economic assistance designed on a cooperative basis between the developed countries and the developing countries. This programme should include a firm commitment by all industrialized countries to put at least 0.7% of their gross national product into a fund to be administered by an appropriate international agency. This money should finance anti-poverty programmes prepared by individual developing countries and chosen for assistance by the representatives of all the developing countries.

ii)   We call upon the churches to speak out boldly:
   a) for land reforms and other measures for redistributive justice;
   b) for the break-up of large privately owned national and international business organizations engaged in monopoly practices and political manipulation.

iii) Recognizing the value of new instruments like the Ecumenical Development Cooperative Society, we propose that churches support more generously the organizations they have created to alleviate hunger and poverty by urging upon individual members to contribute 3-5% of their personal income to this cause. We urge the WCC to explore further a mechanism to allow individual Christians to invest directly in the Ecumenical Development Cooperative Society.

iv)   We recommend that the WCC continue its work on:
   a) identifying the socio-economic roots of injustice, non-participation, and unsustainability;
   b) refining the principles of political economy for a just society through an interdisciplinary group representative of the prevailing socio-economic systems, in order to help the peoples of different countries develop their own designs of society consistent with global interdependence.

v)   We urge countries to examine their own structures and the use of their resources and potentials with reference to the criteria of justice, participation and sustainability.

vi)   We urge churches to examine their own structures and the use of their assets and resources (including land) with reference to the criteria of justice, participation and sustainability—as a response to the latter-day challenge to their stewardship.

IX. Science/Technology, Political Power and a More Just World Order

One of the key issues of modern times is the interaction between politics and technology, especially in the context of the tremendous expansion in the power and functions of states. While centralizing forces that derive from technological changes add new dimensions to the state, such changes also challenge the capacity of the state to maintain control of these processes. The expansion in the power and functions of the state tends to diminish the possibilities of full participation of the people in the processes of decision-making. As the general secretary of the World Council of Churches stated in his address to the conference: "A just and sustainable society is impossible without a society which is participatory. In the present situation of science and technology they are not really participatory, or rather they are forced to be biased on the side of those who wield economic and political power. There is little sign that they are on the side of the oppressed, the deprived and the marginalized or simply the people." This is true within and across nations.

New forces and factors among the nations, facilitated by modern technology, have contributed to a new international situation. Some of these are: big power political and economic domination of smaller powers through advanced technology; the emergence of a global techno-economic stratification system through transnational corporations; and increasing militarization around the globe by rapid advances in military technology.

1. SCIENCE AND TECHNOLOGY AS INSTRUMENTS OF POLITICAL POWER

We affirm the inestimable value of technology in developing new means of meeting the basic needs of all peoples. In light of this purpose, it is important to take into account numerous non-technological factors in order that technology may be so directed as to serve and not exploit humanity.

Science and technology cannot be discussed as isolated entities, they must be seen within the economic, social and political contexts of particular societies. Whereas science and technology have definite positive aspects, for they can enhance the welfare of the people, this section concentrates on their negative aspects, especially in relation to power. All too often science and technology have been used as formidable tools of oppression in the hands of states, military groups and large private or public corporations.

For example, large bureaucracies often reduce people to objects for manipulation, and thus undermine their humanity. States, too, can use technology to achieve their ends. They may use it to keep order, provide welfare services, regulate business practices—or cooperate with corporations in oppressing people and in producing grave ecological destruction.

Science and technology in centralized capitalist countries are used as the primary means of increasing and controlling production. In fact, this configuration of power, the large technological-capitalist state and the global capitalist system based on science and technology, is facing perhaps the most serious crisis in its history. It has been unable to control the problems of resource depletion, environmental damage, mass unemployment, automation, mass transport, energy, nuclear waste disposal and the computerized invasion of privacy. This crisis notwithstanding, some modern states and large corporations will exercise significant power over the world economy and development of markets in other countries through their use and control of science and technology. They can force governments and peoples to conform to their wishes. If dissent arises the corporation can threaten to withdraw and thus effectively undermine the host economy. Making matters worse is the fact that developing countries have become especially dependent upon the transnational corporation for employment, for the production of goods and services and the introduction of the advanced technologies which such companies bring.

The present world economic system with its international division of labour is based on exploitation. This takes different forms, but in many cases it results from an alliance between the purveyors of technology from developed countries and the power elite of the developing countries. It is accompanied by the abuse of science and technology by those in power in the developing countries and suppresses the aspirations of peoples for a just and equitable society. This is sometimes compounded by the introduction of military technology from the developed countries. This exploitation results in many problems, some of which are the following:

i)　extraction of raw materials by foreign companies, which are often kept in control with the help of foreign military power, and the collaboration of local governments;

ii)　sale of agricultural land to foreign companies which introduce mechanized production, creating mass unemployment and under-employment;

iii)　raising crops for export markets, encouraged by foreign companies, instead of crops urgently needed for local consumption;

iv)　relocation of polluting industries by countries whose governments have developed restrictive laws, into countries where such laws do not exist or cannot be enforced;

v)   use of income from exports for the importation of luxury goods which
     only benefit a minority upper class;
vi) introduction of cheap consumer goods from Japan or western countries
     with which local industries cannot compete.

Although in socialist countries the social structures and the way of production are different, problems also arise there relating to the role of science
and technology, e.g. concentration of power within state bureaucracy, lack
of participation in decision-making, ecological damage and some aspects of
consumerism.

The use of science and technology by oppressive powers has to be opposed and the rights to self-determination and appropriate technologies encouraged. The mobilization of countervailing powers in this struggle will succeed through greater international solidarity and communication between
peoples beyond the boundaries of race, class, sex and culture.

2. TRANSFER OF TECHNOLOGY AND ITS IMPLICATIONS

It is undeniable that "developing" countries need a degree of
technological development appropriate to their societies if they are to meet
human needs and participate autonomously in international affairs. Transfer
of technology from industrialized countries, particularly through transnational corporations, has often hindered the development of such appropriate
technology. In fact, "developed" countries have in many cases replaced colonial political control with economic control, now using science and
technology to maintain the traditional relationship of exploitation and
dependence. Certain industrialized countries not only still use developing
countries as a source of resources, labour and markets, but also control their
political structures through a favoured elite.

It is the combination of interests and motivations of the industrialized
countries, transnational corporations and developing countries that determines the present patterns of transfer of technology.

From the point of view of developing countries, several motivations may
operate: the need for technology to meet a growing level of human needs; the
push to develop rapidly in the style of the developed countries; the desire for
parity in international affairs, and the ability to make independent decisions;
the desire of a powerful elite to enjoy the material benefits of association
with the industrialized countries; and the psychological feeling of possessing
and/or sharing power.

The corporation or the industrializing agency which mediates the transfer
of technology is motivated by: the advantages in creating secondary markets
in order to recoup the investment in initial research and development with the
possibility of generating profit through the transfer of old technology which
is already obsolescent in its country of origin; the proximity to sources of raw
materials, cheap labour and less stringent controls.

The governments of developed countries also profit by such transfer because of the strengthening and diversification of their economy by transnational economic links and access to foreign markets. A technical, managerial, bureaucratic and scientific elite which is not in touch with the interests of the general population and which becomes subservient to the developed country is also formed. In addition, governments of developed countries use economic-technological leverage to pressure foreign governments to comply with their political policies and values. Since transfer of technology also implies transfer of values and culture it can thus be used as an ideological tool.

Transfer of military technology is inevitably an expression of economic, political, and cultural interests. In many cases the recipient country becomes part of an overall military strategy. In addition, transfer of military technology tends to reinforce the economic and political dependence of the recipient countries. It fosters militarization and in a large number of cases supports and perpetuates military regimes.

Development of appropriate technology is further hindered in some cases by foreign development advisors. Advisors or consultants from developed countries are often sought by less developed countries as they plan industrial development. Such persons think primarily in terms of classical industrial modes of production, are not likely to appreciate the real needs of the population, maintain contacts only with the political and economic elites, and are most often expert salesmen for development through transnational corporations.

A "technological brain drain" may occur whenever citizens of developing countries receive training in developed countries. The scientific climate may be more attractive in the developed country and therefore large numbers of students do not return to their home countries. On the other hand, technical training in the developed countries is often not suited to the needs of the developing countries. These negative factors have to be weighed against the obvious need of people in the developing countries for training in those scientific and technological fields which might be of use to their countries.

Aid is made available for development of indigenous technologies through loans from individual industrialized countries, the World Bank and other international financial institutions. Because these loans are restricted to countries already developing according to certain patterns and ideologies and because there are strict constraints on their use (e.g. restrictive marketing clauses and contractual obligations), countries which receive them cannot be truly independent.

Transfer of technology under such conditions usually has a detrimental effect because self-reliance is not fostered and the interests of the majority are not served. The claims about creation of more employment and encouragement to development are often dubious. Transfer of technology should be considered inappropriate if:

i)   it leads to absorption or destruction of national industries;

ii)   it suppresses the domestic market for indigenous products;

iii) it redeploys resources and facilities from use by the majority to enhance the prestige and luxury of a few;
iv) it introduces unnecessary hazards and risks through obsolete or harmful designs and products;
v) it encourages the creation of unnecessary desires and urbanization;
vi) it cannot be assimilated or controlled by national technicians but remains an intimidating and alienating force deepening dependence;
vii) it is bureaucratic, capital and energy intensive, and not labour intensive, and discourages participation, decentralization, and employment;
viii) it stifles the national independent research and development which alone can ensure long-term technological self-reliance;
ix) it exploits natural resources without regard to the long-term needs of the country and its environment;
x) it intensifies existing class divisions in the society and entrenches the status quo;
xi) it displaces workers and offers no desirable employment alternative, i.e. if it creates "technological unemployment".

The case of South Africa where an oppressive power structure is undergirded and reinforced by the transfer of technology from the West may be cited in this connection. Transnational corporations are increasingly introducing into South Africa sophisticated technology which replaces black labour by automatically controlled production processes. This development further deprives the black labourers of any possibility of meaningful participation and strengthens the racist nature of the system. We want to draw attention to and reaffirm support for the significant initiatives taken by the World Council of Churches in supporting the liberation struggles in Southern Africa and the programmes for disinvestment.

The alternative to this ill-advised transfer of alien technology is the development of appropriate technology. The word "appropriate" should not be understood as implying some minimal level which will always keep developing countries in a dependent position. Rather, it should represent technology which is in harmony with the needs, culture and environment of a particular society. Certain questions should always be asked in evaluating a particular technology: it is "for whom", "for what" and "by whose decision"? In a political conflict, "by whose decision" becomes the most important and includes the other two questions. If developing countries are to opt for appropriate technologies, they must formulate and enact a coherent system of social goals which serve the interests of the people. The absence of a political system in which people truly participate is the major barrier to this. Decisions are often made by a small elite or false populists. The people themselves may abdicate their role in society, and unfortunately such depoliticization is sometimes supported by the churches. If appropriate technology is to be developed, the people must share in decisions about goals and means of production. They must be educated and politicized so that they become aware of their social situation, can direct themselves through decision-making, and use their dormant collective power. Such representative planning processes are necessary if developing countries are to build a stock of national capabilities making possible independent decision-making.

3. MILITARY TECHNOLOGY: ISSUES OF POWER AND PEACE

The history of industrialized societies reveals intimate and complex connections between military technology and the basic institutions of government, economy and science. These connections require the most competent and thorough analysis if the churches are to be effective instruments of God's justice and peace.

There are three distinct, but always inter-related, aspects of this institutional complex:

i)   relationships between military technology and political institutions;
ii)   military demands on science and technology;
iii)   the churches' challenge to military technology.

Military technology and political institutions

An overview of connections between military technology and political institutions may be sketched by the following propositions which we believe to be true but which invite continuing discussion and research.

1. The advance of military technology has (paradoxically) undermined the capacity of nation-states to defend their own citizens. (The boundaries of the territorial state are indefensible against nuclear bombs and missiles.)

2. The speed of delivery of nuclear weapons has increasingly curbed the capacity of democratic institutions to share in crisis decisions about national security by reducing the time available for decisions and the number of persons making them. (A crisis response to a missile attack in a few minutes hardly permits parliamentary debate.)

3. The managerial structures of military technology have evolved a new form of government in both capitalist and socialist countries: a pattern in which industrial, scientific, military and political elites collaborate in determining national priorities and allocating resources. (The term "military-industrial complex" is too simplistic.)

4. The growing complexity of military technology has expanded the network of vested interests in the development and production of new weapons. (As the variety of technologies and components in modern weapons systems multiplies, the industries and localities affected also tend to multiply.)

5. Early bureaucratic decisions about weapons research and development tend to become increasingly inaccessible to the public and irreversible in the legislative process.

6. The escalating sophistication of military technology tends to alienate the public from any sense of competence in coping with issues, which are

therefore left to "the experts". (No area of public policy is more troubled by a widespread sense of powerlessness than defence and disarmament.)

7. The coopting of intellectual resources by the gross demands of high military technology threatens the autonomy and integrity of academic disciplines and institutions and of public discussion of policy alternatives. (Conflicting loyalties and pervasive secrecy are the lot of many scholars in this field.)

8. Public acquiescence in the production of weapons of mass annihilation threatens mental health by fostering a schizophrenic attitude towards the relation between national security and normal living.

9. The increasing costliness of military technology aggravates the problem of unemployment, not only by diverting government budgets from social programmes but also by reducing the ratio of employees to expenditures.

10. The massive allocation of resources to military research and development undermines the progress of civilian productivity and weakens a nation's position in world trade in civilian products. (The quality and efficiency of industrial engineering are critically affected by military priorities.)

11. The high cost of new military technology in the 1970s has become a growing stimulus to arms exports: the aim is to reduce unit costs by multiplying production.

12. Transfers of advanced military technology to the Third World can increase the capacity of authoritarian regimes to repress and inflict suffering on their citizens, while encouraging militarism.

13. The dynamics of the strategic arms race creates a bureaucratic momentum of military technology independent of the actual behaviour of adversary states.

14. Innovations in military technology increasingly threaten to outrun the technology of disarmament. (Strategic weapons are now being developed in which the characteristics of concealment, deception, and mobility may frustrate available instruments of verification and regulation.)

15. The threat of nuclear weapons technology to the life and habitability of all countries deprives non-nuclear weapon states of political autonomy in matters of their own safety and survival.

16. The assumption of special political prerogatives by nuclear states gives impetus to nuclear options by other states.

17. The more a foreign policy is based on nuclear weapons, the more it tends to substitute technical abstractions for political goals and to become preoccupied with stability and the *status quo.*

18. The technology of mutual terror holds masses of citizens hostage to the narrowly conceived interests of political elites. (The traditional moral doctrine of non-combatant immunity affords no protection to ordinary citizens in a nuclear war.)

Military demands on science and technology

To account for the massive demands of military programmes on science and technology is to survey a wide range of human motives—personal, professional and national.

Unquestionably, many governmental and military persons, together with many scientists and technologists, sincerely believe that their work in weapons research and development contributes to national security and peace. The relationship of such persons to the churches offers a largely neglected opportunity for engagement in these issues through special ministries of the laity.

In many cases, however, the motives of these and other persons include careerist ambitions and the attraction of materialistic life-styles. The result is often personal and family dissociation from any serious moral concern about the consequences of their work. Still more disturbing are the blatant greed and profiteering which often characterize the exploitation and manipulation of public anxiety, fear and national pride in the promotion of new weapons programmes. In some countries, the propaganda of militarism is intended at least as much for domestic consumption as for international impact. Such propaganda is repeatedly unleashed in order to sustain the momentum of research and development, production and deployment which has become the dynamic of military technology and the prime engine of the arms race.

Nevertheless, the very real hostilities between militarized states and the increasing possibilities of nuclear war make concern for national security and survival more legitimate than ever. The issue is whether further escalation of the arms race can make any positive contribution to genuine security. The terrible irony of the nuclear age is that the more the super-powers have committed their resources to the idols of deterrence and defence, the more defenceless they (and all other nations) have become. The final document of the UN Special Session on Disarmament in 1978 declared that nuclear weapons have become "much more of a threat than a protection" for humanity.

Preoccupation with the scenarios of nuclear war has pre-empted the political and scholarly resources which must be devoted to the scenarios of peace-making. Policy-makers, physical and social scientists, the churches and the general public need new strategies to reverse the arms race and to construct institutions to promote global security and survival.

The new scenarios of peace-making must confront the fear, insecurity, ignorance, hate and mistrust which fuel the upward thrust of military technology and the arms race. Such strategies must multiply opportunities for personal encounter across adversary boundaries of political and military leaders, scholars, religious groups and every sector of society. While we are very grateful for the multilateral exchange of views at this conference, we earnestly hope that the next WCC conference of this kind will experience the fullest possible representation of East, West, South and North.

If total trust of any government—others or one's own—is not only difficult but unwise, the works of reconciliation must nevertheless initiate and reinforce relationships of increasing trust and confidence between nations. Disarmament should never be advocated solely on the grounds of "national technical means of verification" and the fictitious claim that no trust is required. Rather, the technology of verification must operate in a political environment in which serious and sustained efforts are made to forge the links of trust.

The possibility of even a minimal degree of trust is frustrated to the extent that weapons production and deployment are captive to "worst case" assumptions. To assume the absolutely worst motives of an adversary is to compound the vicious circle of mistrust and to provide an infinite rationalization for the arms race. In the nuclear era, it is to deny all practical possibility of expressing Christian hope.

The impact of military demands on science and technology not only distorts the priorities and perceptions of "developed" societies: it intensifies the pressures of domination upon "developing" societies. The pattern of domination is one in which economic, military, intellectual and cultural interests are closely inter-related. Some of the poorest "developing" societies are becoming increasingly militarized through collaboration between indigenous elites and the military-industrial-scientific elites of "developed" societies. The distortion of developmental priorities (educational, technological and social) thus increasingly mirrors the misplaced values and interests of richer countries, at the heavy cost of frustrating the most elemental human needs of poor countries and even undermining their own authentic security.

A serious consequence of such distorted priorities and unjust relationships is the disadvantageous position of poorer countries in multilateral disarmament institutions. With the proliferation of UN and other agencies, the richer and more militarized countries can be represented by platoons of experts on weapons systems, nuclear technology, and monitoring devices. The poorer countries cannot easily muster the personnel to represent their governments in all these agencies.

Moral criticism of military technology is often rebutted by citing the benefits of "spin-offs". Among these civilian by-products are 'flu vaccine, jet aircraft, radars for air safety and meteorology, synthetics, nuclear energy, communications satellites, the revolution in astronomy, and urban rapid transit.

It is deeply troubling to ask whether some of these developments would ever have occurred without the high priorities accorded to military technology in research and development. Some of these innovations are clearly ambiguous in their consequences—such as the hazards of nuclear energy and the power of communications to become tools of cultural imperialism. Moreover, the benefits of some spin-offs, such as jet aircraft, tend to be limited to city-dwellers and not to benefit the poor majority. We may also ask whether military technology itself, in economic terms, efficiently produces civilian benefits, especially in view of the enormous wastefulness of defence industries.

Finally, we must ask whether the new generations of strategic weapons which have emerged during the 1970s, such as MIRVs, cruise and mobile missiles, will ever generate substantial civilian benefits. We may well have reached an era of diminishing returns, at best, in which the case for spin-offs will lose its attractiveness altogether.

The role of scientists and technologists in confronting the ethical dilemmas and theological imperatives inescapably embodied in these issues deserves special recognition in the Christian community.

Scientists and technologists must ask themselves whether their careers are instruments of humane service. They must ask themselves the extent to which their very choice of research topics is determined by anticipated funding or rationalized by the hope of spin-offs. They must confront the imbalance of teaching and research resources between the physical sciences with their special claims to costly equipment and the social sciences with their special responsibilities for public policy. More particularly, they must confront the gross disparities between the funding of military research and the funding of disarmament research as well as the tendency of arms control research to focus more on matters of military hardware than on economic and political processes related to disarmament.

4. THE ROLE OF THE CHURCHES

Churches and the power of science and technology

Social, cultural, political and economic factors influence the life of the Church, its theology and its actions within a given society. But whatever its social context, the Church must respond to human needs, as mandated by a full understanding of the Gospel. Churches are too often allied with power structures. They legitimize the *status quo* and sacrifice their prophetic voice.

Churches and Christians in developed countries should actively strive within their own social context:

— to observe and analyse in a critical manner the politics of governments with regard to resources, energy, distribution of their riches, use of scientific and technological knowledge and handling of political power;

— to give a sign and set an example to the world by adopting a new life-style, less wasteful, more concerned about the use of rare resources and the needs of the neighbour;

— to develop educational programmes to make people aware of patterns of domination, excessive consumerism, etc.;

— to influence public policy by precise legislative proposals which would oppose economic and military support for oppressive regimes in the developing regions of the world;

— to participate in protests, economic boycotts or civil disobedience in the active pursuit of justice;

— to examine critically their own investments in order to ensure that they do not support transnational corporations engaged in questionable activities;
— to use their shareholder position to oppose particular policies and to disinvest when necessary;
— to support the WCC Programme on Transnational Corporations and work with the WCC Commission on the Churches' Participation in Development (CCPD) to propose and promote new ways of technology transfer (CCPD has developed a definition of appropriate technology and prepared a directory of appropriate techniques);
— to help in forming a code of conduct for transnational corporations, exporting firms and governments involved in transfer of technology, and to encourage the formation of mechanisms and institutions such as a representative international board which could enforce such a code; elements of the code should require the release of operational information to the public and include a system of sanctions and penalties.

Churches in developing countries should be actively engaged in:
— facilitating development of technologies appropriate to their countries by making their members and the public at large aware of the issues involved in the transfer of technology, and educating the people so they are fully capable of participating in decision-making;
— challenging their own governments and economic institutions to set technological goals which serve the needs of the poorest in society;
— challenging fellow churches which serve existing power structures;
— encouraging regional cooperation of developing countries to decrease dependence on highly industrialized countries.

The churches' challenge to military technology

The churches' witness to this complex arena of military technology and its relationships with science, education, industry and politics can hardly be said to be even adequately envisioned, let alone embodied in the life of congregations, denominations or ecumenical networks.

The WCC Programme on Disarmament and Militarism offers a promising framework for constituent churches to become an active presence in this arena. This programme merits much more substantial support (including funding) if the world Church is to have a significant impact on governments and scientists in disarmament issues. Local and regional ecumenical centres on disarmament and peace can provide a vital link to this programme.

1. The churches must undertake new vocational strategies among the laity, scientists, technologists, industrialists, politicians and others—who have most access to this arena in their daily work. The meaning of their work must be nurtured by a more vocation-oriented learning of the fullness of Christian ethics.

2. Theological education must develop a new cross-professional orientation in which ministers learn about the struggles of the laity for meaningful work and witness as the foundation of their own professional ministry.

3. In addition to fostering personal exchanges across the boundaries of hostility between militarized states, the Church's world mission must give special place to exchanges in which persons from the poor nations most victimized by the injustices of the rich nations' technological priorities and threats may testify to the human consequences as they see them.

4. Local congregations and ecumenical clusters should be prepared to exert strong and competent leadership in the conversion of regional defence industry to civilian purposes.

5. The churches should encourage investments in those enterprises producing products and services for human welfare and not engaged in military production. Thorough and continuing research can provide the information needed for such investment procedures.

6. The churches must celebrate politics as the vocation of all citizens. Humane decisions about the allocation of scientific and technological resources require citizen participation by those most directly affected. In most countries, the political ethics of our churches requires a much more positive development if they are to become redemptive forces in society. The churches can, and do, help to shape the civic values and public opinions which are expressed in governmental decisions about science and technology. Perhaps no other institution can do more to sustain a steadfast public commitment to disarmament and to peaceful and liberating uses of technology.

7. The churches must help their members to understand and support the complex inter-related agreements which improve the prospects for eventual nuclear disarmament. In particular, the churches of nuclear-weapons states must now give forceful emphasis to strategic arms limitations (SALT) and a comprehensive test ban as the indispensable preconditions to halting the spread of nuclear weapons technology. The churches must speak with theological vigour and moral clarity to the injustice and insidious discrimination of the world power structure in nuclear technology. Our colleague from Nigeria, B.C.E. Nwosu, spoke bluntly but fairly to this issue in declaring: "Any country that tells you that nuclear energy is bad but refuses to share with you the secrets of commercial solar energy or other alternative technologies should not be taken seriously. Any country that sits on thousands of megaton bombs and harasses you about the dangers of nuclear proliferation should not be considered a friend."

8. The churches should work cooperatively with other religious communities and with non-religious groups to reverse the direction of military technology and to abolish war itself. The totalitarian nature of weapons of mass destruction has made the whole human family a community of peril which must become a community of hope. Thus have the technical characteristics of the tools of war driven us to acknowledge in our time an ironic fulfilment of prophetic theology: Christ has embraced us all, every people everywhere, people of every religion and of no religion, because we all belong to God in life and death and life again.

X. Towards a New Christian Social Ethic and New Social Policies for the Churches

Section X was composed of representatives from all the other sections of this conference. Our responsibility was to search, among the discussions in plenary and section meetings, for clues to the development of a Christian social ethic and social policies for the churches in our historical era. We did this with an appropriate combination of modesty and boldness. We did not expect to answer hard questions that other sections did not answer or to deliver to the churches (in a few days' time!) a new social ethic. We aimed to clarify some issues that churches all over the world must work at for years to come. Yet we feel ready to make a few affirmations as forcefully as we can.

1. INTRODUCTION

The work of God, enacted in Jesus Christ, is love—a love without limits, a love that seeks justice. The fulfilment of God's love is the purpose of the world; its symbol, the Cross. On the Cross of Christ, the real possibilities of human beings find their limitations and God's power finds its expression.

God is Creator; the world is his creation. We men and women have failed to live the life of love which God intends for us, but Christians testify that the love of God overcomes our human guilt and the superpersonal structures of evil (the "principalities and powers"). Therefore, insofar as we are faithful, we await with confidence the coming of God's Kingdom of love, in which justice and peace and joy will be known by all and God will be all in all.

No human acts can bring God's Kingdom to its perfection, for it is God's work in his own time. We are dependent upon his Spirit. Yet, in the historical reality of God's work in Christ, we have grounds for hope. Hence we Christians can commit ourselves in the Spirit to our work now. Our work will be finite and limited, yet it is a commitment in which we have the real opportunity to live together in love. This is why we want to work together for a just, participatory and sustainable society. This is why Christians—though they themselves often defy God—can experience hope as a present reality, even in the direst suffering and loneliness.

As the Declaration of the Bangalore meeting of Faith and Order (1978) points out: "Our present hope is anchored in God's actions in history and in the eternal life of the age to come... We know that we are accepted by God as forgiven sinners, and therefore we are certain that we can here and now be co-workers with God in pointing to his rule. In Christ as a mirror we see the will of God. Christ will come as the revelation of truth and righteousness."

In this conference we have talked of a just, participatory and sustainable society, and we have found intimations of what such a society might be. We are not ready to define such a society; we expect to continue our venture of discovery of what it can be. But we can at least begin to give meaning to those pregnant words: just, participatory and sustainable.

A *just* society is the kind of society heralded by the prophets and Jesus in the words translated as *justice* and *righteousness*. "Let justice roll down as waters" (Amos 5:24). "Seek first his kingdom and his justice (or righteousness)" (Matt. 5:33). In a just society persons and groups (family, occupational, social, ethnic, national) relate to one another for the benefit of all. Persons and groups have the opportunity to become human in freedom and responsibility. We can give no single universal description of what truly human life is, for that is in part a function of cultural and social situations. Yet we recognize a common humanity among people all created "in the image of God".

We do not expect harmony without conflict. We believe that human beings are created for love and community, but in sin they encroach upon the just rights of others. Individuals find meaning in community, yet must sometimes resist domination from the community. Particular communities can work together in world community, yet must sometimes affirm their particular identities against the domination of the whole. Therefore, justice requires more than good intentions; it requires political and legal structures to hold the powerful accountable and to prevent their exploitation of the weak.

A *participatory* society includes in the process of decision-making all those whom any decision affects. Decisions are thus made by people, with people, for people. The modes of participation are likely to vary in different societies and in different decisions within societies. But everywhere participation is concerned not merely with the making of decisions but also with the sharing of resources, both material and spiritual, and the sharing of the suffering and the benefits. The achievement of meaningful participation in large, complex societies and on a world scale is difficult; we shall say more about this in Part 7 below.

Our awareness of interdependence as partners and competitors has enabled us to recognize that we must see "society" as both particular societies and as the worldwide society of men and women. This leads us to ask about the ways in which human societies settle matters between them. Justice and participation must characterize the relationship between societies as well as the relationships between individuals in society.

A *sustainable* society is one in which people live with each other and the physical environment in ways that lead to continuing life rather than destruction. In recent years much of the world has discovered that its present habits of consumption threaten the physical environment and the resources by which people themselves live. Humanity is one member of the ecosystem (also part of God's creation) and has to live in continuing interaction with it. Practices destructive of the ecosystem will also destroy human society. In this respect justice characterizes a human relationship with the whole ecosystem as well as the relationship with other human persons and groups.

As we explore the dimensions of a just, participatory and sustainable society, we realize that no society—past or present—has achieved this goal in its fullness. Nor do Christians expect the full achievement of such a society within this human history. In fact, new historical achievements open up new possibilities and new perils. But we are capable of more profound justice, fuller participation, and greater concern for sustainability than we now know and practise. God gives us opportunities and calls us to responsibility.

2. THE HISTORICAL AND SOCIAL SITUATION IN WHICH WE LIVE AND MAKE DECISIONS

Gathering in this conference, we realize the uniqueness of our historical situation. Never before has the human race faced the specific opportunities, responsibilities and perils that our generation faces. Whether we think of powers of healing or destroying, of communication on earth or travel in space, of splitting atoms or splicing genes, we today are masters—and victims—of immense technological power. We must make decisions that our ancestors did not make. We feel the force of the Christian belief that God meets his human creation, in grace and in judgment, in the events of history. We believe in a faithful God, a God whose love remains constant, but a God who in freedom does new things and calls on people in freedom to do new things.

Meeting people from many lands, we become aware of how much our diverse social situations affect our experiences, our perceptions of reality, our ethical decisions. Some of us are investing our lives in the scientific enterprise and finding it rewarding. None of us could be at this conference without the achievements of modern technology. Yet some of us are oppressed by technology: our lands have been invaded or our economies distorted by people with more technical power than our own. All of us have fears of technological power misused. Our delights or pains, our picture of the world, our joy, our humour, our sense of moral outrage or guilt depend—not solely but significantly—on our place in society. We struggle to find an ethic more secure and authoritative than our feelings and our social location. But wherever we look, we see what is visible from our location. If, for example, we appeal to conscience, we find that our consciences are largely determined by our societal experiences. If we search the scriptures, we find that the parts that move us most powerfully are those that address us where we are, that the concepts by which we interpret the scriptures are those that we have developed in a given historical context. Sometimes we find with joy that our sensitivities—perhaps as women or as physically handicapped or as economically oppressed people—give the Church insights into biblical meanings that centuries of "official" interpretation have obscured.

Hence we realize that traditional ethical methods have rarely paid enough attention to the social situations of those who try to think ethically. We have to ask of ourselves and all people what the purpose of ethical affirmations is. Are we seeking to justify our own power and pretensions? If so, the most skillful ethical reasoning will only betray our responsibility.

According to our faith, it is not the most brilliant, but the pure in heart who see God. It is to the poor, both in spirit and in material wealth, that the Kingdom is promised. They remind us that all have a duty to seek insight from the exploited and oppressed in order that the whole of society may be liberated. We must remember that women generally are also oppressed; if they are poor or in a minority, they may be doubly oppressed. Faithfulness to the Gospel message warns us against the peculiar distortions and blindnesses that may haunt the powerful.

3. FOR THE CHRISTIAN CHURCH WHAT IS THE RELATION BETWEEN FAITH AND ETHICS?

Faith, for Christians, is more than mere affirmation of truth. It is a response to God, a process, a directing of life, which influences the whole person and the Christian community. Christians are those who are called to realize the essential nature of creation and their own place within it, through Jesus Christ, who is the true image of the invisible God. Thus men and women find their anchor in life and set out to direct their actions and behaviour in relation to God, their fellow men and women, and nature.

Christian behaviour is rooted in the Christian love and understanding of God. The Church, the community of faith, exists to anticipate and celebrate the new era for humanity which God inaugurated in Christ. But this Church, of course, proclaims its faith and lives among people of diverse faith and moral values. In the words of the report to the WCC of the Committee on a Just, Participatory and Sustainable Society (Jamaica, 1979): "Christians believe that all human beings are part of a dynamic pointing to the messianic Kingdom... While Christians claim no monopoly, they live under a special call to obedience, to engage with other people in a search for the common aim: justice on earth, manifested in a peaceful community of all humankind in which every human being finds true fulfilment of life."

Hence there is an obligation on Christians to examine and appreciate ethical insights that come from outside their own community of faith—from people of diverse faiths and ideologies. Christians cannot, should not and must not claim to possess all ethical truth. The ways in which they have tried to live out God's love may have been distorted by any number of misleading influences. Since ethical norms may be influenced by many socio-cultural factors, we cannot assume that there is any simple or fixed language in which to state moral values. Christians are further called to be sensitive to fresh promptings of God's spirit.

We believe that Christian love, as a response to God's love for his creation, has particular relevance to a society which is influenced by scientific and technological innovation. Christians are called to work with all people of good will to build a just and peaceful society, in which the work of human minds and hands may serve the loving purposes of the Creator. They seek a world in which humanity enjoys the fruits of the earth as one family. This hope, set before us by Jesus Christ and signified by his whole community on earth, requires efforts of fortitude, patience and commitment, for it involves the bearing of a cross. In social terms this means that, in the difficult days that we now experience and foresee, Christians have no right to seek protection from the pains that humanity suffers.

4. WHAT IS THE RELATION BETWEEN SCIENCE AND ETHICS?

The authentic scientific enterprise requires honesty, a humility before truth and a willingness to set aside prejudice and accept correction from evidence. These moral values are inherent in science. The violation of them is a betrayal of the meaning of science as well as of ethics. At its best, the scientific openness to truth has sometimes shamed the rigid dogmatisms and prejudices of many religious communities. Furthermore, the scientific enterprise requires a cultural setting that permits freedom to search for truth.

Even so, the values inherent in science are incomplete without the incorporation of humanistic values. Competence in science may or may not be associated with love and passion for justice. The direction and application of scientific research depend largely upon the values in the culture (including its political and economic institutions) surrounding the scientist. The scientists in our midst have made this point forcefully and they are showing how scientists can contribute to the criticism and the shaping of cultural values.

Most policy decisions in our time include both scientific understanding and ethical purpose. Decision-makers (including all who participate in decision-making) must ask both what is possible and what is desirable. They must consult both the scientific evidence and their human purposes. It is sometimes said, erroneously, that scientific data dictate a policy; but what is meant is that, given certain assumptions about values and purposes, the data may point to a policy.

In the words of the WCC consultation on "Genetics and the Quality of Life" (1975): "Churchmen cannot expect precedents from the past to provide answers to questions never asked in the past. On the other hand, new scientific advances do not determine what are worthy human goals. Ethical decisions in uncharted areas require that scientific capabilities be understood and used by persons and communities sensitive to their own deepest convictions about human nature and destiny. There is no sound ethical judgment in these matters independent of scientific knowledge, but science does not itself prescribe the good."

5. WHAT IS THE RELATION BETWEEN TECHNOLOGY AND ETHICS?

We have heard many answers to this question in this conference.

i)   Some have said that technology is a gift of human rationality and imagination, a desirable means of solving human problems. Technologies make possible cures for many diseases, production of more food per hectare, swift communication. Thus, human beings equipped with technology can move some problems from the area of fate to the area of freedom.

ii) Some have emphasized the dehumanizing possibilities in technology. We have not heard in this conference the opinion, sometimes voiced elsewhere, that technology is intrinsically dehumanizing, regardless of its uses and social settings. But we have heard—often—that in the world as we know it, many technologies are in fact inseparable from institutional structures of oppression.

iii) Many have argued that technology, precisely because it is a form of power, is ethically problematic, as is all human power. It may be basically beneficial (e.g. the medical technologies that have apparently eliminated smallpox) or basically destructive (e.g. bacteriological warfare). Some forms of technology are ethically better than others, regardless of social systems, e.g. reliance on renewable energy sources may be better than reliance on non-renewable sources. But the effects of technology depend largely on the social systems within which they function. A society can use technology to relieve poverty or bring new opportunities to the physically handicapped. But in the existing political and economic structures of society, technology often functions to bring more power to the powerful and thereby to increase injustice.

Our section concurs in the judgment that human, social and ethical problems cannot be solved by technology alone. We agree that there are ethical aspects to virtually all technical decisions. It is important to locate these, and make people aware of them, before technical and social processes move to decisions without adequate attention to their ethical implications.

6. WHAT IS THE MEANING/AUTHORITY OF SCRIPTURE AND CHRISTIAN TRADITION FOR CONTEMPORARY DECISIONS ABOUT THE USES OF TECHNOLOGY?

As Christians we bring to ethical decisions faith in God, who is revealed to us in history, and most fully and decisively in Jesus Christ. We believe that this faith confers on humanity a freedom and responsibility in love to make ethical decisions, sometimes without precedent. Christians make these decisions in the light of sensitivity, awakened by Christian revelation, to God and God's creation. Thus biblical images, parables, motifs, principles and doctrines are fundamental to Christian decision, even though often not directly prescriptive.

In these affirmations there is a rejection of two positions sometimes argued. *(a)* We do not regard the Bible as the answer-book to our ethical questions. The Bible and Christian tradition are silent on many decisions that Christians must make today, e.g. about the ethical evaluation of specific discoveries in genetics. *(b)* We do not think that the Bible is made obsolete by new sciences and technologies. We do not live in an age so "enlightened" that we have no need for biblical guidance. In fact, our rising ecological sensitivities frequently make the Bible more, rather than less relevant to our decisions and to the attitudes that underlie those decisions.

7. WHAT IS THE IMPORTANCE OF EXPERT KNOWLEDGE IN ETHICAL DECISIONS, ESPECIALLY IN AREAS OF COMPLEX TECHNOLOGY?

Expert knowledge is an essential aspect of many processes of decision-making. However, the weight of the expert's opinion generally depends on the level of consciousness and awareness of the public. If an issue has been debated both in an academic milieu and among lay people, experts will be called on for highly specific contributions.

But if the issue has been considered only by some specialists or decision-makers, experts are likely to extend their authority to opinions beyond their specific competence.

We can consider two extreme models of decision-making; those of the airline pilot and of the urban planner. The pilot works on a short-term schedule. Knowing the destination, flight plan, and the techniques of operating the plane, the pilot makes continual decisions oriented to the success of the flight and the safety of the passengers. The passengers rely on the pilot's skill. They normally do not want to give the pilot moment-by-moment advice. If the pilot makes wrong decisions, the consequences are immediate and dangerous for all—including the pilot.

The urban planner, on the other hand, deals with long-term issues. Planners make decisions in cases where their information cannot show all the consequences of their choices. Their errors will affect the lives of people in the future in ways not easy to foresee—and they may escape the consequences of their errors.

Of course, these are two emblematic situations, and decision-makers are generally in intermediate situations. It may be said that many urban planners—and other experts—behave like pilots. In short, they make choices without consulting people; they act as if only short-term problems are relevant; they trust the reliability of their methods without considering them critically.

It follows that there is a great need of communication among experts and between experts and the general public. Five aspects deserve particular consideration:

i) The ethical responsibility for scientists to communicate knowledge clearly and responsibly. This implies a will to move information from sanctuaries of knowledge to the people, through channels such as newspapers and magazines, paperback books, TV, etc. possibly in connection with pressure groups and organizations of citizens, workers, and so on.

ii) The ethical responsibility of citizens to inform themselves. This includes the will of citizens to be active members of the society, aware of what is going on and energetic in seeking information. There are both individual and communal strategies to achieve.

iii) The ethical responsibilities of governments to make it physically and economically possible for their citizens to inform themselves on scientific information and the ethical consequences of science and technology, and to support scientists' attempts to socialize scientific knowledge.

iv) The ethical responsibility of international organizations to spread information among different countries and to break down monopolies of information. For example the issue of patents, now under debate in the UN, needs reconsideration.

v) The ethical responsibility and the freedom of non-governmental institutions (including churches, universities, research establishments) to present their views to a wider public.

In a situation characterized by growing participatory processes, the roles of the expert may be to give accurate information, to acknowledge candidly areas of ignorance and uncertainty, and to suggest criteria for decision-making that are coherent with the people's feelings and interests. Such roles can influence the further development of research, e.g. in agriculture or health rather than militarism, research for needed housing rather than unnecessary goods, research in the prevention rather than only the care of disease.

Finally, it should be realized that all people are experts on some subjects. According to the old saying: "I know better than anybody else where my shoe pinches," it is important to develop new participatory processes by which all people can take part in decisions that affect their welfare. A conference like this one allows the sharing of knowledge, insights and experiences among people of diverse skills and backgrounds. Such conferences are necessarily unusual. But there are many opportunities for processes enabling diverse people to enter into the making of programmatic decisions in their own communities.

Genuine participation is not easy to achieve. It is sometimes difficult even within a family. It becomes exceedingly difficult within large and intricate societies. Often decisions of great importance to everyone are delegated to small groups (or even individuals) with great political, economic or technical power. We welcome the many social experiments which are testing new methods of participation, without which justice is incomplete and insecure. Meanwhile we emphasize the importance of access to information as one necessary step towards wide participation in decisions.

8. WHAT CERTAINTIES ARE POSSIBLE IN CHRISTIAN ETHICS?

Both science and ethics often deal with uncertainties. The progress of science during the past century has often meant that old certainties gave way to judgment of probability. Scientific uncertainty often arises from our lack of knowledge, but it may also be the result of the uncertainty intrinsic in natural phenomena. Scientific knowledge may enable us to predict the occurrence of an event, with an indication of the probability associated with our prediction.

In human social decisions there are some possibilities for estimating probabilities and quantifying the extent of possible error. But such decisions depend also upon ethical commitments that are not quantifiable. Decisions of Christians often combine:

i) the certainty of faith in Jesus Christ; this is not the certainty of laboratory verification or mathematical computation; it is—at its most authentic—the certainty by which one is committed to live or die;

ii) the uncertainty of knowing what actions will work to human benefit in a given situation.

There are many occasions, of course, in which Christians—like other people—know what is right; their problem is only the will to do what is right. There are other occasions in which Christians—like other people—are honestly perplexed about the best course of action; they need to learn, especially in new situations, what is right and good.

Such a distinction helps us to realize how easy self-deception is. An emphasis on certainty may be merely a way of escaping the anxiety of uncertainty and the necessity of genuinely listening to people who disagree with us. But an emphasis on uncertainty may be used as a pretext to enable people to avoid responsibility.

In this conference we have discussed many cases of human oppression due to the willing exercise of power by some over other people. The problem was not that the powerful people did not know the harm they were doing; they did not care. And if they did not know, it was because they did not care. We have discussed other cases where Christians of equally good will differed in their opinions of what was best for society and where both sides, if they were honest, realized that they were uncertain.

Like the biblical prophets, we may find occasions to speak with the assurance: "Thus saith the Lord." We may find other occasions when, like those same prophets, we must be silent because we do not have a word from the Lord. And we may find still other times to say: "We are not sure, but it is our best opinion that..."

Christians, responsive to the Cross and the Resurrection, will seek for ways to make love and justice effective in the most complex social situations. We will realize that some of our moral failures are due to our unwillingness—and society's unwillingness—to be born again, and we will look for possibilities of personal and social regeneration. We will realize that some of our perplexities require further exploration—like some of the debates in this conference—on the meaning of love and justice for evaluating the consequences of new technologies, answers to the energy crisis, and the appropriate use of new genetic knowledge. (See Part 14 below for further discussion of this issue.)

9. WHAT ETHICAL CRITERIA CAN GIVE GUIDANCE IN UNDERSTANDING RISK?

The Christian faith can certainly be said to encourage believers to take risks. Jesus said: "Who wants to save his life, will lose it, and who wants to lose it, will save it." The first Christians had to face all sorts of risks in order to spread the Gospel, and they heavily suffered the consequences of defying the rules of the society. During the course of history, and nowadays too, Christians took and take risks in order to be faithful to their commitment.

Each risk-taker accepts the possibility of suffering: in the case of the early Christians, for example, this was overwhelmed by the will to be active witnesses of Jesus. Generally speaking, there is a relation between the risk that is faced and the benefit that is associated with it. The problems of risk-assessment and risk-benefit evaluations are spreading in our societies, and it is important to emphasize several points:

i)   Self-chosen versus inflicted risks. The boundary between these two kinds of risks is difficult to assess. There are some extreme situations, like hazardous or noxious personal habits, which are self-chosen, or externally inflicted risks, like those due to air pollution or radio-active contamination. In many cases the two aspects are connected; for example cigarette smoking is a self-chosen risk, but social and environmental factors (quality of life, stress, mass media) play a role in encouraging or discouraging people to smoke.

ii) Knowledge of the risk by the risk-taker. Lack of knowledge and misinformation in respect to the risk factor are frequently found. This can depend in some circumstances on a general lack of knowledge in that field, but generally it is a matter of distribution, rather than existence, of knowledge. For example, workers are commonly exposed to chemicals whose toxic effects have been known for a long time, but they are given little or no information on the risks they are running.

iii) The existence of alternative choices. The acceptance of a serious risk, without the expectation of a particular benefit, may be due to the lack of alternatives. A typical problem is the "choice" between hazardous work and unemployment.

It can be stated that scientific and technological development have created sensitive tools and methods for risk detection and quantification, but there has not yet been a satisfactory ethical debate on these issues. The focus of such a debate would concern the even or uneven distribution of risks and benefits in the society, in relation to various problems.

The settlement of new factories, the location of nuclear plants, and the introduction of pharmaceutical drugs carry along benefits and risks. It is important, if a correct evaluation has to be made, to assess both the probability and the magnitude of the harmful effects involved, and to find an answer to the question: "Do those who gain from this decision accept the accompanying risks, or do they impose them on others?" The question of participation in society has particular moral significance at this point.

Then come the problems of spreading the relevant information and allowing people or groups at risk to play an active role, possibly resisting inflicted risks. An active, participatory debate on risk assessment and evaluation today may have concrete, positive effects on the planning of towns, factories and the whole environment in the next years.

10. WHAT IS THE ETHICAL SIGNIFICANCE OF PARTICULARISTIC CULTURAL VALUES?

The diffusion of technology usually means the diffusion of the culture that produces it. Today many peoples throughout the world feel threatened by imported technologies that weaken or destroy local cultures. People do not know how to resist the homogenization of culture.

There are some advantages in the adoption of worldwide practices in such areas as safety control at airports, universally recognizable traffic signs, some systems of communication. But the destruction of cultural roots, often swift and violent, is a high price to pay. The phenomenon is often deceptive in that local and regional cultures are expected to yield to more "universal" human ways; but the "universal" is often, in fact, a western particularism masquerading as universal. One especially pernicious effect is the creation in some societies of wealthy elites oriented towards a foreign technologically dominant culture and contemptuous of the people and values of their own societies.

The diffusion of technology and culture requires a reassessment of the ethical significance of particularistic cultural values. It requires also reconsideration of the relation between Christianity—often associated, whether truly or falsely, with the world of elaborate technology and the religions associated with other cultures.

Christianity must accept different cultures and religions; Christians have no monopoly of moral concern or ethical insight (see Part 3 above). For example, the values which Jewish, Hindu, Buddhist or Muslim traditions place upon humanity and nature are illuminating for their own sake. Quite apart from the fact that attention to them may awaken dimly remembered insights of the Christian tradition, it may also enable us to discover new insights and new applications. In a world which is daily becoming smaller our opportunities to learn from these traditions happily increase, and we urge all Christians, not just scholars, to make the most of them.

Furthermore, it is not merely religions but also secular philosophies which have often grasped an element of our human world to which we need to pay attention. In this respect the fact that one third of humanity is governed by a political system which is related to Karl Marx means that Christians should examine with discriminating care the values of Marxism. The worldwide extent of a scientific and technological culture has alerted us now in this conference precisely to the need to examine its motives and values.

The Bible acknowledges cultural differences and celebrates the many ways in which those who are not of the community of faith nevertheless do God's will. We need to be more open to this possibility, for it is often the seeing of difference where no difference really is that frustrates the fulfilment of God's purpose in the world.

The identity of Christians as a separate community is therefore implicitly essential. Others cannot learn of us and we cannot learn of them unless the integrity of each is mutually recognized. This might be seen as an important aspect of participation. Nothing in what is said here destroys the claims which Christians make for the uniqueness of Christ; what is challenged is the uniqueness and priority of the way in which Christians, as individuals and communities, have interpreted the uniqueness of Christ in their own value systems.

An open society is certainly desirable, but this should not be seen to be in conflict with a Christian community standing fast on a particular human concern which may itself be a condition of openness in society. Thus the Black Church in South Africa justifiably stands its ground in favour of an open society in its community.

Technology should be in the hands of those who understand its meaning and can use it within the contexts of their own cultures. The Third World, for example, has the ethical right to choose for itself the purposes to which technology is put, in order to achieve participation in decisions affecting local and regional cultures. The ecumenical church has a responsibility to support the Third World in its struggles for self-determination.

11. WHAT IS THE ETHICAL RELATION BETWEEN JUSTICE AND SUSTAINABILITY?

Justice is a dynamic process, which is already under way. But more constructive effort is required. A theology which accepts the belief that human beings are part of the wider creation is not new, as one can see, for example, in the life of St Francis of Assisi; yet the implications of this belief for our moral concern are not sufficiently appreciated. Sustainability, the appropriate relationship of human beings with their environment, is a long-term goal which must be seen both in economic and in human terms. The Christian impact will be felt through our attempts at an equitable redistribution of present-day resources, so that the whole human world can share the Creator's gifts of food, shelter, power and joy. All men and women should be able to participate as whole persons in the building of a just and sustainable society.

Sustainability is a part of justice also because it is a recognition that God's gifts belong not only to us who are living but also to those who come after us. In this sense the doctrine of the communion of saints—the community of all those who seek God and love God—may be seen to have a new moral significance for Christians. When we see that expanded production is not morally justifiable because it harms the humane relation with the rest of nature, or of one society with another, then sharing is the only possible choice for the Christian. Just how important this moral task is becomes more evident as our knowledge of the physical and psychological world of man grows.

The JPSS Report (Jamaica, January 1979) stated: "In all regions... the sometimes conflicting claims of sustainability and social justice need urgent attention." In their deepest meaning, we repeat, justice and sustainability are intimately related. But there may be immediate conflicts between the two. For example, the use of DDT may prevent deaths from malaria now, while inserting into the ecosystem and the food chain poisons that will harm people and wild life for generations to come. Such tragic conflicts must be acknowledged, while we seek new technological and moral processes to overcome them.

The issue of sustainability may be used hypocritically by the wealthy and powerful as a device to deny the poor the benefits of economic growth. We denounce the immorality of that stratagem and reaffirm that the ecological crisis makes more urgent equity of distribution.

We believe also that sustainability is an urgent issue for all societies, although in widely different ways. The unsustainability of present standards of consumption in the wealthiest nations may mean traumatic changes as people learn to reduce drastically their consumption of petroleum. In other parts of the world, the reliance upon firewood means the desertification of vast areas; already people suffer hunger because of past generations' practices. We are not making a moral judgment against people who in their poverty are unable to reduce consumption for the sake of the future. We say only that sustainability is a problem throughout the world.

It is meaningless to talk about sustainability, especially in relation to justice, unless political and economic forces of transformation are set in motion. Those of us in this conference who advocate sustainability accept the responsibility to struggle in our own countries against those political and economic forces that either oppose sustainability or seek to achieve it without an equally strong concern for justice.

12. WHAT IS THE ETHIC OF THE USE OF SCARCE RESOURCES?

It is the duty of every person and every society to recognize the fact that resources are limited. Further, it is a clear implication of the Christian understanding of the activity of God in creation, that all men and women are to benefit from it and that every person has the same right to use these resources responsibly. Hence no individual or group should be excluded from sharing in them or deciding how they should be used. When resources are scarce, the justice of the market system is most questionable, since it eliminates those who cannot afford the price from benefiting.

Clearly different resources raise the need for different criteria in their distribution, since the needs of individuals and societies will differ. However, it is too easy for both individuals and societies to translate a "want" into a "need". When this happens, the unjustifiable "wants" of one community may deny another community its justifiable needs. As a Christian community we must become more aware of this issue and must attempt some definition of "wants" and "needs" in the wider context of understanding what it is to be human. A just society will attend to needs before it turns to the satisfaction of mere wants. Yet it will recognize that needs are not for mere physical subsistence, but include the expression of the gifts of artistic creation and imagination.

The particular problems raised by the scarcity of medical resources are very difficult. We should do everything possible to preserve the life of any individual patient, yet not without reference to the needs of the society as a whole. And especially as Christians, we should seek to take decisions for the individual in the light of an understanding of resurrection and the quality of human life. There may be times when prolongation of life is unwarranted interference with death.

Since it is clear that the most expensive techniques in medical practice cannot be available to all, we have to give continuing attention to the appropriate ways in which decisions should be taken. The role of the expert is particularly crucial here because of the sometimes unwarranted position in which society has put the doctor. Christian faith has an important contribution to make if it will look for creative moral contexts in which medical expertise may be evaluated. But there are basic medical needs, which we must seek for all; and this has particular relevance for the situation of the Third World, where such needs are far from being met. Again we see the importance of distinguishing between "needs" and "wants", and of looking for a constructive way of recognizing which is which.

It is also worth noting that the rich world's understanding of sophisticated medicine may have blinded it to the insights of the wise traditional medicine in developing societies. In this case we may be greatly helped by discovering that the most technologically sophisticated medicine is not the most humanly creative. Health is wholeness, not mere survival.

13. WHAT IS THE RELATION BETWEEN HUMAN "DOMINION" AND STEWARDSHIP?

Language may by its very structure appear to determine the way in which human beings work out their moral responses. The way in which we conceive of our relation to nature and express it in language will condition what we consider appropriate human action with regard to nature. This is of particular importance to Christians, since it is often argued that the western approach to science and technology is rooted in a Christian understanding of the creation, which sees nature as given to human beings for their exclusive use. It cannot be affirmed too strongly that whatever truth there is in this opinion as a comment on the way some Christians have treated the natural world, it rests on false understandings of the Bible and tradition. We repeat our earlier affirmation (Part 1 above) that justice includes the human relationship with the ecosystem.

Humanity is temporally the last link in God's creation and, therefore, a part of nature, not apart from it. Persons share with the whole of creation in the ultimate purposes which God has for it. What authority they possess, they possess within creation and not over creation; furthermore that authority is a gift of God and one for which men and women will be called to account by God.

The dependence of human beings on non-human nature is becoming only too apparent as the sciences explore the natural world, including the physical and psychological wellbeing of persons and communities. Here the authority of human beings over nature is of an interdependent kind. We should perhaps think of ourselves as the self-conscious intelligence of the whole created order, with authority to act with and for it, not over it. We are therefore to care for nature, as if it were the body of humanity. This is good theologically, and it is good biologically.

Yet having said this, we must recognize that humanity is also called to take responsibility for itself within nature and to make decisions that will protect the lives of individuals and societies. Nature is the context for moral judgment, not a world from which human beings can take their values. Thus, for example, polio viruses may be destroyed in the interests of human life, and the tsetse fly attacked as the carrier of human diseases. It is not obvious that we must all become vegetarians, as the consequences of our respect for nature. What is clear is that the decisions which we take in these respects, as in others, involve considerations of a kind much more fundamental for the ecosystem than we have hitherto thought. Our present choices must be made with due sensitivity in the light of this fact. Our awareness of our participation in nature requires this from us, if we are to act with increasing responsibility and justice. The implications of this need careful attention if we are not to destroy our very humanity.

14. HOW DOES THE ETHIC OF THE KINGDOM OF GOD RELATE TO HUMAN DECISIONS AND POLITICAL ACTIONS?

St Paul emphasizes that the Kingdom of God is characterized by righteousness and peace. The Kingdom of God, moreover, is not a future possibility alone; it is a past and present fact in the life of Jesus Christ. But it is a presence which calls for active effort in the lives of each person and of each society; it cannot merely be assumed. Christians are called to work in society so as to make it more supportive of the values of the Kingdom, more expressive of the purposes of God in Christ. Human fallibility and sin make this a perilous task for anyone, and no less for Christians; yet we dare not refuse the invitation of our Lord to seek his Kingdom.

Christians do not, therefore, bring in from outside history elements which are not present within it; they try to recognize in events—in the movements and ideas around them—the activity of God. Because we believe that God is working for the fulfilment of his purposes, we try to uncover, and to give physical shape to his activity. Our attempts to recognize where God is working have to be put continuously under the radical judgment of Christ, to whom the Bible witnesses. This judgment must be continuous because of the human tendency to prove what we want to prove, to fulfil our purposes, not God's. We can say, then, that the task of the Christian mission and of Christian moral judgment is constantly to point the world to the God who is active within it to bring righteousness and peace. The Christian community does this only when it is itself a community of love, which is prepared to suffer for the sake of its Lord.

Political ethics has the task of translating love into structures, for love is not so much an emotion as a determination of the will. Any form of power in human society tends to serve its own institutional interests independently of the persons and groups it should serve. Hence the Christian sees the neighbour and tries to criticize existing political structures from the point of view of those whom they should serve. In particular, Christians in power must avoid any tendency to preach submissive love to those with less power. They would do better to do whatever they can to empower the powerless. If this seems sometimes to encourage struggle rather than peace, it is actually the unmasking of the false peace that serves injustice.

Laws should have as their purpose the expression of love and the structuring of love into justice. They should give attention to relationships between groups as well as individuals, should attend to the need to promote authentic harmony, should present means of resolving conflicts without violence, should provide a possibility for working out social programmes for justice.

The constant criticism of existing laws and the promotion of a more equitable legal and political structure are requirements on Christians as individuals and communities. This struggle is necessary to enable those who are excluded from society by injustice to participate fully in the service of the Kingdom of God.

15. WHAT SOCIAL POLICIES ARE POSSIBLE AND APPROPRIATE FOR THE CHURCHES IN THEIR VARIOUS CULTURAL SITUATIONS?

Christians believe that the rule of God is already present in nature and history through creation and the redemptive new creation of the whole cosmos (Rom. 8, Cor. 5, Col.). Acknowledging this cosmic new creation and experiencing its "birth-pangs", Christians can and must collaborate with secular groups (including Marxists) and with other religious communities who are participating in and supporting God's new creation of the whole world.

Yet there is a specific calling of the Christian community to respond to God's universal redemptive activity as a faithful, worshipping and actively obedient fellowship—that part of humanity which knows and proclaims what God is about as love, justice and truth for the whole world. In the Christian community there are specific and identifiable acts which illuminate, guide and support Christian action. However, prayer and worship in the Christian community should not isolate but rather, through the Holy Spirit, should be a means of expressing the basic commitment of the fellowship to the ultimate unity of all peoples. Nor is prayer opposite to action; rather it is both the beginning and the resource of political and social action.

When we ask what social policies are possible and appropriate for the churches, we see immediately that different churches in different situations have varying possibilities. The Christian Church in its historical pilgrimage has been a tiny persecuted community; it has established a Christendom in which it gave commands to emperors; it has lived as a community within pluralistic societies. These and many other varieties of existence still persist, as realities or as echoes, in various parts of the world. We cannot prescribe callings for the many churches in many situations. If some churches are powerless to influence national policies in their countries, others would be faithless and irresponsible if they did not exercise such influence. Yet in shaping their particular policies the churches must recognize the universal character of God's coming rule, which transcends the values and determining factors of a particular situation. The Church itself is intended to manifest the justice which every human society should seek. The present brokenness of the churches, which weakens and discredits Christian witness, is one reason for the failures and injustices of societies. The ecumenical movement for unity is indispensable for the validation and influence of the ethical convictions supported by Christian faith. Ecumenical conversations, such as the recent consultation of economists from different social systems, can enable churches to see beyond the limitations of their specific cultural milieu.

Hence we list some callings of the churches, and we invite all churches, acting within the wider ecumenical fellowship, to discover which are possible and appropriate for themselves, and to devise strategies for meeting them:
— the calling of presence in the world, particularly among the lonely and the suffering;
— the calling of witness to God's grace and judgment, both among their own members and among those outside;
— the calling of educator, relating God's revelation to human needs and the perplexities of decision-making in our complex world;
— the calling of explorer in the new world of science and technology, discerning the ways of enhancing humanity in the midst of machines and concentrations of power;
— the calling of advocate, speaking on behalf of those who lack power or have no voice;
— the calling of agent of change and renewal;
— the calling of motivator to elicit and liberate human potentiality in the struggles for justice and truth;
— the calling of model to demonstrate the compatibility of variety and unity in a community with a common cause.

16. RECOMMENDATIONS/RESOLUTIONS

i) This conference, recognizing the crucial influence which technology and science (both natural and social) play in shaping contemporary society, calls on governments, industrial companies, universities and scientists to promote and supplement ways in which scientific and technological information may be made legally accessible and practically available to all citizens. The aim is to enable people to participate fully in decisions affecting their wellbeing.

ii) This conference recommends that the sub-unit on Church and Society of the WCC continue the work begun at the consultation on Political Economy, Ethics, and Theology (Zürich, 1978). We see an urgent need to bring together economists from different social systems to reconsider economic theory and practice in the light of the requirements of a just, participatory and sustainable society. The beginnings of such a reconsideration are in process; some of the first developments have been published in various places including publications of the WCC. But the work is in an early stage. Its continuation, involving the interaction of ethical, economic and political concerns and skills, is an urgent human need.

iii) This conference recommends that the sub-unit on Church and Society and the sub-unit on Education of the WCC bring together social scientists, administrators and people engaged in social action in a consultation on methods, theories, and experiments in participation. The objective of this consultation should be to make the participatory dimensions of JPSS more operational.

iv) This conference, recognizing the crucial need for continued discussions and interactions among scientists, social scientists, theologians and lay people on the ethical aspects of the increasing influence of science and technology on our societies, strongly recommends that the churches initiate such discussions in their own situations.

Part Two
Additional Reports and Resolutions

I. Science for Peace

A Resolution on Nuclear Disarmament

We, scientists, engineers, theologians and members of Christian churches from all parts of the world, participants in the WCC Conference on Faith, Science and the Future, now meeting at the Massachusetts Institute of Technology, acknowledge with penitence the part played by science in the development of weapons of mass destruction and the failure of the churches to oppose it, and now plead with the nations of the world for the reduction and eventual abolition of such weapons.

WHEREAS:
— the arsenals of tens of thousands of nuclear weapons already constitute a grave peril to humankind;
— sharp changes by the super-powers towards a counterforce strategy are so destabilizing that sober scientists estimate a nuclear holocaust is probable before the end of the century;
— there is widespread ignorance of the horrible experience of Hiroshima and Nagasaki, and the even greater implications of limited or global nuclear war with current and projected nuclear weapons;
— we are profoundly disturbed by the willingness of some scientists, engineers and corporations, with the backing of governments, to pursue profit and prestige in weapons development at the risk of an unparalleled destruction of human life;
— the waste of the increasingly scarce materials and energy resources of the world on the instruments of war means further deprivation of the poor whom we are commanded to serve;
— we grieve that so many of the most able scientists, especially the young ones, are seduced away from the nobler aspirations of science into the un-witting service of mutual destruction;
— in a time of radical readjustment of the world economy the intolerable burden of the nuclear arms race creates worldwide economic problems;

AND BECAUSE WE BELIEVE:
— that God made us and all creation;
— that He requires us to seek peace, justice and freedom, creating a world where none need fear and every life is sacred;
— that with his grace no work of faith, hope and love need seem too hard for those who trust him;

WE NOW CALL UPON:
— all member communions of the WCC and all sister churches sending official observers, and through them each individual church and congregation;
— our fellow religionists and believers in other cultures, whether Hindu, Jewish, Buddhist or Muslim, and our Marxist colleagues;
— the science and engineering community, especially those engaged in research and development, together with professional scientific associations and trade unions;
— the governments of all nations and especially the nuclear powers;
— all concerned citizens of the world;

TO EMBARK IMMEDIATELY ON THE FOLLOWING TASKS:
— to support and implement the WCC Programme on Disarmament and against Militarism and the Arms Race, and give special emphasis to issues related to military technology and its conversion to peaceful uses;
— to welcome and give practical support to the initiatives by the UN and its special agencies on disarmament, which affirm the right of all nations to participate in the effort to solve these global problems;
— to press for the full implementation of SALT II, to work without delay for the reduction of nuclear weapons through SALT III, and to complete at long last a comprehensive test ban, all of which are urgent and necessary steps in making the Non-Proliferation Treaty effective;
— to stop the development and production of new forms and systems of nuclear weapons;
— while welcoming the exchange of scientific and technical information made possible through the Pugwash Conferences, other international scientific conferences, and the SALT process, to press for further exchanges of information as a means of reducing international mistrust;
— to educate and raise the consciousness of every constituency to the realities of nuclear war in such a way that people cease to avoid it as an issue too big to handle; in particular we recommend the formation of local study groups on the dangers of nuclear war and approaches to disarmament;
— to use every available means to restore confidence in the sisterhood and brotherhood of all, to remove fear and suspicion, to oppose hate-mongering and militarism, and to undo the policies of any with a vested interest in war;
— to prepare local and national programmes for the conversion to civilian use of laboratories and factories related to military research and production, and to provide for the retraining and re-employment of those who work in them;
— to resolve never again to allow science and technology to threaten the destruction of human life, and to accept the God-given task of using SCIENCE FOR PEACE.

II. A Critical Statement by Participants from Africa, Asia, Latin America, the Middle East and the Pacific

The following statement was presented to the conference by a group of participants from Africa, Asia, Latin America, the Middle East and the Pacific:

We denounce the historical and current use of science and technology by industrialized and technically advanced societies, to serve military and economic interests which have brought about great sufferings to the people of the Third World. This has been done in the guise of an ideology of objectivity and value-free pursuit of truth.

We denounce the use of science and technology by industrialized and technically advanced societies to develop the most sinister instruments of death and total annihilation.

We call for a halt to this situation:

i)   We urge that unilateral steps be taken towards disarmament. This is the only position in harmony with the Gospel—the only way out of the impasse in which we find ourselves.

ii) We call for a global reorientation of the huge amount of funds currently used for military research and war-related industries, towards peaceful purposes. Let the spears be beaten into plowshares and the swords transformed into pruning knives. Our planet can be a friendly place if we have enough courage to make it so.

iii) We denounce the decision to transform the Third World into the sewer for the world, and a dumping ground, by the transfer of polluting industries from the rich to the poor countries.

We urge the WCC to establish a programme of continuing education of scientists and science students on the economic and political implications of their work.

We urge the WCC to encourage and support the holding of regional meetings among third world scientists, theologians and lay persons to plan and implement concrete programmes to carry out the ideas expressed in our document and to continue conversations with our counterparts in the industrialized and technically advanced societies.

We urge all scientists participating in this conference to re-examine their ties with governments, military projects, and transnational enterprises of both East and West, even if these ties are not immediately evident.

We urge scientists of the world to accept as the sole purpose of their work the alleviation of misery of the poor and oppressed.

We call upon scientists in the Third World to give the highest priority to the use of science and technology to improve the quality of the lives of our people.

We proclaim that, for us, God reveals himself in a single tear and in a single sigh of a dying child more than in all the wonders of the physical world.

God in Jesus became the suffering servant, a carpenter, a companion of sinners and prostitutes, an outcast; was judged as a criminal and executed as a subversive.

We urge scientists to leave their ivory towers and wealthy temples and join this humble Man in his service to the suffering people of our world.

WE CHOOSE LIFE.

III. Report on the
Science Students Conference

"What is needed is a new vision of a global community, a new society in which the horizons of moral concern and accountability extend not only to every human, but also to every other aspect of the natural order. Christian communities of the past and present have been guilty of unwillingness fully to comprehend the radical nature of the Gospel, and the Christian witness has thereby become an instrument of political and economic oppression. Nevertheless, in the present economic and political situation, the vision and norms of the Christian faith serve as a judgment upon the western abuse of the power provided by science-based technology. One aspect of such a vision is the recognition that the world in all its parts is truly one and that a parochial vision is no longer acceptable. The transition to an international community would seem to imply a need for the attainment of some measure of national self-reliance for all peoples and an end to the present unjust patterns of domination and dependence between nations. Another important aspect of this vision is that a main purpose (some would argue it is the sole purpose) of science and technology is to alleviate the misery and suffering of human beings and their fellow creatures. Therefore the greatest part of scientific research and the development and use of technology should be directed towards meeting basic human needs and, insofar as we can discern them, the needs of the rest of creation."

(from a statement on "Science and Ethics",
conference of science students)

Introduction: the dynamics of the meeting

About one hundred students—official participants, stewards and coopted staff—representing the natural sciences, engineering, social sciences and theology, many of them with experience far beyond their academic studies, assembled at Wellesley College, Wellesley, Mass., USA, from 6 to 11 July 1979. Coming from 55 countries, they represented a wide range of cultures and confessional denominations. About two-thirds of them came from the Third World, and approximately 35% were women. For most of the

---

● This presentation of material from the science students, participants at the MIT conference and at their own preceding conference at Wellesley College, was prepared by Mr Peter Scherhans, the organizing secretary for this part of the programme.

participants it was the first time they had been involved in the adventure of a world ecumenical conference. They gathered in advance of the WCC conference at MIT, to which they were invited as full participants, in order to prepare their contribution to it.

Attempting to capture the spirit and findings of this conference is an almost impossible undertaking. The statements which were prepared by the participants for consideration at the subsequent world conference at MIT expressed some of the most urgent student concerns regarding a world increasingly dominated by science and technology and the powers that control them. They could hardly reflect the wide scope of the innumerable debates in plenary, in small working groups and in personal encounters. Nor could they reflect much of the mood of the meeting, the conflicts, the humour, the sharing and the passion which helped this diverse group of participants to grow together. An official conference report is an inadequate medium to record the impact which informal gatherings, worship, singing and dancing have on the general atmosphere of a student meeting; and yet this impact has an important bearing on the quality of the human encounter in more formal discussion sessions.

In some time, even the participants may hardly remember the details of what was said about the issues discussed or the conclusions and findings of their deliberations. But they will recall the depth and intensity of personal encounters and experiences. As many have already remarked in their evaluations, for them "nothing will ever be the same again", even though they often find it difficult to define the exact nature of the change.

Speaking of the first great ecumenical youth meeting forty years ago, one participant said: "Invisible seeds were sown" which were later to grow into "an enduring vision". It is obviously too early to know what was sown at Wellesley and MIT and what it will produce. This report can only present some of the main issues, challenges and answers the student group wrestled with, and try to give a faithful record of the discussions which took place.

The programme of the Wellesley conference was prepared by students. The preparatory process began at a five-day meeting at Reading University, Great Britain, in July 1978. The issues identified by this international group of twenty students were circulated for comment and submitted to a further preparatory group convened at Cambridge, Mass., in January 1979, which completed a *Prospectus* for the conference. This *Prospectus* was sent to all WCC member churches, national Christian councils, and student Christian movements around the world. With their help, and that of the WCC Youth Department and the World Student Christian Federation, the participants were chosen. The Vatican Secretariat for Promoting Christian Unity and the Pontifical Commission Justice and Peace also showed keen interest in the preparations, and as a result of the advance in ecumenical fellowship at the local and national levels a comparatively large number of Roman Catholic students were involved in the conference planning from the very beginning.

A preliminary programme was drawn up at a final preparatory meeting bringing together about 15 students from different national and scientific backgrounds at the Ecumenical Institute, near Geneva, March 1979. This was shared with all participants, and their comments and suggestions were invited and incorporated in revised versions of the programme.

Yet, once at Wellesley, the participants became aware that the four working days of the conference were too short for an adequate treatment of the wide range of issues on the agenda. As the time pressure increased, the lack of sufficient opportunity for a thorough and extended informal exchange of views created a growing uneasiness. The students became painfully aware that their own high expectations could hardly be met within the limited time available. One working group therefore observed with a certain resignation:

"It is inevitable that world conferences will always fall short of their goals. Time is short, work is too tightly packed, we come from different backgrounds, and we do not know one another. As a result, the conclusions are often superficial, and the documents do not represent any real progress in the understanding of the problems."

The starting point of the conference—the debate on the seemingly contradictory basic patterns of thought about science and faith—sparked comparatively little enthusiasm. In an introductory presentation, Dr Wang Hsien-Chi, a physicist and theologian from Taiwan Theological College, traced the several transitions in the thinking of scientists about the world, and concluded that the tensions between science and faith are perennial and there is no panacea. He pointed to the danger of the compartmentalization of reality by modern science and pleaded for an integral world-view. This call was readily accepted by the student conference which concluded:

"Truth is not contained within any one discipline, but throughout all disciplines; and this must include theology... We must not make science an idol, as in scientism: the unquestioning belief in science, as the final arbiter of truth and the source of solutions to all problems; rather we must consider it an instrument, useful to humanity."

More controversy was aroused when Prof. Rubem Alves of Brazil led the students into an examination of the relationship between faith, ethics and technology. He stated the problem sharply:

"Science and technology have lost their freedom. Once they were tools for creativity. Now they have become cages. Once they were instruments of life. Now they have become limits and threats to life... The future is not a blossoming of the present; it is its denial. It is not the present in its mature and full developed form; it is its death and reversal. The present is not to be improved. It is to be brought to an end."

On the basis of this assumption, he challenged the science students to be vigilant regarding the social context of their vocational role: "To whom are you delivering power? Science, for whom? Research, for whom? Knowledge, for whom? Power, for whom?"

The question of power, aggravated by the enormous means of advanced science and technology, and the role of scientists and technologists within these power constellations remained the key problem throughout the student meeting. Once the problem was stated, the discussions intensified significantly. An Australian student wrote after the conference: "The series of tensions and debates challenged my whole being, including my understanding of myself, our technological world, and my faith."

The new awareness of the social and political context of their scientific endeavours also marked a turning-point in the personal perspectives of many of the participants. As an Egyptian student remarked in his evaluation:

"Before the conferences, I tended to separate my scientific 'personality' from social and ethical criteria. Unfortunately, most scientists do the same thing. There has to be a serious reconsideration of this attitude if science is to play its rightful role in the advancement of humanity."

This new awareness was not just an individual response; it was shared by a clear majority of participants. The student presentation to the MIT meeting records: "Science and technology always exist in a social and ideological context, and they therefore have inescapable moral and ethical implications."

The intensity of the debate increased when, on the third day of the conference, a group of four students presented a paper entitled "As We See It—An Alternative Perspective". Its focus was an analysis of the third world negative experience of western science and technology and it suggested that this perspective be the starting-point for the remainder of conference discussions. The paper also claimed that the proceedings and organization of the conference itself had been dominated by western cultural assumptions which had limited the subjects under discussion. Because of the significant impact of this paper on the subsequent conference proceedings, it is quoted here in full:

As We See It—An Alternative Perspective

1. In our experience western science and technology have been used to oppress and exploit poor countries for the benefit of rich countries. This oppression has been perpetuated by means of:

a) transnational corporations which:
— exploit cheap labour;
— wantonly exploit natural resources;
— create artificial consumer markets;
— market inappropriate technology;
— locate their most polluting processes in poor countries;
— use the people of these countries as guinea-pigs for testing drugs and pesticides;

b) super-power strategies which use our countries as pawns by:
— tied financial aid which creates dependence;

— the sale of weapons which encourages local conflicts and reinforces repressive régimes;

— playing out their rivalries in our regions which involves us in the proliferation of nuclear technology (the arms trade is the West's most profitable business);

— trade protectionism which ensures massively unequal trading patterns.

2. In our experience institutions which support these negative features of western science and technology include:

a) governments;
b) universities and schools;
c) churches and other religious establishments;
d) international aid and finance agencies.

3. Some of the consequences of the incursion of western science and technology are:

a) unemployment;
b) the creation of élites;
c) an increase in the gap between rich and poor;
d) ecological catastrophe;
e) national economic subservience;
f) the isolation of the majority from real participation in decision-making;
g) the depletion of natural resources for no local benefit.

4. Our expectation is that western science and technology will continue to produce these effects as long as industrialized countries seek profit and their own self-interest above human values and obstruct the development of a science and technology with human ends and means. This necessarily manifests itself in imperialist, paternalist, racist and sexist perceptions of the world.

5. Acknowledging the opportunities for learning and the hospitality of this conference, we nevertheless feel compelled to look carefully at our situation. Only a clear awareness of our context here will enable us to make the most use of this opportunity. We therefore make the following observations:

a) This conference was organized in a pattern derived from normal western bureaucratic practices: the way material is dealt with, the way topics are phrased, the conference format, the cultural assumptions on how arguments progress and what conclusions constitute "results". These cultural assumptions derived from the West are one factor in determining what can come out of this conference. Such factors also ensure that people are forced to contribute within the limits of this way of meeting.

b) Another aspect is the constituency of this conference. Inviting students who have a natural vested interest in the continuation of the prevailing systems of science and technology is rather like asking the South African government to examine alternatives to apartheid.

It would seem important to include a substantial number of people who have suffered from the competitive education system and the negative effects of western science and technology, e.g. school drop-outs, women, minorities, youth, unemployed, factory workers, labourers, farmers...

c) The reality is that those who paid for this conference control the starting directions and also have wider political directions which may include a students' conference as a public relations exercise for the main MIT conference.

6. Such factors are likely to limit this conference by:
a) restricting the range of issues and the depth;
b) leaving the basic assumptions and inadequacies of western academic methods unchallenged;
c) ignoring the need to recognize or develop alternative ways of doing science;
d) relegating to second place first-hand experience of the negative effects of western science and technology;
e) restricting the "results" to pieces of paper describing the effects of western science and technology; possible strategies for action will be entirely within the limits of this same science and technology.

* * *

During the evening following the presentation of this paper, many regional groups convened and considered their reactions until late at night. Most of them formulated responses which were brought to the next plenary session and led to a passionate debate. Unfortunately, lack of time prevented a substantial encounter or dialogue between the positions of the different regions. However, a fire had been lit and was kept burning, inspiring the work of the five sections proposed by the programme. Excerpts from the findings of these five sections are presented below. They do not reflect comprehensively the mood and content of the discussions which took place. But they are characteristic snapshots. Snapshots of a debate.

I. Science education for a just, participatory and sustainable society*

"Education is a critical link between science, technology and the future, because it is a primary vehicle in the preservation, transmission and transformation of values. Education is a process of crucial importance to the welfare of any society." In line with this assertion from the Prospectus of the science

---

* The explanatory notes in italics are by Mr Scherhans.

students conference, the participants focused their discussions in this section on the underlying values of science education. An examination of these values, however, proved to be intimately linked with the need for an analysis of the social, political, economic and cultural context within which present patterns of science education are set. If universities have rightly been describ-ed as the "nerve centres of societies", students have a special responsibility to ensure that the perspective of their views does not remain unheard in this discussion. It was therefore not surprising that students contributed con-siderably to the proceedings of Section III of the conference at MIT on "Science and Education".

1. THE FAILURE OF PRESENT SCIENCE EDUCATION

Throughout their working life, scientists are called upon to make deci-sions which involve moral and ethical questions. The present science educa-tion system denies any help and guidance in approaching these questions. It produces scientists who are morally detached from their subjects, and who fail to assume responsibility for the results of their work. They do not ques-tion the overall structure and approach which are often geared towards specific economic interests. Science education produces another élite group that is separated from the rest of the people and hence is unable even to con-sider their needs.

As a consequence, the students' motivations for studying science are too often geared towards self-oriented goals, e.g. social mobility, prestige and material wellbeing. However, these motivations need to be seen within the context of the driving forces of existing social systems. These systems are geared to using the West as a model for advancement, thereby perpetuating the vicious circle of cultural, political and economic domination. It appears that one of the tools of this domination is the educational establishment.

2. THE DILEMMA OF THIRD WORLD STUDENTS STUDYING ABROAD

Often because of the inadequacy or unavailability of appropriate educa-tional institutions in their home countries, an increasing number of students from third world nations aim at studying abroad. The two main problems which have been created by this development need to be given more atten-tion. Too many students return to their home country equipped with skills which are alien to their societies and inappropriate to the needs of their peo-ple. Furthermore, there are a large number of third world students who choose to remain in their country of study abroad, which causes an apparent-ly serious brain-drain problem.

3. THE ROLE OF WOMEN IN SCIENCE AND TECHNOLOGY, PARTICULARLY AS RELATED TO EDUCATION

Women within science more often choose life sciences rather than physical sciences. This stems from educational processes which involve a con-ditioning for women to be more concerned with community and human concerns and for men to be channelled into "rational, objective" mathematical fields. This has led to a situation where women are not only excluded from positions of influence (e.g. professors, administrators), but are also under-represented in all scientific fields. This sort of division needs to be recognized and changed in order that:

a) women may have more influence and power than at present; and
b) both men and women get a more complete and broader view of life by a closer integration of the "objective" and "subjective".

The pressure on women to conform, stay quiet and submit to educational authority in order to obtain a degree has been even stronger than on men students. This is a result of women being a minority and very often not having a supportive community to share feelings of discrimination and to organize protests about educational structures.

Two traditional roles of women scientists have been perpetuated:

a) as a research assistant or similar subsidiary position; quite often women are not given due recognition for work done in scientific papers, or are not given promotion when it is due;
b) as the exceptional woman who by determination or by obvious brilliance has managed to make it to the top on men's terms, which often means moving out of relationships of solidarity with other women.

The seeds of discrimination are sown through the educational system itself; they are also sown through the history of science which recognizes only few women scientists with whom a woman student might identify.

While the churches themselves have only few women in positions of teaching and authority, refuse ordination and, in some cases, even place restrictions on those women who *are* ordained, it is hoped that they might still be a potential supportive community for women scientists by:

a) promoting justice in scientific and technical institutions which currently discriminate against women;
b) promoting participation of women in positions of influence and power in decisions that affect the lives of all people, women and men;
c) promoting sustainability through encouraging a holistic education for all people so that full human potential might be reached.

4. THE POLITICAL AND ECONOMIC CONTEXT OF SCIENCE EDUCATION

Science education cannot be separated from its political and economic framework. A fundamental change of this framework is essential in order to establish an educational system which will lead to a just, participatory and sustainable society. This quest for change was spelled out most clearly in the report of the regional group of Latin American students:

In Latin America, foreign interests and, along with them, imported philosophies have blocked the development of our culture, ideologically as well as practically. In spite of increasingly more acute domination and repression the Latin American people struggle for their identity, their own values and basic human rights.

Science and technology have been used as the means of domination of some nations by others. At the national level, the same kind of domination is exerted by minority groups on the rest of the people in order to uphold their power positions. Science and technology cannot be blamed for such misuse; the responsibility is to be found within the social context.

The present educational system in scientific, technological and other fields reflects the marks of this context. It operates in an impersonal way, lacks human values, and stimulates individual rather than community goals. This educational system, motivated by particular interests of a small section of the population, is inadequate to educate ethically aware and responsible scientists and intellectuals.

We do not believe in the solutions offered by the prevailing exploitative system. We know that humanity can be freed from oppression only by radically changing that system. This change should emerge from a critical analysis of our present reality, an analysis which needs to be developed on an individual as well as a collective basis.

5. TECHNOLOGICAL DEVELOPMENT AND CULTURAL ALIENATION

As science and engineering students examine the interests they will be serving in their future professions, they need to be particularly aware of the kind of technological development which is fostered by present institutions of technical education.

It appears that at present there is a tendency to make technology more specialized and more inaccessible to the people who bear its consequences. Technology must, however, be appropriate to the culture and society in which it is used, and implemented with a concern for human values. Alienation will occur if the pace of change is too quick for society to deal with the consequences. This is illustrated by the phrase: "The soul cannot catch up with the body." A materialistic attitude leading to consumerism, which is often closely connected with the application of new technologies, represents a further major source of alienation. Materialism is the result of the dominant economic system and, along with consumerism, is gradually infiltrating the Third World. The poor countries should have the power to decide how and to what extent they want to use a particular technology, in order to be able to examine whether it can be integrated into their value system. Participation is a vital aspect of this decision.

A statement by the regional group of Pacific students at the science students conference called attention to an example of grave violation of the right of this kind of participation in decision-making, regarding vital aspects of development of a whole world region:

The Pacific has become a new zone of exploitation. The incursions of the nuclear weaponry of major powers and the penetration of transnational corporations are but the beginning of the plundering of Pacific nations. As countries with small populations spread across a vast ocean at a great distance from centres of world power, we are very vulnerable to exploitation and domination. Already we are on the way to becoming a radio-active paradise choked with nuclear weapons and waste. Our cultures are assaulted by the indiscriminate marketing of western technology. This technology is not ours and we do not choose it freely.

Our ability to live off the riches of our island environments has already been undermined by the pollution of the sea, by foreigners taking our land, by the introduction of a cash economy, and by our scarce raw materials being swallowed by the voracious appetites of unseen powers.

As a first step in repelling these invasions of our sovereignty, we call on all peoples to support a Nuclear Weapon Free Zone in the South Pacific.

6. RECOMMENDATIONS OF THE SCIENCE STUDENTS CONFERENCE REGARDING SCIENCE EDUCATION

In view of the urgently required change of orientation of present science education patterns, we offer the following proposals:

a) Local permanent task forces could be organized to study science education in its socio-economic context.

b) Community level programmes should be set up within the educational structures to make students more aware of their cultural and social environment. These programmes should stress appropriate technology, self-help schemes, etc.

c) Educational programmes must be planned for the users of technology in order to evolve participatory decision-making in scientific issues.

d) Interdisciplinary studies to ensure awareness of science students about their socio-political environment are essential.

e) Ethical studies should be an integral part of science education.

f) The setting up of universities and colleges for the specific study of science and technology should be discontinued, because contact with students of other disciplines is impeded. Adequate mixing of the student population should be ensured in all educational institutions.

g) Students should be encouraged to have practical work experience prior to and during their university education.

II. The scientists' responsibility in view of the dynamics of militarism

Alarmed by the accelerated process of militarization in many parts of the world, the participants of this section attempted to examine the major features of contemporary militarism. They gave particular attention to:

— *the recent significant shift from a quantitative to a qualitative arms race where more and more sophisticated technologies are employed;*

— *the military research and development activities which greatly influence the direction and the momentum of a country's scientific and technological development;*

— *the military apparatus which influences research policy decisions;*

— *the military-industrial complex which represents a significant force in the determination of national and foreign polices of industrialized nations;*

— on the international level, the evolution of dominance-dependence relationships in military affairs, parallel to the dominance-dependence relationships in economic matters;
— the transfer of military technology, especially to third world countries,
  which involves the transfer of a whole social and economic system.

A special focus of the discussion was the relationship between civil
nuclear energy programmes and worldwide nuclear proliferation. This resulted in the adoption of a number of recommendations which proved to be of
significance for the students' role in the MIT conference debates on disarmament and the proposal for a five-year moratorium on the construction of
nuclear power stations.

1. THE DYNAMICS OF CONTEMPORARY MILITARISM

Militarism is not a new phenomenon, although its tools have changed
throughout history. The militarism of today is characterized by an increasing
use of more and more sophisticated technology. This is readily provided by
big profit-oriented industries and, at the global level, also by the sale of
military apparatus to other governments. In this way, an international
military system has evolved.

Scientists and engineers often cooperate with the military powers.
Sometimes this occurs without the knowledge of scientists themselves or
others who are involved in the process of technological innovation. Science
and technology present findings and methods which might later, often in-
cidentally, be applied for military production. The fate of the first physicists
researching in the field of civil nuclear technology has been a tragic example.

However, there is also a much more direct support of military powers by
laboratories and industries. A large percentage of the budget for scientific
research in industrialized countries goes into research and development for
military purposes. It has been estimated that $400,000 million are spent each
year on military activities. In many of the industrialized countries 50-60% of
all scientists are directly or indirectly involved in these activities.

The arms race has gained a momentum of its own. Industrialized countries which produce most of this armament anticipate further improvements
in the quality of other countries' military products. Consequently, they
themselves keep on developing more and more advanced weapons and other
military products. The accuracy of new missiles is stressed over their ex-
plosive power. Submarines exist (e.g. Trident) which can destroy four hundred large cities with one load of weapons, while cruising in deep waters
without being detected with present technology. The super-powers are com-
peting to achieve the so-called first-strike capability.

This process has gained such momentum that it is increasingly difficult
for society to control the military establishment. The gigantic dimensions of
the military complex are a further complicating factor: in some societies it
uses up to ¾ of the Gross National Product. It employs a large number of
people and at the same time the production processes are highly capital inten-

sive. Consequently, capital accumulation is possible, from which large profits and further investment capital can be realized.

The military establishment can operate on the basis of an ideology which conditions people all over the world to accept the possibility of enemy attack. Since people are thereby led to believe that militarism is in the best interest of their own country, ever increasing amounts spent on military-related activities can be justified. Gradually the military structures have gained a substantial influence not only on society as a whole, but also on governments. This facilitates smooth cooperation between military and technological establishments which makes it unlikely that science and technology will ever succeed in breaking through the deadly embrace of their military misuse. It is therefore our urgent responsibility to be stewards of human inspiration and knowledge in order to bring about justice instead of wars, participation instead of oppression, and sustainability instead of military waste of science, technology and natural resources.

2. NUCLEAR POWER AND NUCLEAR PROLIFERATION

a) Civil nuclear power evolved from the nuclear weapons programmes of the industrialized countries. Since some segments of the nuclear fuel cycle for civil nuclear power plants (i.e. enrichment, reprocessing) facilitate the overt or clandestine production of nuclear weapons (for example in the cases of India, Pakistan and South Africa), we believe that the increasing proliferation of civilian nuclear power cannot be divorced from governmental or military attempts to achieve nuclear weapons capability.

b) Because of the increased security needed to maintain a civil nuclear programme that would minimize the danger of proliferation, increased military and police control of the civilian population becomes necessary. Civil nuclear power therefore contributes to the militarization of a society.

c) No adequate means exist to prevent the diversion of nuclear materials from civil programmes to the production of nuclear weapons.

With the above points in mind, the participants of the science students conference call for:

— the complete elimination of nuclear weapons and nuclear weapons technology in all countries;

— an end to all further nuclear proliferation occurring via weapons programmes and/or civil nuclear power programmes;

— a moratorium on future construction of nuclear power plants;

— the phasing out of all existing nuclear power plants over a period of transition such as to minimize social disruption;

— the transfer of subsidies for nuclear power to alternative sources of energy.

3. STRATEGIES FOR ACTION

a) We recommend that science students:

— critically examine the military components of their research and be willing to refuse such projects;

— challenge universities and other institutions which engage in research and development of military technology;
— join activist groups that work for international peace;
— be informed about current problems related to militarism and technology.

b) We recommend that the WCC member churches:
— examine their investments and withdraw their funds from companies which are involved in research and development of military technology and put pressure on other institutions with similar investments;
— cooperate with international peace movements and encourage their members to support these organizations;
— develop economic strategies to combat militarism;
— accept primary responsibility for unmasking deceitful military doctrines such as "national security", and "mutual defence" which obscure the reality of militarism;
— initiate educational programmes for their members which clarify the connection between militarism and technology.

III. The control of technology by transnational corporations and its international implications

Much of today's science-based technology is owned and controlled by transnational corporations (TNCs). Science and technology facilitate the exploitation of the world's non-renewable resources and human labour by TNCs. The benefits from this process of exploitation go to the dominant and ruling classes rather than to the masses. In this way TNCs have succeeded in preserving the world capitalist domination at all costs and sometimes even at the expense of immediately profitable or commercial programmes.

The arguments which TNCs would claim in favour of their existence are that they provide the most efficient means of large-scale production. They transfer new technologies to third world countries and create new employment. They contribute funds to research and cultural activities and act as innovators.

TNCs invest enormous funds in scientific research and in training personnel which possesses scientific expertise. Existing businesses expand in all directions, creating new areas of investment and positions for their highly trained employees. Monopolies have a natural tendency to expand. One criterion for expansion is to pursue investments in areas that will yield maximum profits. The central motivation of profit maximization can well be illustrated by the example of the textile industry. A good part of this industry has been transferred from Europe and the United States to developing countries, especially the Free Trade Zone where labour is abundant and cheap and labour unions are repressed. This has caused unemployment in Europe and the USA. At the same time, the newly created textile industry in the Free

Trade Zone has not supplied useful employment opportunities, since it has been concentrating on the exploitation of women and youth.

In their attempt to control and dominate the world, superpowers and TNCs use technology as a tool of political and military power. This can best be exemplified by the overthrow of the Chilean democratic government in 1973, and by the perpetuation of apartheid in South Africa. When the Chilean people began to develop a socialist system, TNCs began a systematic sabotage of the Chilean economy. This led to the overthrow of the democratically elected government under Allende and the installation of one of the most repressive and brutal of military juntas of today, led by Pinochet.

Due to their control of technology, the TNCs have also played a central role in ensuring that the white racist minority régime in South Africa has the power capacity to sustain the apartheid system and to control effectively the economies of neighbouring countries. US and European TNCs and banks enabled South Africa to develop the industrial capacity to produce its own weapons or to import necessary weapons and oil from abroad to safeguard its economic and military hegemony. Furthermore, TNCs have licensed South African firms to produce military equipment and machinery such as fighter aircraft, missiles, tanks, large fighting ships, etc. It is important to note that no such right has been given to any other African country.

Whereas the international community under the leadership of the United Nations has made efforts to support forces struggling against apartheid, the TNCs and western imperialism have increased their support of the South African economy. Between 1960 and 1970, for instance, TNC investments increased greatly because of the demand for military expansion in South Africa. It is significant to note that during this period South African military expenditure increased from $65 to $405 million. By 1978 it had grown to $1.9 billion.

The implications of the economic support of South Africa by TNCs were also summarized in a report of the regional group of African students at the science students conference. Surveying the impact of science and technology on a large number of African countries, the report states in relation to South Africa:

Transnational corporations facilitate the transfer of military technology to South Africa, including nuclear technology and instruments of torture. This has enabled the racist minority government to obtain the potential for producing nuclear weapons.

American and European TNCs and banks have played and continue to play a major role in sustaining apartheid and helping South Africa to gain both military and economic hegemony vis-à-vis the rest of Africa.

Through heavy capital investment and wanton exploitation of cheap labour, western and Japanese TNCs have helped South Africa to emerge as a comparatively highly developed industrial economy in Africa. As a result South Africa today plays the role of a sub-imperialist state in Southern

Africa. The implications this phenomenon has for liberation struggles and economic development in Southern Africa are obvious.

In the light of these considerations we call on the WCC member churches to:

— collaborate with and facilitate the work of local groups organizing against the exploitation by TNCs;

— facilitate study and research by organizations that try to gather information and analyse the operations of TNCs;

— create their own appropriate institutions to gather information on TNCs and to disseminate it in their own constituencies for the purpose of furthering awareness and conscientization.

IV. Technology and labour: a quest for workers' participation in technological decision-making

One of the most challenging presentations to the science students conference was made by Peter Kelly, an automobile worker and union representative from Detroit. He urged the students to take a close look at the specific problems which arise in factories through the development of new technologies. In a special section on the relationship between technology and labour he involved the participants in one of the most intense encounters of the conference. On the same occasion, George Mathew, a political scientist from New Delhi, examined the issue from an Indian perspective. Yet his presentation appeared to have the same focus. As he said:

"The biggest asset of the Third World is its people. The thrust of my argument is that people are forgotten when we make a choice of technology... Workers must take control of technology, and labour is to be put at the centre of decision-making... Science and technology are not neutral, they represent a concealed ideology. Therefore the question before us is, how to bring about a workers' control of technology, thereby a technology for the people and a people's science."

1. THE NEED TO EVALUATE CONCRETE TECHNOLOGIES

As students we often confine ourselves to abstract discussions about conflicting ideologies, the nature of science, or the nature of power and domination, etc., while at the same time we exclude from our discussion the very people who are being dominated (in this case the worker) and the very tools of that domination (in this case specific technologies and specific means of production). We are now aware of the need to relate ideological discussions about technology to *concrete technologies* and to *concrete* and everyday experiences of the working class. Cheap discussions about revolutions or "reforming the system" are of little value to the worker, because they lead to no agenda for actual social change. However, rebellion against a specific technology that is about to replace a worker's job or a worker's skill can be a matter of life or death. It was therefore suggested that we ask questions, for example, about a particular machine, a particular worker, a particular management, and that from there the ideological questions involved in the current social relations of production will become clear, and in addition an agenda for specific social change, specific action, will become possible.

We must take care that opposition to a specific technology does not take the form of an "anti-technology" protest *per se*. Technology itself is not the enemy, but it reflects the social relations of production that act to maintain dominance and control over the worker by the holders of capital. Maximum productivity or a computerized shop floor is not the primary objective of corporations in relation to the worker; they aim at *total control* over the labour force.

The advent of computer numerically controlled machine tools threatens to replace millions of skilled workers in the western world. Recent Fiat automobile advertisements, for example, read: "Designed by a computer, silenced by a laser, and built by a robot." The new machines, which are a reality *now*, will essentially create a new production process, eliminating skilled workers entirely. The unskilled workers who remain as "attendants" of the machines will have drastically diminished bargaining power with corporate management, since they will have no flexibility in controlling the productive process as a result of this technology.

The importance of assessing, as scientists and theologians, *concrete* technologies, lies in the fact that the design of the technology itself is reflected in the social relations of production. New technologies reflect the worker's total lack of control and decision-making power. No worker, for instance, were he in control of the design of a new technology, would design himself out of a job. It is therefore our responsibility as scientists and theologians to form new alliances with labour. In the words of a worker: "Don't walk ahead of me, I may not want to follow you. Don't walk behind me, I may not want to lead. Walk beside me, and we'll be partners."

2. IMPACT OF TECHNOLOGY ON LABOUR

The impact of technology on labour is a complex issue, raising various open problems:

a) The workers, who are the fraction of population most directly concerned with technology and technological changes, are increasingly absent from the phases of decision-making.

b) The effects of new and changing technologies on labour are relevant and serious; at the same time they are difficult to assess, except in extreme situations, such as sudden reductions in the number of employed workers, or severe accidents.

c) A better understanding of the impact of technology on labour would allow proper risk-benefit evaluations to be made with respect to risks and hazards related to work.

So far the workroom environment has been a laboratory in which new technologies and new chemical compounds were tested on people, and in some cases removed if they had caused a particularly high number of deaths and injuries. Every human activity has associated with it a certain amount of risk, which may be "weighted" against the benefit it causes. Risk-benefit evaluations are currently done for self-administered risks (connected, for example, to life-style, use of drugs, recreational activities, etc.) but in the case of occupational exposures to hazards, it is the workers who suffer from the risks, and the companies who have the benefits in terms of increases in profit. Decisions concerning acceptance of these risks belong to the workers and are not to be delegated to companies, agencies, governments, etc.

d) Some elementary mechanisms of technology distribution deserve particular attention. In the same country, skilled and unskilled workers, besides having different occupations, often face diverse levels of hazard or discomfort. This also happens in the case of groups with different levels of political consciousness and organization. The weaker ones (e.g. immigrants or prisoners) are more likely to suffer from dehumanizing or hazardous work.

e) There seems to be a significant role for the churches, in emphasizing two basic rights of people, which in the past have been especially supported by non-Christian people or organizations:
— the *right to work*, which also means the right to realize fully one's capacities through one's professional life;
— the *right of the worker to physical and psychological wellbeing*.

3. TECHNOLOGY AND DOMINATION

Technology in the hands of capital has been used in the industrialized countries to *dominate, control* and *appropriate* products of labour.

The expansion of capitalism with the aid of science and technology in developing countries has not only facilitated the control, exploitation and domination of the workers who are directly affected, but has also led to the incorporation of countries and peoples of the Third World into colonialism and continued control by the international finance capital. Thus, this process today goes beyond the control of the labour force to subjugation of total societies.

4. STRATEGIES FOR ACTION

It is necessary for the problems related to the struggle between capital and labour, as exemplified in the field of technology in both industrialized and developing countries, to be understood and dealt with concretely and specifically. We therefore suggest:

a) that the participants of this conference, in their respective countries and situations, address themselves to the questions raised by the impact of capital-controlled technology on labour; this is a call for most of us to descend from the Mount Olympus of knowledge and abstraction and engage in the struggle of translating theory into practice in the interests of those who are excluded from decisions which affect the production and application of science and technology;

b) that international and national solidarity between those dominated and controlled by capital-technology (working people) is imperative if the transnational corporations are to be dealt with effectively at the level they operate; we recommend that multinational trade unions be established;

c) that nationalization which should be followed by responsible and worker controlled management could be an answer to the profit oriented TNCs which ignore the needs of the workers;

d) that the interaction of intellectuals and the working class movement is necessary for the struggle of labour over against the stranglehold exercised by capital and technology;

e) the history of the contributions made by labour to technological advance, and indeed the whole struggle of labour has been ignored in many countries; the educators must remedy this falsification of history and knowledge if the contribution of working people is to be fully realized.

V. The role of the Church in technological decision-making

The starting-point of the discussions of this particular section was a paper prepared by Christoph Stückelberger, a Swiss theologian and pastor. He examined the conditions for a fair dialogue between faith and science, and encouraged the participants to enter into an enquiry as to what might constitute the specific contribution churches could make with regard to technological policy.

1. God loves his creation. To the extent that science and technology affect this creation and have a bearing on the quality of life of humanity, the churches are called to hold forth their vision of man as being created in the image of God. The implications of this are spelled out in the report by the Orthodox participants within the Eastern European regional group:

"The Church should always remind people of the good gifts of Creation, of the sacred nature of human life and the right of man and peoples to the realization of these good gifts on the basis of the ontological solidarity of humanity, established according to the image of the Holy Trinity. The Church should always act out of love for man. Siding with the poor, the marginalized and hungry, it recognizes the image of Christ in every particular man."

2. Siding with the poor, the marginalized and hungry will mean in the context of technological decision-making that Christians attempt to ensure that the voices of those who are most affected by the consequences of a particular technological choice will be heard. This implies that all processes of technological policy-making will have to involve non-experts who represent the hopes, fears and aspirations of the concerned communities.

3. Since many church members do not realize the direct connection between faith and an ethical concern for technological development, there are many tensions inside the churches about whether the churches should speak as social institutions or only through their members as individuals. It appears to us that churches should not hesitate to speak as bodies, but they need to

realize that this may cause disunity and tension within themselves. They should, however, recognize the possibility of such conflict and attempt to deal with it constructively.

4. In order to contribute to the process of highlighting ethical considerations in relation to technological decision-making, churches should engage in dialogue with appropriate responsible institutions and attempt to communicate their ethical perspective. The churches need to make a special effort to involve their lay members, especially those who are scientists and technologists, in these consultations.

5. In cases where new technologies are being introduced which are clearly disadvantageous or even harmful to a certain section of the population, the churches might have to initiate forms of active protest in solidarity with the people concerned.

Appendices

Officers of the Conference

Presidents

Prof. D. Enilo AJAKAIYE (Nigeria)
Dr James HAM (Canada)
Archbishop KIRILL (USSR)

The Rt Rev. Hugh MONTEFIORE (UK)
Bishop SAMUEL (Egypt)

Moderator   Metropolitan Dr Paulos GREGORIOS (India)

Vice-Moderator   Prof. Charles BIRCH (Australia)

Conference Steering Committee

Moderator, Vice-Moderator, Presidium, two Officers appointed from each Section

Officers of the Sections

Section I	Moderator:	Prof. Philip HEFNER (USA)
	Vice-Moderators:	Prof. D. Enilo AJAKAIYE (Nigeria)
		Mr Israel Belo DE AZEVEDO (Brazil)
	Rapporteur:	Prof. Yoshinobu KAKIUCHI (Japan)
Section II	Moderator:	Prof. Rubem ALVES (Brazil)
		(Substitute: Prof. John COBB (USA)
	Vice-Moderators:	Protopresbyter Vitaly BOROVOY (USSR)
		Dr Dan-Ilie CIOBOTEA (Romania)
	Rapporteur:	Dr Kenneth WILSON (UK)
Section III	Moderator:	Dr Manuel THANGARAJ (India)
	Vice-Moderators:	Prof. Manuel SADOSKY (Venezuela)
		Ms Marie-Christine RAKOTONIRINA
		(Madagascar)
	Rapporteur:	Dr John HOWIE (UK)
Section IV	Moderator:	Prof. Charles BIRCH (Australia)
	Vice-Moderators:	Dr Wangari MAATHAI (Kenya)
		Mr Joseph VARGHESE (India)
	Rapporteur:	Dr Joan VENES (USA)
Section V	Moderator:	Prof. Richard ODINGO (Kenya)
	Vice-Moderators:	Prof. G.W. DIMBLEBY (UK)
		Ms Charlotte SAMUEL (Malaysia)
	Rapporteur:	Dr Kamal GIRGIS (Switzerland/Egypt)
Section VI	Moderator:	Dr Albert VAN DEN HEUVEL (Netherlands)
	Vice-Moderators:	Mrs Suliana SIWATIBAU (Fiji)
		Mr Ragui ASSAAD (Egypt)
	Rapporteur:	Prof. Bernard PICINBONO (France)
Section VII	Moderator:	Mr Pentti MALASKA (Finland)
	Vice-Moderators:	Dr B.W. GARBRAH (Ghana)
		Mr Rudy PRUDENTE (USA)
	Rapporteur:	Dr John FRANCIS (UK)
Section VIII	Moderator:	Mr Thomas P. MATTHAI (India)
	Vice-Moderators:	Prof. Dr Helmut HESSE (FRG)
		Mr Kabiru KINYANJUI (Kenya)
	Rapporteur:	Dr Diogo DE GASPAR (Brazil)

Section IX	Moderator:	Prof. Anwar BARKAT (Pakistan)
	Vice-Moderators:	Ms Chris LEDGER (Australia)
		Dr Young Gul KIM (Korea)
Section X	Moderator:	Prof. Roger SHINN (USA)

Bible Study Leaders

Canon John Austin BAKER (UK)   The Rt Rev. John HABGOOD (UK)
Canon Burgess CARR (Liberia)   Dr Albert VAN DEN HEUVEL (Netherlands)
Prof. André DUMAS (France)   Prof. Dr Klaus KOCH (FRG)
Metropolitan Paulos GREGORIOS (India) Dr Günter KRUSCHE (GDR)

Officers of the Communications Committee

Moderator, Press Conference: The Rt Rev. Hugh MONTEFIORE (UK)
Vice-Moderator, Press Conference: Ms Betty THOMPSON (USA)

Local Arrangements Committee (Boston)

Prof. David ROSE, Convenor   Ms Mary MORRISEY
Mr Robert BYERS   Dr James NASH
Fr Peter CONLEY   Prof. J. Robert NELSON
Rev. James CRAWFORD   Dr Richard NESMITH
Rev. Jessica CRIST   Prof. D. NOBLE
Dr Nicholas HERMAN   Rev. Scott PARADISE
Prof. Robert J. HOLDEN   Prof. George W. RATHJENS
Ms Diane KESSLER   Rev. Gordon SCHULTZ
Prof. Jonathan KING   Prof. Max STACKHOUSE
Ms Kathryn LOMBARDI   Prof. Leon TRILLING
Prof. Louis MENAND   Rev. John TURNBULL
Fr Robert MORAN   Ms Barbara WEINBLATT

Conference Staff

World Council of Churches: General Secretariat

Dr Philip POTTER   Prof. Todor SABEV
Dr Konrad RAISER

Organizing Secretaries

Dr Paul ABRECHT   Ms Christa STALSCHUS,
Rev. William PERKINS   Administrative Assistant
Rev. Gordon SCHULTZ

Administration

Mr Don NEWBY, Coordinator   Ms Dorothy BERRY, Registration
Rev. Karen BOCKELMAN, Housing   Ms Julie KELLER

Sections

Section I:	Dr Lukas VISCHER, Rev. Gordon SCHULTZ,
	Dr Constantin PATELOS
Section II:	Prof. Charles WEST, Dr Stanley SAMARTHA, Rev. Peter HAMEL
Section III:	Mr Peter SCHERHANS, Fr John LUCAL
Section IV:	Dr Robert NELSON, Prof. Ion BRIA
Section V:	Mr Pascal DE PURY, Mr Medard HILHORST, Prof. Thomas DERR
Section VI:	Mr Janos PASZTOR, Dr David GOSLING, Dr Keith ROBY
Section VII:	Mr Samuel KOBIA, Dr Donald SHRIVER
Section VIII:	Dr Richard DICKINSON, Dr Karl-Heinz DEJUNG,
	Ms Agnes CHEPKWONY
Section IX:	Mr Ninan KOSHY, Dr Konrad RAISER, Prof. Nicolas ZABOLOTSKY
Section X:	Dr Keith BRIDSTON, Prof. Todor SABEV

Worship and Bible Study Staff
  Dr Geiko MÜLLER-FAHRENHOLZ   Mrs Eileen FRANCIS
  Ms Jessica CRIST

Science Students Conference
  Mr Peter SCHERHANS   Ms Agnes CHEPKWONY

Typing and Documentation
  Mr Trevor DAVIES

Typing Pool
  Ms Barbara ASCHWANDEN   Ms Micheline RAOELIMALALA
  Mrs Renee HABIBI   Mrs Marillyn SCHULTZ-ROTHERMEL
  Ms Helga KAISER   Ms Audrey SMITH
  Ms Verena PENSINI   Ms Evelyn TRACEY

Administrative Staff
  Mr Hamid HABIBI   Ms Marjorie SHANE
  Rev. Yuk Kim JONG   Ms Donna TAKACS
  Ms Nancy SCHULTZ

Communications and News Media
  Mr Jürgen HILKE   Ms Lani JOHNSON
  Mr Wesley ADAMS   Mr Freddy KLOPFENSTEIN
  Mr Jean-Jacques BAUSWEIN   Mr Jan KOK
  Ms Harriet BLAKE   Mr Bruno KROKER
  Mr John BLUCK   Mr Günter LORENZ
  Ms Joan CAMBITSIS   Mr Williams McCLURKEN
  Mr Gilbert CUDRÉ-MAUROUX   Ms Ishbel MACLELLAN
  Mr Jacques DENTAN   Ms Nancy NOLDE
  Mr Frank DEVINE   Mr Yushi NOMURA
  Mr Helmut FALKENSTÖRFER   Mr Anibal SICARDI
  Mr Robert FRIEDLY   Ms Frances SMITH
  Mr Gil GALLOWAY   Ms Heather STUNT
  Ms Wendy GOLDSWORTHY   Mr John TAYLOR
  Mr Robin GURNEY   Ms Anna THEILIG
                                     Ms Sara WINTER

Translation and Interpretation Services
  Mrs Tomoko EVDOKIMOFF   Ms Ingrid JONAS
  Ms Elisa BENBASSAT   Ms Cornelia KERKHOFF
  Ms Dorothea BENES   Ms Irina KIRILOVA
  Ms Sigrid BONNEWITZ   Ms Nelly LASSERE
  Mr Antony CARTER   Ms Karin LEBBE
  Mr Jorge Soto CHAVEZ   Mr David LEWIS
  Mrs Donatha COLEMAN   Ms Carol MEREDITH
  Mr Martin CONWAY   Mr Paul MISNER
  Mr Lino D'ALESSANDRI   Mr Anatole NALPANIS
  Ms Vicky DIADIUK   Ms Margaret PATER
  Ms Rosemarie DÖNCH   Mrs Françoise POTTIER
  Mr Mark ECKMANN   Ms Joan REILLY
  Mr Robert FAERBER   Ms Madeleine RICHTER
  Mrs Nicole FISCHER   Ms Nimet SALEM
  Mrs Roswitha Poulet-GINGLAS   Mrs Helga VOIGT
  Ms Natalia GORINA   Mr Mstislav VOSSKRESENSKY

Accredited Visitors Programme
Dr Robert THORNBURG

Dr Thomas OKUMA

Finances
Mr Herman DE GRAAF

Mrs Jean SCHMIDT

Information Office
Mrs May NEWBY

Mrs Anna Brita PERKINS

Travel Office
Ms Brigitte THALER

MIT Conference Coordinator
Ms Barbara WEINBLATT

Stewards

Ms Tamara KUNANAYAKAM
Mr David PEEL
Ms Stephanie ABBOTT
Mr Joe Set AJI-MVO
Mr Harold ANDREWS
Ms Ros BANGUN
Ms Susan BLACK
Ms Inge BLASCHKE
Ms Ilse BONOW
Mr Frans BOUWEN
Mr Milton BROUWER
Mr Marcus BRUCE
Mr Jean-Philippe BUJARD
Ms Katrin BURGER
Ms Audrey CARR
Mr K.B. CARR
Mr Barry CARLSON
Mr Mark CHATER
Mr Li Li CHUNG
Ms Kirsten CLEMENT
Mr Peter DEGEN
Mr Moïse DJOULO
Ms Lydia DOERBAND
Mr George ERUMALA
Mr Peter FELBER
Mr Innocent FEROZE
Ms Fabienne FISCHER
Mr André DE GASPAR
Ms Linda HARTKE
Mr Robin HENRY
Mr Vincent HERMANS
Mr Reinhard HERRENBRÜCK
Ms Eva HORSTMANN
Mr Duncan JEFFREY
Ms Cynthia JENSEN
Ms Deborah JONES
Mr Mathew KAMITSUKA-FOSTER

Mr Chiharu KIKUCHI
Mr Ingo KOLL
Mr Stuart KORSHAVN
Mr Gary LEE
Ms Cheryl LEGGE
Mr Petri LEHTONEN
Ms Joan LOFGREN
Mr Arthur LOVELL
Ms Nathalie MARTIN
Ms Laura MOTZ
Ms Rosemarie NEFF
Ms Priscila DEL NERO SILVA
Mr Peter NEWBY
Mr John OLSON
Mr Ricardo ORDOÑEZ
Mr Sunny PANITZ
Mr George PERERA
Ms Ingrid PERKINS
Mr Alan PREVITO
Ms Leny RASQUINHA
Mr Mitchell RICHARDSON
Mr Matthias RIEMENSCHNEIDER
Mr Bruce ROBINSON
Mr Michael ROTHERMEL
Mr Jan SANDEN
Mr Fernando DE SANTA ANA
Mr Nestor SANTILLAN
Ms Maaria SEPPÄNEN
Mr Doddy SLAMET
Ms Pamela SUDDENDORF
Mr Wolfgang TRAUMÜLLER
Ms Julie TUERS
Mr Michael WILEY
Mr Michael WILLIAMS
Mr Ruud WITTE
Mr Rinze Marten WITTEVEN

Other WCC Staff
Mr Fred BRONKEMA

List of Participants

ABRAHAMSON, Dr E. W.
Professor of Chemistry
University of Guelph, Canada
(Orthodox)   USA

ACEVEDO, Mr Fernando
Graduate Student, Biochemistry
(Roman Catholic)   Colombia

ADEBIYA, Dr George A.
Principal, Federal Polytechnic
(Baptist)   Nigeria

ADEGBOLA, Mr Tunde
Student of Electrical Engineering
(Methodist)   Nigeria

AICHELIN, Rev. Helmut
Director, Research Institute on
Contemporary Ideologies
(Evangelical)   FRG

AJAKAIYE, Prof. (Mrs) D. Enilo
Dean, Faculty of Science
Ahmadu Bello University
(Anglican)   Nigeria

ALBECKER, Mr Christian
Student, Ecole nationale du Génie
rural et des Eaux et Forêts
(Lutheran)   France

ALLORERUNG, Mr Frans
Student of Biology
(Protestant)   Indonesia

ALTNER, Prof. Dr Günter
Professor of Theology
(Evangelical)   FRG

ALVES, Prof. Rubem
Professor of Philosophy
(Protestant)   Brazil

ANAMINYI, Mr Peter
Student of Sociology of Education
(Pentecostal)   Kenya

ANER, Ms Kerstin
Under-Secretary of State
(Lutheran)   Sweden

ANI, Rev. Timo
Minister
(United)   Papua New Guinea

*DE ANTUÑANO, Dr Jorge S.
Professor of Design
(Roman Catholic)   Mexico

ARIGA, Mr Seiichi
Student of Physics and Theology
(United)   Canada

ARULAMPALAM, Mr Genga
Student of Industrial Chemistry
City University, London
(Methodist)   Sri Lanka

ARUNGU-OLENDE, Dr Shem
Energy Expert, UN
(Anglican)   Kenya

ASARE, Ms Augustina
Student of Biological Sciences
(Methodist)   Ghana

ASSAAD, Mr Ragui
Student of Engineering and Physics
(Coptic Orthodox)   Egypt

AUKES, Mr Tim
Student of Sociology and Religion
(Reformed)   Netherlands

AZAR, Mr Abdallah
(Greek Orthodox)   Lebanon

DE AZEVEDO, Mr Israel Belo
Professor of Church History
(Baptist)   Brazil

AZINGE, Canon Dr N. O.
Chief Consultant Physician
and Canon
(Anglican)   Nigeria

*BACHTIAR, Dr Harsja W.
Faculty of Letters
University of Indonesia
(Muslim)   Indonesia

BAKER, Canon John Austin
Sub-Dean of Westminster
Chaplain to the Speaker of the
House of Commons
(Anglican)   UK

BALCOM, Rev. Margaret
Associate Pastor
(Presbyterian)   USA

---

*Observer-consultant   **Guest

BALL, Dr John R.
Senior Policy Analyst
Office of Science and Technology
Policy, Executive Office
of the President of the USA
(Presbyterian)   USA

BARBOUR, Prof. Ian
Professor of Religion and Physics
Carleton College, Minn.
(Presbyterian)   USA

BARKAT, Prof. Anwar
General Secretary
Church of Pakistan
(Anglican)   Pakistan

*BATTRO, Prof. Antonio
President
Centre of Philosophical Inquiry
Buenos Aires
(Roman Catholic)   Argentina

BEAUMONT, Mr Olivier
Ingénieur des Mines
(Reformed)   France

BEKHEET, Prof. (Mrs) Inaam Abdou
Professor of Botany
Alexandria University
(Coptic)   Egypt

BENA-SILU, Mr
Teacher of Physics
(Kimbanguist)   Zaïre

BENEDYKTOWICZ, Prof. Witold
President, Ecumenical Council
(Methodist)   Poland

BERGER, Mr Justice Thomas R.
Judge, Supreme Court
of British Columbia
(Anglican)   Canada

BERRY, Prof. J. R.
Professor of Genetics
University College, London
(Anglican)   UK

BERTAZZOLI BELLUCI, Ms Silvia Brandao
Physician
(Roman Catholic)   Brazil

BERZONSKY, Fr Vladimir
(Orthodox)   USA

BEST, Prof. Ernest E.
Professor of Religious Studies
University of Toronto
(United)   Canada

BIGGS, Dr John
Lecturer in Chemistry
(Baptist)   UK

BIRCH, Prof. Charles
Challis Professor of Biology
University of Sydney
(Uniting)   Australia

BLONDEL, Mr Jean-Luc
Assistant, Institute for Social Ethics
Swiss Federation of
Protestant Churches
(Reformed)   Switzerland

BOLALAILAI, Ms Amelia
Student of Education
University of the South Pacific
                Fiji

BONSU, Ms Adwoah Seiwaah
Student of Building Technology
(Presbyterian)   Ghana

BOONSTRA, Mr Azing
Student of Mathematics, History
and Social Aspects of Science
(Reformed)   Netherlands

BOROVOY, Protopresbyter Vitaly
Representative
Russian Orthodox Church, WCC
(Russian Orthodox)   USSR

BOUEVSKY, Dr Aleksy
Secretary, Department of
External Church Relations
(Russian Orthodox)   USSR

BROWNLEA, Prof. Arthur
Professor of Epidemiology
University of Toronto
(Uniting)   Australia

*BRUNGS, Fr Robert, S. J.
Director, Institute for
Theological Encounter
with Science and Technology
(Roman Catholic)   USA

BUESO MADRID, Mr Gustavo A.
Student of Medicine
(Reformed)   Honduras

BUNDE, Dr Terry A.
  Professor of Biochemistry
  Maryville College, Tenn.
  (Presbyterian)   USA

*BURTON, Mr Lawrence
  Analyst, Genetics and World
  Population Group, Office
  of Technology Assessment
  US Congress   USA

CARIOCA, Prof. J. O.
  Energy Specialist   Brazil

CARPENTER, Mr R. C.
  Research Officer CISIR
  (Organic Chemistry)
  (Church of South India)   Sri Lanka

CARR, Canon Burgess
  General Secretary, All Africa
  Conference of Churches
  (Episcopal)   Liberia

CASTELLS I FERRER, Ms Edith
  Student of Biology
  (Evangelical)   Spain

*CHAGAS, Prof. Carlos
  Dean, Faculty of Health Sciences
  Federal University of Rio de Janeiro
  (Roman Catholic)   Brazil

CHERRY, Dr Neil
  Senior Lecturer
  in Agricultural Meteorology
  (Baptist)   New Zealand

CHKADUA, Bishop David
  Bishop of Batumi
  (Georgian Orthodox)   USSR

CIOBOTEA, Dr Dan-Ilie
  Candidat au doctorat
  en théologie
  (Orthodox)   Romania

CLARK, Mr Harold
  Student of Material Science, MIT
  (Lutheran)   USA

COBB, Prof. John B.
  Professor of Theology
  School of Theology, Claremont, Cal.
  (Methodist)   USA

COMBA, Mr Pietro
  Student of Biology, Research
  in Occupational Health
  (Waldensian)   Italy

CONNER, Mr Richard
  Vice-President, Business Department
  Control Data Corporation
  (Lutheran)   USA

COOLEY, Rev. Bruce
  Minister
  (Disciples)   USA

COUNELIS, Dr James
  Professor of Education
  University of San Francisco
  (Greek Orthodox)   USA

CRAWFORD, Ms Linda
  Student of Biology
  (Methodist)   USA

CREIGHTON, Mrs Phyllis
  Editor
  (Anglican)   Canada

CUMMINGS, Ms Katina
  Student of Urban Studies
  and Planning
  (Greek Orthodox)   USA

DALY, Prof. Herman
  Professor of Economics
  Louisiana State University
  (Methodist)   USA

DEATS, Dr Paul
  Professor of Social Ethics
  Boston University School of Theology
  (Methodist)   USA

DEMPSTER, Dr J. R. Hugh
  Associate Professor
  of Computer Science
  University of British Columbia
  (Anglican)   Canada

DIMBLEBY, Prof. G. W.
  Professor of Human Environment
  Institute of Archaeology
  University of London
  (Reformed)   UK

DIYAMANDOGLU, Mr Vasil
  Ecologist
  (Greek Orthodox)   USA

DOI, Dr Masatoshi
  Director, NCC Center for the
  Study of Japanese Religions
  (Kyodan)   Japan

DOMETIAN, Bishop
General Secretary of the Holy
Synod, Bulgarian Orthodox Church
(Orthodox)   Bulgaria

DOUHE, Mr Ignace
Licencié en recherche de chimie
(Roman Catholic)   Ivory Coast

DUMAS, Prof. André
Professeur de Morale et Philosophie
Protestant Theological Faculty, Paris
(Reformed)   France

DYKSTRA, Dr D. Ivan
Professor of Philosophy
Hope College, Mich.
(Reformed)   USA

EDWARDS, Mr Gordon
National Chairman, Canadian
Coalition for Nuclear Responsibility
                                     Canada

EGAN, Mr Joe
Student of Nuclear Engineering,
Technology and Policy, MIT
(Roman Catholic)   USA

*EL-KHOLY, Dr O. A.
Assistant Director General
Science and Technology
Arab Educational, Cultural and
Scientific Organization
(Muslim)   Egypt

EL-KHOURY, Ms Nour Farah
Student of Electrical Engineering
(Greek Orthodox)   Syria

ENGELEN, Dr. O. E.
President, Christian University
(Evangelical)   Indonesia

ENGLEVAKIS, Dr Benedict
(Orthodox)   Cyprus

FABINI, Dr Hermann
Architect
(Lutheran)   Romania

FALCKE, Dr Heino
Propst
(Evangelical)   GDR

FARRIS, Prof. W. J. S.
Professor of History and Philosophy
of Religion, Knox College
(Presbyterian)   Canada

FERNANDO, Mr Clinton
Teacher
(Methodist)   Sri Lanka

FERNANDO, Rev. Duleep R.
Minister
(Methodist)   Sri Lanka

FERRE, Dr Frederick
Charles A. Dana Professor
of Philosophy
(Methodist)   USA

FINTEL, Mr William A.
Student of Biology
(Lutheran)   USA

FORSTER, Mr Peter
Theological Research
(Episcopal)   UK

FRANCIS, Dr John M.
Government Administrator
(Anglican)   UK

FREUDENBERGER, Dr C. Dean
Clergyman, Tropical Agronomist
(Methodist)   USA

FURUYA, Prof. Keiichi
Professor of Science
University of Tokyo
(Kyodan)   Japan

FYODOROV, Priest Vladimir
Teacher at Leningrad
Theological Academy
(Russian Orthodox)   USSR

GALINSKY, Hieromonk Feofan
Teacher
(Russian Orthodox)   USSR

GAMBORG, Dr Oluf
Research Scientist
(Lutheran)   Canada

GARBRAH, Dr B. W.
Scientific Coordinator
(Methodist)   Ghana

GARCIA HEREDIA, Ms Irma
Language Teacher
(Roman Catholic)   Colombia

GARCIA, Dr Neftalí
Scientific Adviser
Puerto Rican Industrial Mission
(Episcopal)   Puerto Rico

DE GASPAR, Dr Diogo
World Food Council
(Roman Catholic) Brazil

GEORGE, Dr K. M.
Professor of Systematic Theology
Orthodox Theological Seminary,
Kottayam
(Orthodox Syrian) India

GEORGY, Ms Nawal Emeel
Assistant, Coptic Evangelical
Organization for Social Services
(Coptic Orthodox) Egypt

GEYER, Dr Alan
Professor of Political Ethics
Center for Theology and Public Policy
(Methodist) USA

GIRGIS, Dr Kamal
Oberassistent, Institut für
Kristallographie, ETH Zürich
(Orthodox) Switzerland/Egypt

GOODRIGE, Dr Sehon
Principal, Codrington College
(Anglican) Barbados

*GOTTSCHALK, Dr Stephen
Editor
(Christian Scientist) USA

DE GRAAF, Rev. Arent I.
Parish Minister
(Reformed) Australia

GRAEWE, Dr Wolf-Dieter
Agriculturalist,
Humboldt-Universität, Berlin
(Evangelical) GDR

GREGORIOS, Metropolitan Paulos
Metropolitan of New Delhi
(Orthodox Syrian) India

GREVEN, Drs J.
Director, IKON
(Reformed) Netherlands

GROSS, Ms Tracy Ann
Student of Biology, MIT
(Episcopal) USA

HABGOOD, Rt Rev. John
Bishop of Durham
(Anglican) UK

HAGGMARK, Ms Nancy
Lutheran Brotherhood
(Lutheran) USA

HAIGLER, Ms Candace
Student of Cell
and Molecular Biology
(Southern Baptist) USA

HAJJAR, Mr Youssef
Associate General Secretary
World Student Christian Federation
(Roman Catholic) Syria

HALL, Dr Charles
Professor of Religion
Beaver College, Pa.
(Presbyterian) USA

HAM, Prof. James
President, University of Toronto
(Anglican) Canada

HAMAMDJIAN, Mr Gilbert
Assistant in Physics
Faculty of Science, Cairo
(Roman Catholic) Egypt

HANBURY BROWN, Prof. Robert
Chatterton Astronomy Department
University of Sydney
(Anglican) UK/Australia

HARAKAS, Dr Stanley S.
Dean and Professor of Christian
Ethics, Holy Cross Greek
Orthodox School of Theology
(Greek Orthodox) USA

HAUGE, Prof. Jens G.
Professor of Biochemistry
Norwegian Veterinary College
(Lutheran) Norway

HEADLEY, Dr Oliver
Lecturer in Chemistry
University of the West Indies
(Adventist) Barbados

*HECKEL, Rev. Roger, SJ
Staff, Pontifical Commission
Justice and Peace
(Roman Catholic) France

HEDLIN, Dr Charles
Research Officer
National Research Council
(Lutheran) Canada

HEFNER, Prof. Philip
Professor of Systematic Theology
Lutheran School of Theology, Ill.
(Lutheran)   USA

HEINTZELER, Dr Wolfgang
Industrialist
(Evangelical)   FRG

HESSE, Prof. Dr Helmut
Professor of Economics
University of Göttingen
(Evangelical)   FRG

VAN DEN HEUVEL, Dr Albert
Secretary General
Netherlands Reformed Church
(Reformed)   Netherlands

HIDEAKI, Dr Itoh
Research Assistant
Department of Applied Chemistry
Nagoya University
(Kyodan)   Japan

*HIGDON, Rev. William
Minister
(Latter Day Saints)   USA

HOFFMANN, Mr Ralf
Chairman, Board of Hoechst
(United)   Canada

HONEY, Rev. Colin
Theologian   Australia

HOWIE, Dr John
Professor of Mathematics
St Andrews University
(Church of Scotland)   UK

HUBER, Mr Felix
Medical Student
(Roman Catholic)   Switzerland

HÜBNER, Prof. Dr Jürgen
Scientific Consultant, Evangelical
Churches' Research Working Group
(Evangelical)   FRG

HULBERT, Mr Philip
Hydrographer
(Uniting)   UK/Australia

HUSZTI, Dr Kalman
Professor and Pastor
(Reformed)   Hungary

HUTTON, Dr Miriam
Associate Professor
University of Manitoba
(Anglican)   Canada

IISAKA, Prof. Yoshiaki
Professor of Political Science
Gakushuin University
(Kyodan)   Japan

ITAIA, Rev. Maunaa
Lecturer in Biblical Studies
(Protestant)   Gilbert Islands

JACOB, Rev. J.
Pastor
(Church of South India)   India

JENSEN, Prof. Ole
Professor of Theology
(Lutheran)   Denmark

JOHANSSON, Mr Lennart
Student of Biomedical Engineering
(Baptist)   Sweden

JOHN, Metropolitan
Metropolitan of Helsinki
(Orthodox)   Finland

JOSHUA, Rt Rev. Dr. S. B.
Bishop of Bombay
(Church of North India)   India

KAA, Rev. Hone T. K.
Priest
(Anglican)   New Zealand

KAKIUCHI, Prof. Yoshinobu
Professor, International
Christian University, Tokyo
(Episcopal)   Japan

KANGSEN, Rev. J. C.
Moderator
(Presbyterian)   Cameroon

KAREFA-SMART, Dr John
(Methodist)   Sierra Leone

KAREFA-SMART, Mrs Rena
Professor of Christian Ethics
Howard University, Va.
(Episcopal)   USA

KATOPPO, Ms Marianne
Theologian, Journalist   Indonesia

KEMAYOU, Mr Claude
Hydraulic Engineer
(Evangelical)   Cameroon

KESTERTON, Ms Margaret
Student of Soil Chemistry
and Pesticides
(Anglican)   UK

KIBICHO, Dr Samuel
Senior Lecturer, Religious Studies
University of Nairobi
(Presbyterian)   Kenya

KIEMSTEDT, Dr Hans
Professor, Institut für
Landschaftspflege und Naturschutz
(Evangelical)   FRG

KIM, Prof. Young Gul
Vice-President and Professor
Korea Advanced Institute of Science
(Presbyterian)   South Korea

KIMURA, Dr Rihito
Lawyer
(Kyodan)   Japan

KING, Prof. Jonathan
Associate Professor
of Microbiology, MIT   USA

KINYANJUI, Mr Kabiru
Student of Educational
Planning and Social Policy
(Presbyterian)   Kenya

KIRILL, Archbishop
Rector, Leningrad
Theological Academy
(Russian Orthodox)   USSR

KISHIMOTO, Rev. Kazuyo
Pastor, Fukuoka Kego Church
(Kyodan)   Japan

**KISTIAKOWSKY, Prof. George
Professor Emeritus in Chemistry
Harvard University   USA

**KLOMPE, Dr (Mrs) M. A. M.
Chairman, National Justice
and Peace Commission
(Roman Catholic)   Netherlands

**KOBEISSI, Dr Hafez
Secretary-General
Arab Physical Society
(Muslim)   Lebanon

KOCH, Prof. Dr Klaus
Professor of Old Testament
and History of Ancient Religions
University of Hamburg
(Evangelical)   FRG

KOFFI KOUASSI, Mr Guillaume
Student of Mathematics
(Roman Catholic)   Ivory Coast

KOH, Dr Bum Soe
President, Soong Jun University
(Presbyterian)   South Korea

KOLLEK, Dr Regine
Student of Biology
(Evangelical)   FRG

KOUWENHOVEN, Dr A.
Teacher of Social Ethics
Free University Amsterdam
(Reformed)   Netherlands

KRIVOHLAVY, Dr Jaro
Psychologist
(Brethren)   CSSR

KRUSCHE, Dr Günter
Seminary Dean
(Evangelical)   GDR

KUO, Dr George
Associate Plant Physiologist
(Presbyterian)   Taiwan

KURIEN, Dr C. T.
Director, Madras Institute
of Development Studies
(Church of South India)   India

KYSKA, Pastor Miroslav
Secretary, Slovak Evangelical
Church of the Augsburg Confession
(Evangelical)   CSSR

LALISANG, Drs W.
Director, Development Centre, NCC
(Protestant)   Indonesia

LANG, Dr Wilfried L.
Assistant, Institut für
Religionswissenschaft, Vienna
(Roman Catholic)   Austria

DE LANGE, Dr H. M.
Director, University Institute
for Value Research
and Training, Rotterdam
(Remonstrant)   Netherlands

LAUFFER, Prof. Max A.
Professor of Biophysics
University of Pittsburgh
(Presbyterian)   USA

LAY, Rev. Arthur Ko
Pastor
(Baptist)   Burma

LEBACQZ, Dr Karen A.
Associate Professor of Christian
Ethics, Pacific School of Religion, Cal.
(United)   USA

LEDGER, Ms Chris
ASCM Worker
(Anglican)   Australia

LEE, Prof. (Mrs) Yang-Cha
Associate Professor of Nutritional
Sciences, Yonsei University
(Presbyterian)   South Korea

LEGGE, Dr Russel D.
Assistant Professor of Religious
Traditions in South East Asia
University of Waterloo
(Disciples)   Canada

LEHTONEN, Ms Eeva-Maria
Ph.D. Student, Organic Chemistry
(Lutheran)   Finland

LEITE, Dr Rogerio de Cerqueira
Professor, Institute of Physics   Brazil

*LEJEUNE, Prof. Jérôme
Professor of Fundamental Genetics
(Roman Catholic)   France

LELON, Dr Thomas
President, Hellenic College/
Holy Cross Greek Orthodox
School of Theology
(Greek Orthodox)   USA

LEUENBERGER, Prof. Theodor
Professor of Contemporary
Social and Economic History
University of St Gallen
(Reformed)   Switzerland

LIEDKE, Dr Gerhard
Pastor
(Evangelical)   FRG

LINDAMAN, Dr Edward
President, Whitworth College, Wash.
(Presbyterian)   USA

LINDELL, Dr Bo
Chairman, National Institute
on Radiation Protection   Sweden

LØNNING, Bishop Per
Professor, History
of Christian Thought
University of Oslo
(Lutheran)   Norway

LUCAL, Fr John, SJ
Director, SODEPAX
(Roman Catholic)   USA

MAATHAI, Dr (Mrs) Wangari Muta
Associate Professor of Anatomy
University of Nairobi   Kenya

MACKENZIE, Mr Papa Oyeah
Musician   Ghana

MAHARADZE, Archbishop Nikolas
Archbishop of Sukhumi and Abhazia
(Georgian Orthodox)   USSR

*MAJKA, Msgr Jozef
Dean, Pontifical Theological
Faculty, Wroclaw
(Roman Catholic)   Poland

MALASKA, Mr Pentti
Professor of Mathematics
and Statistics
Turku School of Economics
(Lutheran)   Finland

MALHERBE, Prof. Jean-François
Assistant, Catholic University
Louvain
(Roman Catholic)   Belgium

MALONE, Ms Annie
Social Worker
(Lutheran)   USA

MALVAR, Mr Felix A.
Retired Naval Officer
Businessman
(Independent)   Philippines

MANGELSDORF, Prof. Paul C.
Professor of Physics
Swarthmore College, Pa.
(Friends)   USA

MANOOGIAN, Archbishop Torkom
Primate, Diocese
of the Armenian Church
(Armenian)   USA

MAPOMA, Ms Carol
  Student of Zoology, Botany
  and Chemistry
  (Methodist)   Zambia

MARASCHIN, Dr Jaci Correia
  General Secretary, Association of
  Evangelical-Theological Seminaries
  (Episcopal)   Brazil

MARCOTTE, Fr Roger, SJ
  Teacher of Philosophy
  (Roman Catholic)   Canada

MARKHOFF, M. Gerhard
  Director, Villemétrie Centre
  (Reformed)   France

MARSTON, Mr Peter
  Food Technologist
  (Uniting)   Australia

MASILO, Mr Mabeta
  Student of Sociology of Development
  (Anglican)   South Africa

MATHEW, Dr George
  Student of Sociology
  and Social Change
  (Mar Thoma)   India

MATHEW, Rev. Dr K. V.
  Professor of Old Testament
  Mar Thoma Theological Seminary
  (Mar Thoma)   India

MATSUGI, Dr Nobuhiko
  Novelist
  (Buddhist)   Japan

MATTHAI, Mr Thomas P.
  Journalist
  (Indian Orthodox)   India

MATTSSON, Mr Bertil
  Electrical Engineer
  (Covenant)   Sweden

MAYSONAT, Mr Carlos
  Puerto Rican Industrial Mission
                             Puerto Rico

MBOGORI, Mr Ezra T.
  Student of Mathematics and Physics
  (Methodist)   Kenya

MCGREGOR, Dr Donald
  Associate Professor of Zoology
  University of Otago
  (Anglican)   New Zealand

**MEDEIROS, H. E. Humberto Cardinal
  Archbishop of Boston
  (Roman Catholic)   USA

MEDINA, Mr Ricardo   Mexico

MEHANEY, Dr Makram
  Student of Pharmacy
  (Coptic Orthodox)   Egypt

MENDELSOHN, Dr Everett
  Professor of History of Science
  Harvard University
  (Quaker)   USA

MEZEMIR, Mr Aklilu
  Student of Electrical Engineering
  (Ethiopian Orthodox)   Ethiopia

MICA, Mr J. Hunter
  Student of Sociology
  (Lutheran)   USA

MILLER, Dr David
  Health Physicist
  (Brethren)   USA

MILLER, Rev. Ms Elizabeth
  Director, Issue Development
  National Ministries
  American Baptist Churches
  (Baptist)   USA

MINIAN, Mr Isaac   Mexico

MITCHELL, Mrs Sheila
  Radio Education Unit
  University of West Indies
  (Anglican)   Jamaica

MMARI, Prof. G. R. V.
  Teacher, University of Dar-es-Salaam
  (Lutheran)   Tanzania

MNJOKAVA, Mr Michael
  Teacher, Lutheran Junior Seminary
  (Lutheran)   Tanzania

MONTEFIORE, Rt Rev. Hugh
  Bishop of Birmingham
  (Anglican)   UK

MORCOS, Prof. Sabry
  Professor, National Research Centre
  (Coptic Orthodox)   Egypt

MORGAN, Prof. Karl
  Professor of Health Physics
  Georgia Institute of Technology
  (Lutheran)   USA

** MORRISON, Prof. Philip
   Professor of Physics, MIT   USA

* MURPHY, Msgr William
   Staff, Pontifical Commission
   Justice and Peace
   (Roman Catholic)   USA

MUSTAFIN, Archpriest Vladimir
   Head, Post-Graduate Course
   of Moscow Theological Academy
   (Russian Orthodox)   USSR

NAGAMI, Prof. Isamu
   Assistant Professor
   Hiroshima University
   (Independent)   Japan

NAHAS, Dr Gabriel
   Director of Research, INSERM, Paris
   (Reformed)   France

NANKIVELL, Dr Owen
   Business Economist
   (Methodist)   UK

NASERI, Mr Utufua
   Student of Social Science   Samoa

NASHED, Dr W. N.
   Industrial Management
   Training Adviser, UNIDO
   (Coptic Orthodox)   Egypt

NEBELSICK, Prof. Harold
   Professor of Doctrinal Theology
   (Presbyterian)   USA

NELSON, Dr David
   Professor of Physics
   Luther College, Iowa
   (Lutheran)   USA

NEWSOME, Mr William
   Student of Neurobiology
   (Baptist)   USA

NGATIRI, Dr George
   Medical Doctor
   (Baptist)   Kenya

NIKITIN, Hegumen Augustin
   Teacher, Leningrad
   Theological Academy
   (Russian Orthodox)   USSR

NINAN, Prof. C. A.
   Professor of Genetics
   Head, Department of Botany
   Kerala University
   (Syrian Orthodox)   India

NJOYA, Dr Timothy
   Lecturer, PCEA Pastoral Institute
   (Presbyterian)   Kenya

NOKO, Rev. Dr Ishmael
   Head, Department of Theology
   University of Botswana
   (Anglican)   Botswana

NOLLAU, Dr Volker
   Assistant Professor, D.Sc.
   (Evangelical)   GDR

NWOSU, Dr B. C. E.
   Chief Education Officer (Science)
   Federal Ministry of Education
   (Anglican)   Nigeria

NYEMA-JONES, Dr A. E.
   Geologist
   (Episcopal)   Liberia

NYORMOI, Mr Okoth
   Cell Biologist   Uganda

ODHIAMBO, Dr Thomas
   Director, International Centre
   of Insect Physiology and Ecology
                                      Kenya

ODINGO, Prof. Richard
   Associate Professor of Geology
   University of Nairobi
   (Anglican)   Kenya

OKE, Prof. Segun
   Lecturer, Chemistry Department
   University of Ife
   (Methodist)   Nigeria

* OLDSHUE, Dr James
   Chemical Engineer
   (Reformed)   USA

OMARI, Prof. Cuthbert
   Associate Professor of Sociology
   University of Dar-es-Salaam
   (Lutheran)   Tanzania

ORLOV, Mr Ilia
   Union of Evangelical
   Christian Baptists
   (Baptist)   USSR

OSIPOV, Prof. Alexy
   Professor
   Moscow Theological Seminary
   (Russian Orthodox)   USSR

OTUBELU, Bishop Gideon
Bishop of Enugu
(Anglican)   Nigeria

OYANAGI, Dr Yoshio
Assistant Professor
Information and Computer Sciences
(Roman Catholic)   Japan

PAK, Dr Chong Min
Professor of Chemistry
Soong Jun University
(Presbyterian)   South Korea

**PALIHAWADANA, Prof. Mahinda
Professor of Sanskrit
University of Kelaniya
(Buddhist)   Sri Lanka

PARRENT, Dr Allan
Professor of Church and Society
Virginia Theological Seminary
(Episcopal)   USA

PEACOCKE, Dr Arthur
Dean, Clare College, Cambridge
(Anglican)   UK

PEAT, Dr Stanley
Parish Minister
(Church of Scotland)   UK

PECK, Dr Jane
Assistant Professor
Religion and Society
Andover Newton Theological School,
Mass.
(Methodist)   USA

PETRIC, Dr Ernest
Professor, Faculty of Sociology,
Political Science and Journalism
                            Yugoslavia

PHAILBUS, Mrs Mira
Principal, Kinnaird College
for Women
(Church of Pakistan)   Pakistan

*PHINNEY, Mr A. W.
Church Administrator
(Christian Science)   USA

PICINBONO, Prof. Bernard
Professor, University Paris-Sud
(Reformed)   France

PISUTHA-ARNOND, Ms Supaporn
Student of Geology
(Buddhist)   Thailand

POLLARD, Dr William
Priest; Consultant,
Institute of Energy Analysis
(Episcopal)   USA

POPOVIC, Prof. Vladan
Professor, St Sava Seminary
(Serbian Orthodox)   Yugoslavia

PORTER, Mr David
Vice-President
Council of Yukon Indians   Canada

PRÖHLE, Rev. Prof. Dr Karoly
Professor of Theology
(Lutheran)   Hungary

PRUDENTE, Mr Rudy
Student of Engineering
(Methodist)   USA

RACKOW, Dr (Mrs) Sabine
Chemist, Government Institute
for Drug Control, Berlin
(Evangelical)   GDR

RAIFORD, Dr Maurice
Solar Energy Consultant
(Friends)   USA

RAKOTONIRINA, Ms Marie-Christine
Student of Biology and Pedology
(Church of Jesus Christ)   Madagascar

RAMOS, Mr José Guillermo Castro
Student of Electrical Engineering
(Baptist)   El Salvador

RANDALL, Dr (Ms) Claire
General Secretary
National Council of Churches USA
(Presbyterian)   USA

RASEROKE, Mr B.
Lecturer in Biology
University of Botswana and Swaziland
(Roman Catholic)   Botswana

RASSKAZOVSKY, Mr Sergey
Student of Theology
(Russian Orthodox)   USSR

RAVETZ, Dr Jerome
Reader in History
and Philosophy of Science
University of Leeds   UK

**REITZ, Mr Rüdiger
Aide to Vice-Chairman of SPD
(Evangelical)   FRG

RENDER, Mr Peter
Students of Aeronautics
(Methodist)   UK

RENDTORFF, Prof. Trutz
Professor of Systematic Theology
(Evangelical)   FRG

RENNIE, Ms Pat
Student of Biology
(Anglican)   Canada

ROLLMANN, Mr Michael
Student of Mechanical Engineering
(Roman Catholic)   FRG

ROSE, Prof. David
Professor of Nuclear
Engineering, MIT
(Episcopal)   USA

ROSE, Rev. Lois
Minister
(United)   USA

ROSSEL, Prof. Jean
Professor of Physics
University of Neuchâtel
(Reformed)   Switzerland

ROY, Prof. Rustum
Director, Materials Research
Laboratory, Pa.
(Episcopal)   USA

RUETHER, Dr Rosemary
Professor of Theology
Garrett Evangelical
Theological Seminary
(Roman Catholic)   USA

RUTGERS, Dr Erik
Manager, Nuclear Engineering
Division, Motor-Columbus
(Reformed)   Switzerland

RYNNE, Mr John
Student of Chemistry
(Roman Catholic)   Ireland

SABER, Mr Tony
Student of Medicine
(Greek Orthodox)   Lebanon

SADOSKY, Prof. Manuel
Professor of Mathematics
Central University, Caracas
                              Argentina

SAID, Dr Mufeed
Professor of General Surgery
Cairo University
(Presbyterian)   Egypt

SAMUEL, Bishop
Bishop of Public, Ecumenical
and Social Services
(Coptic Orthodox)   Egypt

SAMUEL, Ms Charlotte
Student of Zoology
(Anglican)   Malaysia

SANDSTROM, Dr Donald
Nuclear Engineer
(Lutheran)   USA

SCOTT, The Most Rev. Edward
Archbishop
Anglican Church of Canada
(Anglican)   Canada

SCOTT, Rev. Fr Olof
Priest
(Antiochian Orthodox)   USA

*SCHNEIDER, Dr Maxyne, S. S. J.
Professor of Physics
(Roman Catholic)   USA

SCHOLZ, Dr Günter
Plant Biochemist
(Evangelical)   GDR

SCHROEDER, Prof. Dr Traute
Professor, Institute
of Human Genetics
(Evangelical)   FRG

*SCHROTENBOER, Rev. Paul
General Secretary
Reformed Ecumenical Synod
(Christian Reformed)   USA

SCHWARZ, Dr Hans
Professor of Systematic Theology
Trinity Lutheran Seminary, Ohio
(Lutheran)   USA

SEITE, Dr Berndt
Veterinary Surgeon
(Evangelical)   GDR

SELLER, Dr Mary
Lecturer in Experimental Biology
Guy's Hospital, London
(Anglican)   UK

SETTERWALL, Dr Max
President, Swedish Electrical
Manufacturers' Association
(Lutheran) Sweden

SHERIDAN, Prof. Thomas
Professor of Mechanical
Engineering, MIT
(United) USA

SHILALUKEY, Ms Mary
Student of Medicine
(Baptist) Zambia

SHINN, Prof. Roger
Professor of Social Ethics
Union Theological Seminary
(United) USA

SHIRAHATA, Mr Lucas
Student of Economics
(Episcopal) Brazil

SHRIVER, Mrs Peggy
Assistant General Secretary
Research, Evaluation and
Planning, NCC/USA
(Presbyterian) USA

SIEBERT, Rev. Udo
Superintendent
(Evangelical) GDR

*SIEGHART, Mr Paul
Chairman, Executive Committee
"Justice", London
(Roman Catholic) UK

SIMIONESCU, Mr Constantin
Architect
(Orthodox) Romania

SIMON, Dr K. M.
Priest, Educator
(Syrian Orthodox) USA

SIPAHUTAR, Mr Marulam
Civil Engineer
(Protestant) Indonesia

SIRAIT, Mr Sabam
Member of Parliament
(Protestant) Indonesia

SIREGAR, Mr Tunggul
Student of Political Development,
Sociology and Political Science
(Lutheran) Indonesia

SISWOHARDJONG, Ms Ariatmi
Director, Guidance and
Counselling Centre, Satya
Wacana Christian University
(Reformed) Indonesia

SIWATIBAU, Mrs Suliana
Former Research Fellow
University of the South Pacific
(Methodist) Fiji

SODZI, Dr Nathaniel
Senior Lecturer in Engineering
Kumasi University
(Evangelical) Ghana

SOKOLOV, Mr Anatoly
Assistant Director, International
Department, Baptist Union USSR
(Baptist) USSR

SOMMERS, Mr Davidson
Consultant, World Bank
(Unitarian) USA

SOMPLATSKY-JARMAN, Rev. William
Amalgamated Clothing
and Textile Workers Union
(Disciples) USA

STACKHOUSE, Prof. Max
Theologian
(Baptist) USA

STAELIN, Prof. David
Professor of Electrical
Engineering, MIT USA

VAN STEENBERGEN, Dr Bart
Visiting Fellow
Princeton University Netherlands

STIVERS, Dr Robert
Professor of Religion
Pacific Lutheran University, Wash.
(Presbyterian) USA

STOIKOV, Archpriest Vasily
Professor, Leningrad
Theological Academy
(Russian Orthodox) USSR

STRIEGNITZ, Mr Meinfried
Physicist and Director
Evangelische Akademie Loccum
(Evangelical) FRG

STUECKELBERGER, Mr Christoph
Vicar
(Reformed) Switzerland

SUHARSO, Dr
  Director, National Institute of
  Economic and Social Research
  (Presbyterian)   Indonesia

**SUKAPANPOTHARAM, Dr Sukhum
  Assistant Professor
  Faculty of Engineering
  Chiang Mai University
  (Buddhist)   Thailand

SUMBELE, Mr Abel
  Principal, Kumba Presbyterian
  Secondary School
  (Presbyterian)   Cameroon

SUNARINGSIH, Ms Dwiworo
  Student of Post-Harvest Technology
  (Protestant)   Indonesia

SUNG, Rev. Kap Shik
  General Secretary
  Presbyterian Church of Korea
  (Presbyterian)   South Korea

SVEHLA, Dr Gyula
  Reader in Chemistry
  Queen's University
  (Presbyterian)   Northern Ireland

*SWIFT, Dr Nancy
  Professor of Theology
  (Roman Catholic)   USA

TAEAO, Rev. Ioane Venitura
  Pastor
  (Protestant)   Samoa

TAMAS, Rev. Bertalan
  Pastor
  (Reformed)   Hungary

TAMTHAI, Dr Mark
  Assistant Professor of
  Mathematics/Philosophy
  Chulalongkorn University
  (Church of Christ)   Thailand

TAYLOR, Rev. R. F.
  Senior Industrial Chaplain
  Diocese of Lincoln
  (United Reformed)   UK

**TEMPLETON, Mr John
  Businessman and Philanthropist
                                 Bahamas

TEWARI, Dr Sharat
  Engineer, National
  Aeronautical Laboratory   India

THANGARAJ, Dr Manuel
  General Secretary
  All India Association
  for Christian Higher Education
  (Church of South India)   India

THAWNG, Mr Smith Ngulh Za
  Executive Secretary
  University Christian Work
  (Baptist)   Burma

THUNG, Mrs Mady
  Reader of Sociology of Religion
  Theological Faculty,
  Leyden University
  (Reformed)   Netherlands

THURAISINGHAM, Dr Ranjit
  Lecturer in Chemistry
  University of Colombo
  (Church of South India)   Sri Lanka

TOMB, Mr François   Lebanon

TRAITLER, Dr Helmut
  Research Assistant
  (Organic Chemistry)
  (Lutheran)   Austria

TREMEWAN, Mr Chris
  Student of Social Anthropology
  (Anglican)   New Zealand

TRICKETT, Mr David
  Teaching Fellow
  Perkins School of Theology, Tex.
  (Methodist)   USA

TUCKER, Dr W. Henry
  Chairman
  Department of Chemical Engineering
  Tri-State University, Ind.
  (Methodist)   USA

TUININGA, Mr Eric-Jan
  Lecturer, Applied Science Institute
  (Reformed)   Netherlands

TUN THAN, Mehm
  Youth Secretary
  Burma Council of Churches
  (Baptist)   Burma

TURKEVICH, Dr John
  Professor of Chemistry
  Chaplain to Eastern Orthodox
  Students, Princeton University
  (Orthodox)   USA

UDARBE, Dr Proceso
Vice-President for Academic
Affairs, Silliman University
(United)   Philippines

UI, Prof. Jun
Sanitary Engineer
Department of Urban Engineering
University of Tokyo   Japan

VALENA, Ms Rahima
Student of Economics
(Muslim)   Afghanistan

VANDERHOFF, Mr Franz
(Roman Catholic)   Mexico

VARGHESE, Mr Joseph
Student of Genetics
and Plant Breeding
(Orthodox Syrian)   India

VARUGHESE, Mr Raj
Professor of English
(Mar Thoma)   India

VEDANAYAGAM, Dr (Ms) Edith
Professor and Head
Department of Education
University of Madras
(Church of South India)   India

VAN VEEN, Drs Jan
Executive Secretary
Department on Church and Society
Netherlands Reformed Church
(Reformed)   Netherlands

VAN DER VEKEN, Prof. Jan
Professor
Catholic University of Louvain
(Roman Catholic)   Belgium

VENES, Dr Joan
Doctor of Pediatric Neurosurgery
Children's Medical Center, Dallas
(Lutheran)   USA

* VEREB, Fr Jerome-Michael
Attaché, Secretariat for
Promoting Christian Unity
(Roman Catholic)   USA

VERHEUL, Prof. Henk
Professor of Physics
Free University Amsterdam
(Reformed)   Netherlands

DE VRIES, Prof. Egbert
Professor of Public
and International Affairs
University of Pittsburgh
(Methodist)   USA

WAGLEY, Dr Mary
Executive Director
Episcopal Social Services
Diocese of Maryland
(Episcopal)   USA

** WAKABAYASHI, Prof. Hiroaki
Associate Professor, Nuclear
Engineering Research Laboratory
University of Tokyo   Japan

WALTAR, Dr Alan
Advisory Engineer
(Presbyterian)   USA

WANG, Dr Hsien-Chih
Associate Professor
Tainan Theological College
(Episcopal)   Taiwan

WARNER, Dr Cynthia
Research Scientist
Emory University, Ga.
(Methodist)   USA

WATTANACHANTRAGUL, Rev. Pakdee
Student of Christian Ethics
(Church of Christ)   Thailand

WEAVER, Ms Barbara
Director, United Methodist
Law of the Sea Project
(Methodist)   USA

WEIZENBAUM, Prof. Joseph
Professor of Computer Science
and Engineering, MIT   USA

WHALEY, Ms Birgitta
Student of Mathematics
(Roman Catholic)   UK

WHITE, Ms Valerie
Student of Mechanical Engineering
(Anglican)   Jamaica

WHITNEY, Rev. Dr Norman
Professor of Biology
University of New Brunswick
(United)   Canada

WHITTEMORE, Mr Gilbert
Student of History of Science
(Roman Catholic)   USA

WICK, Dr Ruth C.
Secretary for Social Concerns
Lutheran Church in America
(Lutheran)   USA

WICKHAM, Ms Lynda
Student of Agriculture
(Adventist)   Trinidad

WICKREMASINGHE, Dr O. C.
Research Chemist
(Methodist)   Sri Lanka

WIDJAJA, Dr Albert
Lecturer and Researcher
Institute of Economic and Social
Research, University of Indonesia
(Mennonite)   Indonesia

WILARDJO, Dr Liek
Satya Wacana Christian University
(Protestant)   Indonesia

WILKES, Dr James
Psychiatrist
(Anglican)   Canada

WILLIAMS, Prof. Preston
Houghton Professor of Theology
and Contemporary Change
Harvard Divinity School
(Presbyterian)   USA

WILSON, Dr Francis
Director, Southern Africa Labour
and Development Research Unit
University of Cape Town
(Anglican)   South Africa

WILSON, Rev. Dr Kenneth
Tutor in Philosophy
Wesley College
(Methodist)   UK

*WINTER, Fr F. X., SJ
Theologian
(Roman Catholic)   USA

WONG, Mr James Kin On
Student of Chemistry
(Methodist)   UK/Hongkong

WOODWARD, Ms Jimmie
YWCA Secretary   USA

YOUNGER, Mr Dana R.
Policy Analyst
US Department of the Interior
(Baptist)   USA

**ZAKARIA, Dr Fouad
Chairman, Department of Philosophy
Kuwait University
(Muslim)   Egypt

ZELEALEM, Mr Yiheyes
Student of Economics
(Ethiopian Orthodox)   Ethiopia

ZILLESSEN, Dr Horst
Director, Social Science Institute
Protestant Churches in Germany
(Evangelical)   FRG

ZIMMERMANN, Rev. Peter
Student, Sociology of Religion
and Social Ethics
(Evangelical)   GDR

Inside front cover:
Above, at the plenary session on "The Nature of Science", the conference heard (left to right) Prof. H. Verheul, physicist and Rector of the Free University of Amsterdam, Prof. M. Maathai, professor of animal anatomy at the University of Nairobi, Prof. R. Hanbury Brown, astronomer, and Prof. Charles Birch, biologist, both of the University of Sydney, Australia

Below: Students from the Boston area dramatize for conference participants the human and social problems from the misuse of modern science and technology

Inside back cover:
1. Prof. Enilo Ajakaiye (left) of Ahmadu Bello University, Nigeria, presided the plenary session at which Prof. Carlos Chagas, President of the Pontifical Academy of Science, Rome, spoke. With them is Dr Paul Abrecht, Organizing Secretary of the conference

2. Ms Adwoah S. Bonsu, a science student from Ghana, presented part of the report from the science students conference

3. The conference gathered for coffee, tea and discussion every morning and afternoon outside Kresge auditorium

4. Bishop Hugh Montefiore (left), of Birmingham, UK, well-known Anglican theologican, was an active conference participant and served as Chairman of the press briefings. Dr Shem Arungu-Olende of Kenya (right) spoke to the conference on "Energy for the Future". He is on the staff of the UN Centre for Natural Resources, Energy and Transport

5. Prof. Rubem Alves, social philosopher from Sao Paulo, Brazil, and Dr Roger Shinn, professor of social ethics, Union Theological Seminary, New York City, engage in discussion

6. Dr John M. Francis, a British nuclear physicist and public administrator, addresses the conference on the technological future of the industrialized countries

7. Prof. David Rose of MIT (left), Chairman of the Boston Preparatory Committee, discusses the conference programme with the conference Moderator, Metropolitan Gregorios (centre) and Dr Abrecht

Photos: Wendy Goldsworthy, Greg Moyer and John Taylor